D1643213

Life

UPPER INTERMEDIATE
STUDENT'S BOOK

Paul Dummett

John Hughes

Helen Stephenson

Contents Split Edition A

Listening	Reading	Critical thinking	Speaking	Writing
three people talking about important relationships in their lives a radio extract about animal friendships	an article about changing attitudes in China an article about immigrant families in New York	identifying the main aspect	your friends the generation gap family influences	text type: an informal email (1) writing skill: greetings and endings
a conversation about different accounts of Ayrton Senna's life an interview with a film critic	a true story about dangerous animals an article about the brothers Grimm	close reading	the film of the book a famous writer or filmmaker narrow escapes storytelling	text type: a story writing skill: using descriptive words
three people making predictions about the future a presentation about overpopulation	an article about augmented reality an article about appropriate technology	balancing arguments	global problems overpopulation information age predictions technological solutions	text type: short email requests writing skill: being polite
a conversation about two people who do artistic things in their free time an extract from a radio programme about what's on in Melbourne an artist's opinion about what art is	an article about unusual street art an article about the origins of rap	analysing contrasts	participation in the arts an art competition music and values	text type: an online review writing skill: personalising your writing
three speakers talking about different types of development someone talking about redevelopment in their city an interview with a journalist talking about social development in southern India	an article about urban development in Dubai an article about a hydropower dam project in Laos	fact or opinion	changes in your town a happy society sensitive development evaluating a development project	text type: an opinion essay writing skill: linking words
someone describing their stay at an ice hotel an interview about volunteer vacations	a blog about holidays at home an extract from a travel magazine about historical hotels	claims and justifications	local knowledge planning a staycation opinions about travel ideas for an unusual hotel	text type: a letter of complaint writing skill: formal language

Contents Split Edition B

Listening	Reading	Critical thinking	Speaking	Writing
an ecologist describing how we can avoid wasting natural resources four people talking about saving water	an article about Ecuador's plan to protect resources an article about Madagascar's unique ecology	emotive language	how we use water conservation wishes	text type: a letter to the press writing skill: giving vivid examples
a radio news report about the parents of Chinese university freshmen television news report of four good news stories	an article about an iconic image an article about the power of the press	different perspectives	the ethics of taking photographs good news stories reputations	text type: minutes from a meeting writing skill: impersonal language
a description of a mahout's job two friends discussing an astronaut's extraordinary career an interview about Emerging Explorers	an article about an extraordinary career an article about a woman who was king	weighing the evidence	a career path personal qualities women at work	text type: an online profile writing skill: writing in note form
an anthropologist's explanation of the quote 'manners maketh man' an extract from a radio programme about a tribe with an unusual diet	an article about the *tiger mother* approach to parenting an article about body language	sources	typical behaviour food and eating habits customs in your country wedding traditions	text type: an informal email (2) writing skill: elision in informal writing
a psychologist describing a situation in which you have to use your intuition a talk by a psychologist on memory	an article about an ethnobotanist an article about a parrot	reinforcing ideas	acquiring knowledge memory tests why you forgot types of learner	text type: an email about a misunderstanding writing skill: linking contrasting ideas
extract from a radio programme with an economist giving definitions of poverty and wealth an interview with the author of *The Servant Economy*	an article about Norway's riches an article about an alternative economic model	signposts to key information	the economy in your country getting things done gift giving and exchange	text type: a report writing skill: sub-headings and bullet points

Video in Split Editions A and B

Life around the world

Unit 1 Immigration

The history of immigration in the United States.

Unit 2 History of film

A history of film, from its early beginnings in the 19th century to the Hollywood blockbusters of today.

Unit 3 Augmented reality

Learn about a system that allows the user to see 3-dimensional images of everyday locations.

Unit 5 Aquarium on Wheels

A special aquarium that gives its student teachers lessons in life.

Unit 4 Urban art

Discover the world of graffiti and innovative music.

USA

Ecuador

Paraguay

Unit 10 Eating insects

Discover why eating insects could be good for you, and why one man is on a mission to change our tastes.

Unit 7 Galapagos energy

Find out about the impact of humans and tourism on the Galapagos Islands.

Unit 11 Paraguay shaman

Find out why it's essential to record plants from the rain forests of Paraguay before they disappear.

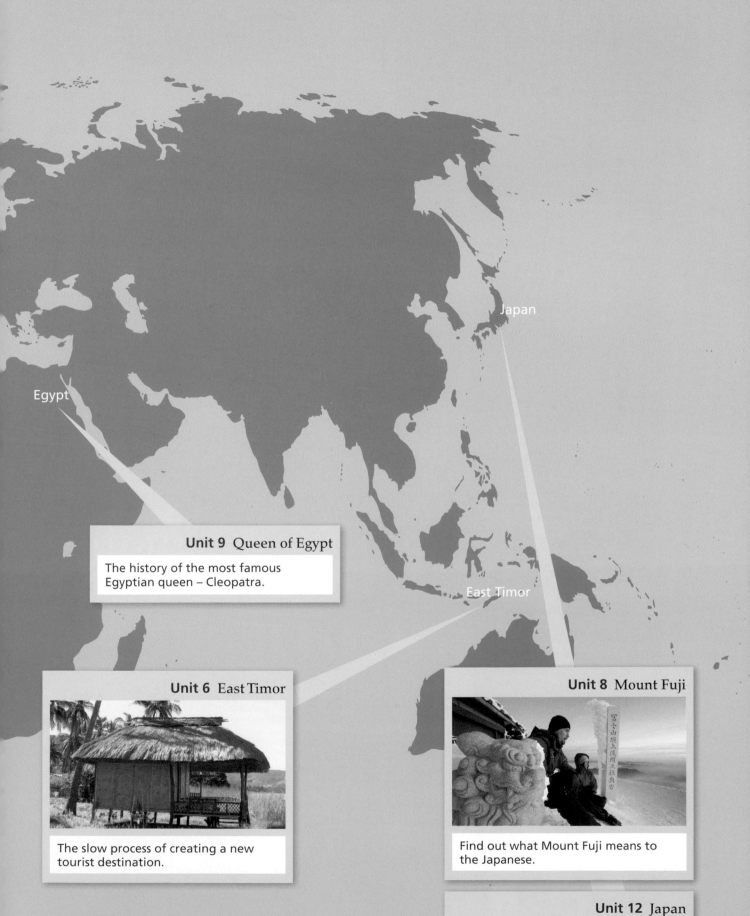

Japan

Egypt

Unit 9 Queen of Egypt

The history of the most famous
Egyptian queen – Cleopatra.

East Timor

Unit 6 East Timor

The slow process of creating a new
tourist destination.

Unit 8 Mount Fuji

Find out what Mount Fuji means to
the Japanese.

Unit 12 Japan

Learn more about the history and
traditions of Japan.

Split Editions A and B

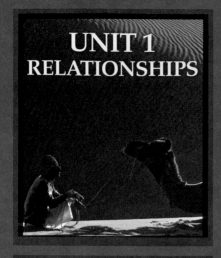

UNIT 1
RELATIONSHIPS

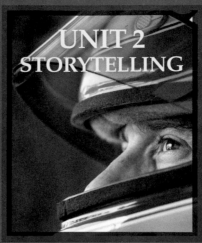

UNIT 2
STORYTELLING

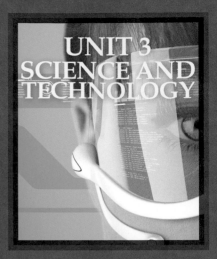

UNIT 3
SCIENCE AND TECHNOLOGY

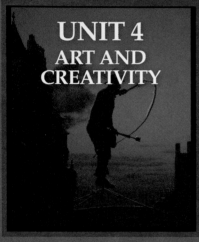

UNIT 4
ART AND CREATIVITY

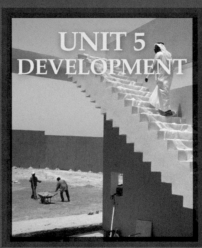

UNIT 5
DEVELOPMENT

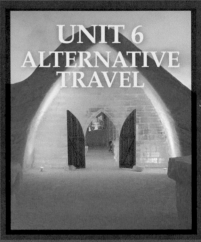

UNIT 6
ALTERNATIVE TRAVEL

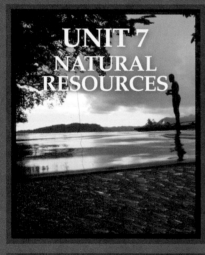

UNIT 7
NATURAL RESOURCES

UNIT 8
THE NEWS

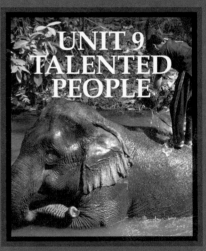

UNIT 9
TALENTED PEOPLE

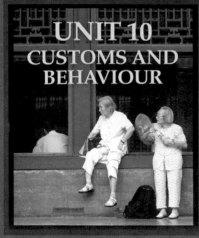

UNIT 10
CUSTOMS AND BEHAVIOUR

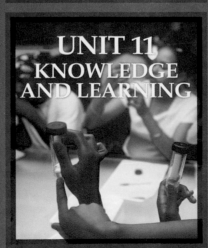

UNIT 11
KNOWLEDGE AND LEARNING

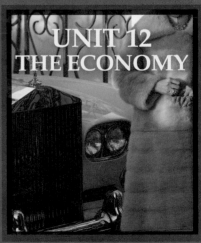

UNIT 12
THE ECONOMY

Unit 1 Relationships

A camel and his driver take a break in the desert, Rajasthan, India.
Photograph by Shivji Joshi

FEATURES

10 Unlikely friends

Two animals that enjoy each other's company

12 A confused generation

Changing attitudes among China's young generation

14 Bloodlines

Two accounts of how family has shaped people's lives

18 Immigration

A video about how immigrants have helped build America

1 Work in pairs. Look at the photo and the caption. Choose the phrase you think best describes the photo.

> a faithful companion   blood relatives
> a passing acquaintance   mutual respect   a strong bond
> true friends   an odd couple

2 Look at these English sayings about relationships. What do they mean? Do you have a similar saying in your language?

1 Blood is thicker than water
2 A friend in need is a friend indeed
3 Like father, like son
4 No man is an island

3 🔘 **1.1** Listen to three people talking about important relationships in their lives. Put the number of the speaker (1, 2 or 3) next to the person they are talking about.

a husband ☐   a fiancé ☐   a colleague ☐
an old friend ☐   a brother ☐   a grandparent ☐

4 Think of a person a) you have been meaning to contact for ages; and b) you have shared a travel experience with. Tell your partner about these people.

1a Unlikely friends

Image by Stevi Calandra for the
National Geographic Channel

Listening

1 Work in pairs. Look at the photo. Discuss the questions.

1   What are the two animals in the photo?
2   Are they normally working animals, pets, wild animals or something else?
3   What does the photo suggest about these animals' characters?

2 🔊 **1.2** Now listen to an extract from a radio programme about an unlikely friendship between these two animals. What things do they do together to enjoy each other's company?

3 🔊 **1.2** Listen again and choose the right word to complete each statement.

1   Co-operation between animals of different species is not
    _____ .
    a natural   b easy   c usual
2   Dogs are usually _____ apes.
    a suspicious of   b frightened of   c aggressive towards
3   This particular dog and orang-utan behave like _____ .
    a old friends   b children   c people
4   Their behaviour has attracted the interest of a lot of _____ .
    a TV viewers   b scientists   c psychologists
5   Orang-utans are very _____ creatures.
    a physical   b naughty   c kind
6   Their relationship is based on a need in both animals to
    _____ .
    a share new experiences   b hunt together   c be sociable

4 Do you believe animals can have friendships? Or do they form relationships only for practical reasons? Do you know other examples of sociable animals? Discuss.

Grammar present tenses review

> **PRESENT TENSES REVIEW**

Present simple
Suriya lives with his keepers.

Present continuous
The two animals are fulfilling a basic social need in each other.

Present perfect simple
Suriya has understood that the hound dog is very hungry.

Present perfect continuous
They have been doing this every day since they first met.

For further information and practice, see page 84.

5 Look at the grammar box. Match the tenses (1–4) with their uses (a–d).

1 present simple   a highlights a recent activity
2 present   b describes a situation in progress
   continuous   or happening around now
3 present perfect   c describes a permanent / usual
   simple   situation
4 present perfect   d highlights the present result of a
   continuous   recent past action

6 Choose the correct tense to complete this passage about animal friendships.

> A number of recent videos on YouTube showing unlikely animal friends [1] *have started / have been starting* a debate about animal friendships. Lately many people [2] *have discussed / have been discussing* a particularly moving film which shows a dog making friends with an elephant. Elephants often [3] *show / are showing* concern for their social group, but there is one extraordinary scene where the elephant becomes distressed when the dog gets injured. The dog [4] *has recovered / has been recovering* now and the two animals have been inseparable. The question scientists [5] *ask / are asking* is: is such behaviour normal, or do we just want it to be? Some say it happens when animals [6] *have lived / have been living* close to humans. No one [7] *has provided / has been providing* a definite answer, but it seems some animals are just naturally sociable. Others, like giant pandas, [8] *live / are living* more independent and solitary lives.

7 Work in pairs. Explain to each other the use of the verb forms in bold in sentences 1–10 using a–d from Exercise 5.

1 We're not close friends – we'**re** just **studying** French at the same evening class.
   This sentence describes a situation in progress.
2 I **live** with Sarah, but each of us **has** our own group of friends that we hang out with.
3 Olivia and I went on a trip to Peru together ten years ago and we'**ve kept up** with each other ever since.
4 I wouldn't say we were friends really. We'**ve met** a couple of times at parties.
5 Oh, **do you know** Tom? He's a good friend of mine too. We should all meet up some time.
6 Jacob **always hangs around** when he's bored, but he **never comes round** when he's got something better to do.
7 Kate **has always stood by** me in times of difficulty. If ever I'm in trouble, I **know** I can rely on her for help.
8 Colin and I **have been teaching** at the same school for years. We get on very well, even though we **never really see** each other socially. I think I've been round to his house once.
9 Barney and I **have known** each other since we were at school. It doesn't matter if we **haven't seen** each other for a while; we just seem to pick up where we left off.
10 Jessica and I are going to go for a medieval-style wedding. Themed weddings **are becoming** very fashionable.

Vocabulary friends: nouns and phrasal verbs

8 Work in pairs. What type of friend or person is each person talking about in Exercise 7? Match each sentence with a person from the box.

> acquaintance   fair-weather friend
> fellow student   flatmate   girlfriend
> mutual friend   old friend
> travel companion   true friend
> workmate

9 Find the following phrasal verbs in the sentences in Exercise 7. Which ones contain two prepositions, rather than one? Discuss what each verb means.

- 1 verb with *get*
- 1 verb with *stand*
- 2 verbs with *hang*
- 2 verbs with *round*
- 3 verbs with *up*

10 Choose the correct phrasal verbs to complete these sentences.

1 We come from different backgrounds but we _____ really well.
2 We don't have to do anything special, like going to a show. It would just be nice to _____ each other for a bit.
3 I made a lot of really good friends at university, but I haven't _____ with many of them.
4 Why don't you _____ to my house for supper tonight?
5 Some friends are great just to have a good time with, but real friends are the ones who _____ you when you're in trouble.
6 I'm busy at six o'clock but we could _____ later, if you like. Say, eight thirty?

Speaking

11 Work in pairs. Think about three of your friends. What kind of friend are they? Choose from the types in Exercise 8. Think also about how often you see these people and what things you do together. Discuss if your friendships are similar in any way.

1b A confused generation

Reading

1 Work in pairs. Look at the photo accompanying the article below. Discuss the questions.

1 What does it show?
2 What do you think the matter is with the young girl?
3 Is this situation familiar to you?

2 Discuss what effects you think China's recent economic boom has had on the attitudes of the younger generation and the older generation.

3 Read the article and compare your answers.

4 Look back at the article and find examples of the following to show how attitudes are changing in China.

- language use
- caring for the old
- the relationship between parents and children
- shopping
- knowledge of the world

5 Do Bella's parents seem to accept the changes that are happening in China or not? Do you think the changes are difficult for Bella too? Why? / Why not?

Grammar the passive

6 Work in pairs. Look at the examples of passive verbs from the passage (1–6). Then look at uses of the passive (a–d). Which are true and which are false?

1 Bella is the name that she **has been given** by her English teacher.
2 But at the same time these new values **are** also **being questioned**.
3 '**Have** our lives **been made** richer by all our new possessions?'
4 **Is** Chinese culture **being supplanted**?
5 When they go shopping Bella makes sure that the 'right' western brands **are selected**.
6 'Our advice **is not listened to** and it **is not wanted**,' her mother says.

a The person doing the action – the agent – is not the main focus of the sentence.
b We use *from* to introduce the agent in a passive sentence.
c The agent is often unimportant or unknown – it is the action that interests us.
d The passive is often used because we want to start a sentence with something that has already been mentioned.

Change brings problems. Bella lives with her parents in a brand new apartment in Shanghai. Her real name is Zhou Jiaying – 'Bella' is the name that she has been given by her English teacher. Her parents are representative of a confused generation in a confused time. In modern Chinese society different ideologies are fighting against each other. Enormous material benefits have been brought by China's economic boom, but the debate is not about these; it's about family life and values. Old values – the respect of family and the older generations – are being replaced by new ones which place money as the critical measurement of one's position in society. But at the same time these new values are also being questioned. Have our lives been made richer by all our new possessions? Is Chinese culture being supplanted? As in all changing societies people are trying to find the right balance between the 'new' and 'old'.

Recently, Bella's family put their grandfather into a nursing home. It was a painful decision. In traditional China, caring for aged parents has always been an unavoidable duty, but times are changing. Bella's ambition? 'I want one day to put my parents in the best nursing home' – the best that money can buy, she means.

'When she told us that' Bella's father says, 'I thought – is it selfish to think she will be a dutiful and caring daughter and look after us? We don't want to be a burden on her when we get old. This is something my daughter has taught us. Once it was parents who taught children, but now we learn from them.' The family can buy many more things these days, and when they go shopping, Bella makes sure that the 'right' western brands are selected. (Pizza Hut is her favourite restaurant.) She also teaches her parents the latest slang.

Her parents want to be supportive, but they no longer help with Bella's homework; in spoken English she has surpassed them. She has already learnt much more about the world outside than them. 'Our advice is not listened to and it is not wanted,' her mother says. 'When she was little, she agreed with all my opinions. Now she sits there without saying anything, but I know she doesn't agree with me.' Bella glares, but says nothing. 'I suppose our child-raising has been a failure.' In China there is no concept of the rebellious teenager.

▶ THE PASSIVE

Present simple passive
I am given, you/we/they are given, he/she/it is given

Present continuous passive
I am being given, you/we/they are being given, he/she/it is being given

Present perfect simple passive
I/you/we/they have been given, he/she/it has been given

For further information and practice, see page 85.

7 🔊 **1.3** Look at the grammar box. Which of the verbs in bold in 1–6 below also sound natural in the passive? Transform the sentences from active to passive. Listen and check.

> There are many children like Bella in China. They ¹ **admire** western brands. Their parents ² **have spoiled** them a little perhaps. Often these children ³ **receive** a better education than their parents. Their parents ⁴ **send** them to private schools and they ⁵ **encourage** them to go to university. In China the new economy ⁶ **is raising** everyone's hopes.

▶ WORDBUILDING forming adjectives from nouns

There are various endings in English: *-ful, -ish, -ent, -ious, -ive*, used to form adjectives from nouns.
support → supportive, rebel → rebellious

For further information and practice, see Workbook page 107.

A confused
generation

8 Pronunciation weak forms in passive verbs

a 🔊 **1.3** Work in pairs. Listen again to the passive verbs used in Exercise 7. Which parts of the verb are stressed? Which are not stressed?

b Practise saying these sentences, putting stress on the main verbs and un-stressing the auxiliary verbs.

1   A lot of changes **have been introduced** in China.
2   As a result, the average Chinese person **has been given** a better standard of living.
3   Couples **are only allowed** to have one child.
4   A lot of money **is invested** in each child's future.
5   But changes in this policy **are being discussed**.
6   The government **has been concerned** by the growing number of people over 60.

9 Complete the sentences by putting the verb in the correct tense, active or passive.

1   'Children _____ (grow) up much too quickly today. Girls of twelve _____ (dress) as if they are eighteen.'
2   'We _____ (leave) behind by all the new technology they use.'
3   'Our grandparents _____ (probably / work) harder than us, but they _____ (not / have) so much fun.'
4   'They _____ (live) longer and longer and we _____ (expect) to look after them. It's not fair.'
5   'Our parents aren't so different to us: they _____ (listen) to the same music, for example.'
6   'In recent years respect for wisdom and knowledge _____ (replace) by respect for money.'
7   'I rebelled against my parents. My children feel that they _____ (expect) to rebel, but in fact they have nothing to complain about or rebel against.'
8   'We _____ (often / criticise) for being selfish and having no moral values, but that's our parents' fault: we _____ (spoil) by them.'

Speaking

10 Work in groups. Discuss whether it was a young person or an older person that said each of the items in Exercise 9. Which of the statements do you agree with?

11 Do you think the 'gap' between your generation and your parents' generation is greater than the one between your generation and the next generation?

1c Bloodlines

Reading

1 Work in pairs. Why do you think people emigrate? What difficulties do you think they face when they settle in a new country? Compare your ideas with another pair.

2 Read the article about immigrants in New York. Answer the questions. Then compare your answers with your partner.

1 What is special about the area of Queens in New York?
2 What do Richard and Tanja's families have in common?
3 What are the differences between Richard's and Tanja's stories as immigrants?

3 Are the sentences true (T) or false (F) according to the article?

1 Immigrants in Queens feel attached to their new country.
2 People are much more interested in learning about distant ancestors than recent generations.
3 Some years after immigrating to America, Tomas met his brother in New York by accident.
4 Richard's grandmother has kept the family history alive.
5 Tanja's mother wasn't able to balance work with looking after her children's education.
6 Tanja and her sister have chosen to have similar careers to their parents.

4 Look at the article and choose the correct explanation of each phrase.

1 *a melting pot* (para 1)
   a a place of conflict
   b a place where all mix together
   c a place which attracts
2 *their ancestral roots* (para 2)
   a where their family came from originally
   b how they got to America
   c their parents' character
3 *one recurring theme* (para 3)
   a sad fact
   b common story
   c unusual quality
4 *seeking his fortune* (para 4)
   a hoping to get lucky
   b looking for the right job
   c looking for a way to get rich
5 *a must* (para 5)
   a a good thing
   b a right
   c a necessity

Critical thinking identifying the main aspect

5 Work in pairs. This article deals with different aspects of emigration. Identify the aspects in each of the first three paragraphs. Compare your answers with another pair to check you have identified the same themes.

6 Read the personal accounts of the immigrants again. Which of the aspects do their stories pick up on? Which aspects are not really mentioned again?

7 Discuss what the main aspect, or message, is of this article. Then ask other pairs if they have reached the same conclusion.

Speaking

8 Look at these phrases from the passage describing family characteristics or traits and discuss what they mean.

'He was clearly something of a free spirit.'
'My parents have a strong work ethic.'
'We've both inherited that desire to get ahead.'

9 Look at the questions below and note down your answers. Then ask your partner about their answers. Does family have a similarly strong influence in your lives?

HOW DOES FAMILY SHAPE YOU?

Would you say you are a close family?

How much time do you spend with family:
• out of a sense of duty?
• because you choose to?

Is family a consideration for you in choosing where to live?

How conscious are you of your family's history?

Is there a strong family trait? Have you inherited it?

Is there a 'head of the family'? How important is it to have this person's approval?

Is there someone in the family you particularly admire? Why?

Has your family influenced the career path that you have chosen?

When seeking advice, are you more likely to turn to friends or family?

How important is it to you that your family approves of your partner?

Would you say your family members have the same attitude to:
• money?
• bringing up children?

BLOOD LINES

America itself is well-known for being a melting pot of different ethnic groups and cultures, but nowhere is this diversity more pronounced than in Queens, New York. Here, second-generation Puerto Ricans live alongside third-generation Greeks and first-generation Koreans, all united by a common feeling of pride in their American identity.

However, they are also proud and curious about their ancestral roots. *National Geographic's Genographic Project*, known also as the Human Family Tree, set out to trace the origins and common ancestry of the various immigrants in this community by examining their genetic makeup using a simple DNA test. The study was well supported by local residents, but often what was of more immediate interest to people was something which intrigues us all: the history of our recent ancestry. In other words, how their grandparents and great-grandparents arrived in America, and what brought them there in the first place.

One recurring theme among immigrants seems to be the hard work and sacrifices that went in to building a new life and how their descendants now feel a duty to honour their efforts by working hard too. Here are two Queens residents' stories.

Richard, 38

My great-grandfather Tomas came to America from Poland when he was fifteen. His mother had become ill and died, and his father remarried to be able to take care of his seven children. Tomas didn't like his stepmother, so he ran away to Belgium, where he boarded a ship to America – without a ticket. He was clearly something of a free spirit. Arriving in America with nothing, he got a job on the railroads in California. Then one day he saw an announcement in a newspaper that was read by immigrants. It was from his brother in New York who was also seeking his fortune in America and was looking for him. Tomas got in touch and they had an emotional reunion in New York, where Tomas subsequently settled. This is the story that my grandmother has passed down to us, to my parents and all my aunts and uncles. She is an amazing woman and the head of the family, I suppose; the one who holds us all together. She's actually quite forgetful now, but she never forgets family details. What that has meant is that all of us – brothers, aunts, cousins – have a strong family bond and a strong sense of belonging to a group that has struggled and fought together to succeed here.

Tanja, 29

I'm a first generation American. Both my parents came here from Jamaica, where getting a good education is a must. My mother always says that people may take everything away from you, but they can never take away your education. My father was a nurse in Jamaica, but he had an ambition to be a doctor in the US; when he first came here, he studied during the day and went to work at night. My parents have a strong work ethic. My mum has always worked as a nurse, but at the same time has always been very involved in our lives also, helping with our studies and following our careers with interest. Both my sister and I have followed them into the medical profession and now I'm working as a doctor at the Mount Sinai hospital in Queens. I don't know if that kind of dedication is genetic or just something that you learn from your parents, but that desire to get ahead … we've certainly both inherited it. The great thing about America is that it gives you the opportunity to live those dreams too.

1d A face from the past

Real life meeting people you know

1 Work in pairs. Discuss the questions.

  1 When was the last time you bumped into someone that you hadn't seen for ages?
  2 What did you talk about?
  3 Had they changed a lot?

2 🔊 **1.4** Listen to a conversation between two people, Tim and Greta, who meet by accident in the street. Answer the questions.

  1 What have they been doing since they last met?
  2 What future arrangement do they make?

3 🔊 **1.4** Listen again and tick the expressions in the box the speakers use.

4 Find the ticked expression that matches sentences 1–6.

  1 how Greta expresses her surprise at meeting Tim
  2 how Greta asks Tim for his news
  3 what Tim says about Greta's appearance
  4 how Greta describes her business
  5 what Greta says about Amanda, their other friend
  6 how Greta says she can't carry on the conversation

5 Pronunciation expressive intonation

a 🔊 **1.5** Emotion (surprise, excitement, etc.) is often conveyed by expressive or exaggerated intonation. Flat intonation often suggests a lack of emotion or interest. Listen to these phrases and say if the intonation is expressive (E) or flat (F).

		E	F
1	Hello. Fancy seeing you here.	☐	☐
2	Oh, busy as ever.	☐	☐
3	How's it all going?	☐	☐
4	Sorry, I'm in a bit of a hurry.	☐	☐
5	Do you see much of Amanda?	☐	☐
6	You're looking well.	☐	☐

b Work in groups. Choose a phrase from the box and say it either with expressive intonation or with flat intonation. Ask the others in the group to say which intonation you used.

6 Imagine you are in a large shopping centre during your lunch break from work. Walk around and 'bump into' other people that you have met before. Find out what each person has been doing, and make a future arrangement. Then move on until you bump into someone else. Use the box to help you.

▶ **MEETING PEOPLE YOU KNOW**

Fancy meeting / bumping into / seeing you here!
What a (nice) surprise!

How are things?
What have you been up to?
How's it all going?

Busy as ever.
I've been completely snowed under.
It has its ups and downs.

You're looking well.
It obviously suits you.

Do you see much of Amanda?
How's Amanda getting on?
She was asking after you the other day.

Do give her my regards.
Say hello to her from me.

Well, I should probably go and …
Sorry, I've got to rush. / I'm in a bit of a hurry.
I don't mean to be rude, but I need to …
It was really nice to see you. / Great to see you.
Good luck with …

TALK ABOUT ▶ YOUR FRIENDS ▶ THE GENERATION GAP ▶ FAMILY INFLUENCES ▶ MEETING PEOPLE YOU KNOW
WRITE ▶ AN INFORMAL EMAIL

1e News from home

Writing an informal email

1 How often do you send news to friends and family? Do you communicate by letter, email, text message?

2 Read the email below from Ben to his friend, Fergus. Where is Ben and what is he doing there? How would you summarise the contents of each of the three paragraphs?

Dear Fergus

I hope all's well with you. I've been meaning to write for ages, but my journal takes up a lot of my time. Please don't think it's because I haven't been thinking about you all – I have and I'm getting quite homesick. But I have to remind myself of why I am here, which is to try and get established as a freelance journalist and photographer.

I'm now in Sri Lanka visiting some tea plantations and talking to people about how their lives have changed in the last 20 years or so. The countryside here is amazing. At the moment I'm in the hills just outside Kandy which are so lush and green, you wouldn't believe it. I'm trying to get an interview with one of the plantation owners that I can make into a feature for a magazine. Fingers crossed!

So, my plan is to stay here until the end of September and then get a plane back to the UK to see if I can find someone who will publish some of this stuff. It would be great to get together with you then. How is the family? Is Sarah still working for that horrible estate agent? Do give them all my love. I'll write again soon.

All the best,

Ben

---

3 What features of the language in this letter tell you that it is in an informal style?

4 Writing skill greetings and endings

Which of these other phrases for greeting and ending would be appropriate in an informal email to a friend or relative?

> All my love   Best wishes   Dear Mr Franks
> Dear Sir or Madam   Hello   Hi John
> Kind regards   Love   Regards   Warm regards
> Yours   Yours faithfully   Yours sincerely

5 Word focus *get*

a The verb *get* is used often in spoken or informal written English. Find five phrases / sentences in the letter where it is used. What does it mean in each case? Think of a synonym for *get* in each case.

b Read the sentences. Match the uses of *get* to a word with a similar meaning in the box.

> be (in passive sentences)   catch   do / manage
> persuade   reach   receive

1 Did you get my last letter?
2 How have you been getting on in your new job?
3 I got a virus which kept me in bed for two weeks.
4 We got delayed for four hours at the border.
5 I'm going to try to get him to come with me.
6 I'll call you when I get to London.

c Write three sentences of your own with *get* giving recent news about yourself. Work in small groups and read them to each other.

6 Imagine you have been away from home for some time. Write an email (200 words) to a friend or family member to ask them for news from home and to give them your news. Try to use the verb *get* at least twice.

7 Work in pairs. Exchange letters. Check for the following:

- Is the use of tenses correct?
- Is the style not too formal?
- Did they use the correct greeting and ending?

1f Immigration

Fleeing economic and political hardships, many millions left their homelands in Europe and Asia in search of a better life.

Before you watch

1 Work in groups. Look at the photo and discuss the questions.

1 Where are the people in the photo?
2 What do you think they are doing?
3 What does the caption tell us about the people?

2 Work in pairs. Write down five images you think you will see in the video.

An immigration officer checking the documents of a person arriving in the US by boat.

While you watch

3 Watch the video and check your ideas from Exercise 2.

4 Watch the first part of the video (to 02.30). Find and underline eleven errors. Write the correct information below the text.

Large numbers of immigrants have come to the United States since the early 17th century. Europeans settled mainly in the western half of the country. Immigrants from Asia and from Mexico settled mostly in the east and the northwest. Between 1892 and 1954, Ellis Island in Los Angeles Harbour admitted seventeen million immigrants. In 1907, as many as eleven thousand people a week were processed. And today, four out of every five Americans can trace part of their family history directly back to Ellis Island. Many of these immigrants settled on the Upper East side of Manhattan. The Tenement Museum shows how harsh their living conditions could be. Families of eleven people lived in small apartments with just two rooms. On the other side of the country, families arrived at Devil's Island in California, where conditions were more relaxed for Asians.

1 ....
2 ....
3 ....
4 ....
5 ....
6 ....
7 ....
8 ....
9 ....
10 ....
11 ....

5 Watch the second part of the video (02.31 to the end). Answer these questions.

1 How many legal immigrants arrive in the US each year?

2 What particular challenge is there along the US–Mexico border?

3 What have foreign-born citizens brought with them to the US?

4 How is the US economy affected by immigration?

5 What do immigrants usually share with people already living in the US?

6 How does this help the immigrants?

After you watch

6 Roleplay arriving at Ellis Island

Work in pairs.

Student A: Imagine you are an immigrant to the US arriving at Ellis Island. Read the information below and make notes.

Student B: Imagine you are an immigration officer at Ellis Island. Student A wants to enter the country as an immigrant. Read the information below and prepare questions to ask the immigrant.

- where you come from
- your journey
- why you want to come to the US

Act out the interview, then change roles and act out the interview again.

7 Lavinia Limon says, 'We're in a much better position because we have maintained our immigration flows.' What do you think she means? Do you agree with her?

8 Work in groups and discuss these questions.

1 What kind of problems do you think immigrants faced when they arrived in the United States in the 1920s?
2 Do you think immigrants face similar problems today?
3 Do you think immigrants should try to keep the customs and values of their home countries, or adopt those of their new country?

---

contend with (v) /kənˈtend wɪð/ deal with a difficult situation
discrimination (n) /dɪskrɪmɪˈneɪʃən/ treating a group of people in an unfair way
diverse (adj) /daɪˈvɜːs/ varied
flee (v) /fliː/ escape from
hardship (n) /ˈhɑːdʃɪp/ something that makes life difficult

harsh (adj) /hɑːʃ/ unpleasant and difficult to live in
leap (n) /liːp/ jump
partition (v) /pɑːˈtɪʃən/ divide
shore (n) /ʃɔː/ coast
tenement (n) /ˈtenəmənt/ a large building divided into apartments in a poor area of a city

Grammar

1 Read the article below about families. Answer the questions.

   1 What is the difference between a nuclear and an extended family?

   2 What are the benefits of an extended family?

2 Underline the right present tense form to complete the text. Then check your answers with your partner.

3 Work in pairs. Make a list of other advantages and disadvantages of living in an extended family. Then compare your answers with another pair.

When talking about family, a distinction [1] *is making / is made* between extended family and nuclear family. The nuclear family is the basic family unit of parents and children. The extended family is all the other members who [2] *are related / have been related* by blood and by marriage: aunts, uncles, grandparents, nieces, nephews, in-laws, etc. In the West, the importance of extended family [3] *has decreased / has been decreased* greatly in the last 50 years. But the extended family has many economic benefits. Grandparents [4] *help / are helped* with childcare and in turn they [5] *are looked after / have been looked after* when they are old by younger members of the family. Also, when houses and domestic chores [6] *are sharing / are being shared* by many, living costs are naturally lower. But in recent years more and more young people [7] *are choosing / have been choosing* to live in nuclear families and so the economics [8] *have changed / have been changing*. The older generation say that traditional family values [9] *are losing / are being lost*; but the more serious economic issue is that everyone's network of support [10] *has been taking / has been taken* away.

I CAN	
use present tenses	
talk about events in present time using active and passive forms	

Vocabulary

4 Read each definition and then put in the correct word.

   1 Someone who is also studying, like you = a _____ student

   2 Someone you go on a trip with = a _____ companion

   3 Someone who you can really depend on = a _____ friend

   4 Someone you and another friend both know = a _____ friend

   5 Someone you share an apartment with = a _____

   6 Someone you know but is not really a friend = an _____

   7 Someone you are related to by birth = a _____ relative

5 Work in pairs. Give details about one of the people in Exercise 4:

- who you hang out with regularly
- who you haven't kept up with
- whose house you go round to regularly

I CAN	
describe different types of friends and acquaintances	
use phrasal verbs that describe relationships	

Real life

6 Put the sentences below into the right order to complete the conversation between Karen (K) and Jim (J).

K: Hello Jim. Fancy bumping into you here. *1*

K: Great. Well, I should probably go. I'm in a bit of a hurry to get to the bank.

K: Of course I will. We should get together some time.

K: You know – busy as ever. He's working for BP now in London.

K: You too. Good luck with the work in New York.

K: Not bad, thanks. What have you been up to?

K: Have you? That sounds exciting. You're looking well.

J: Thanks. You too. How's David getting on these days?

J: Well, do give him my regards.

J: Yes, that would be nice. I'll get in touch when I'm back next month.

J: Well, it was great to see you.

J: I've been working in New York for the past month.

J: Oh hello, Karen. What a nice surprise! How are things?

7 Work in pairs. Imagine you meet each other in the street by accident. Act out a similar conversation.

I CAN	
have a conversation with someone I haven't seen for some time	

Speaking

8 Work in pairs. Tell each other about a relationship with a family member or friend that is important in your life.

Unit 2 Storytelling

Ayrton Senna at his last race, Imola, Italy, 1994.
Photograph by Dario Mitidieri

FEATURES

1 🎵 **1.6** Work in pairs. Look at the photo and the caption. What do you know about this man? Listen to a conversation about different accounts of his life. Answer the questions.

　1　What facts about his life do the speakers mention?
　2　How are the film and book different?

2 🎵 **1.6** What are the opposites of these adjectives? Which ones did the speakers use to describe the documentary and the biography about Senna? Listen again and check.

> accurate　biased　fair　objective　partial　sympathetic truthful

3 Match the adjectives (1–5) with the genres (a–e).

1	sentimental, touching	a	thriller
2	creepy, scary	b	historical drama
3	fast-moving, gripping	c	science fiction
4	original, thought-provoking	d	romantic comedy
5	powerful, authentic	e	horror

4 Describe to your partner a book or film you have enjoyed recently. Would you like to see the film or read the book your partner has described?

2a The film of the book

Vocabulary books and films

1 Work in pairs. Look at the photo below. What kind of film do you think this was a location for?

2 Do the words in the box relate to books, films or both? Put them into three categories.

> audience   author   best-seller
> blockbuster   box office   cast   chapter
> characters   director   location   plot
> portrayal   producer   publisher   readers
> scene   screenwriter   script   setting
> storyline   theme   trilogy

3 Match words from the books list and the films list to make pairs of words that are related. What is the difference between the words in each pair? Compare your list with another pair.

Example:

author and screenwriter – the author is the writer of a book, a screenwriter writes the script of a film

---

> ▶ **WORDBUILDING synonyms**
>
> There are often words which are close in meaning but not exactly the same. Or they have the same meaning but differ in use.
> *author* and *screenwriter*
>
> For further information and practice, see Workbook page 115.

Speaking and listening

4 Work in pairs. Ask each other the questions.

  1 Do you like to see film adaptations of books you have read?
  2 Do you sometimes read a book because you have seen the film?

5 🔊 **1.7** What do you think is the secret of making a good film adaptation of a book? Tell your partner if you agree with a, b or c. Then listen to an interview with a film critic and say which answer he gives.

  a to remain completely faithful to the details of the story and the characters in the book
  b to remain faithful to the spirit and main themes of the book
  c to create a story that works on film, even if it is not faithful to the book

6 🔘 **1.7** Answer the questions. Then listen again and check.

1 What do people generally think are the ingredients for a box office success?
2 What does the critic say about the success of film adaptations of books?
3 What are *Sense and Sensibility* and *The Shining* examples of, according to the critic?
4 What does the critic compare making a good film from a book to?
5 What is the central theme of *The Lord of the Rings*?
6 Why was it difficult to reproduce the world J.R.R. Tolkien created?
7 How did director Peter Jackson compensate for leaving out elements of the story in the book?

7 Work in groups. Discuss the questions.

1 Have you seen any good film adaptations of books? And any bad ones?
2 What made them good and bad?
3 Were the reasons similar to the ones described by the critic?

Grammar past simple and present perfect simple

8 Work in pairs. Match each sentence from the listening text (1–5) to one of the uses of the past simple (a–e).

1 Some film adaptations **have worked**, others **have flopped**.
2 'What is the secret?' That **was** the question I **put** earlier to Mark Mowlam.
3 He **has followed** the progress of many book-to-film adaptations in his time.
4 The author, Tolkien, **created** a magical world.
5 It **has become** one of the most successful films of all time.

a When the action is clearly linked to a specific time in the past we use the past simple.
b When the experience is more important than the time and the time is not stated we use the present perfect.
c We use the present perfect to talk about people's life experiences.
d If the person is dead we must use the past simple to talk about their lives.
e When we talk about a period of time that is not finished we use the present perfect (e.g. over the past few weeks, this year) even if the action itself is finished.

> ▶ **PAST SIMPLE and PRESENT PERFECT SIMPLE**
>
> **Past simple**
> *I visited / He visited ...*
> *I didn't visit ...*
> *Did you visit ... ?*
>
> **Present perfect simple**
> *I have visited / She has visited ...*
> *I have not visited ...*
> *Have you visited ... ?*
>
> For further information and practice, see page 86.

9 Look at the grammar box. Then put each verb in these pairs of sentences into the correct form, past simple or present perfect simple.

1 I first _____ (read) *The Hobbit* when I was twelve years old. What about you?
No, I _____ (never / read) *The Hobbit*, but I know a guy who _____ (read) it 24 times. He never gets tired of it.
2 There _____ (be) a lot of film adaptations of Stephen King books over the years.
Yes, I know. There _____ (be) a great adaptation of *The Green Mile* a few years ago.
3 _____ you ever _____ (write) a play or a screenplay?
No, but my great grandfather _____ (write) a play for radio.
4 _____ you _____ (see) *2001: A Space Odyssey* on TV last night?
No, but I _____ (see) it before. It's amazing, isn't it?

10 **Pronunciation the letter *l***

a 🔘 **1.8** Listen to three words which contain the letter *l*. Notice how *l* is pronounced in three ways. Listen again and repeat.

1 as a clear *l* before a vowel sound *location*
2 a dark *l* before a consonant sound *film*
3 silent *l* *would*

b 🔘 **1.9** Listen to these words and say which *l* sound you hear (1, 2 or 3). Compare your answers with your partner. Then practise saying each word.

> best-seller calm child details faithful to
> felt half loyal plot screenplay
> should told trilogy walk

Writing and speaking

11 Think about a living writer or filmmaker. Make notes about their life and work. Then describe this person's work to your partner. Ask questions.

2b A close shave

Reading

1 Work in pairs. Discuss how you would react if faced with the following dangerous situations. What do you think would be the right thing to do?

- a snake showing its teeth at you
- a shark swimming near you
- a bear approaching when you are eating a picnic

2 Have you had any 'close shaves' with dangerous animals? What happened? Tell the class.

3 Read the story below about three encounters two *National Geographic* reporters had with rhinos on the same day. What did the rhinos do in each case and how did the people react?

4 Look at the eight highlighted verbs in the article and guess their meaning from the context. Then check in a dictionary to see if you were right.

5 What effect does the use of these verbs have on the story?

KAZIRANGA National Park in India is home to two of the world's most endangered species: the tiger and the single-horned rhino. Photographer Steve Winter and writer Douglas Chadwick had only been working there a few days when they had a rather frightening close shave with some rhinos.

They were driving into the park to start filming, when their guide stopped the jeep to move a turtle from the middle of the road just ahead of them. Winter, Chadwick and their guard got out to stretch their legs and watch. But when Chadwick turned to look up the road, he saw something terrible.

About 50 metres away, a rhino was charging at them. Rhinos can sprint at more than 40 kilometres an hour, so there was no time to leap back in the car. Instinctively, the guard fired a shot into the ground just in front of the rhino. The crack of the rifle and the dirt that the bullet kicked up was enough to distract their attacker and he veered off into the grass seconds before reaching them.

Shaken, but relieved the incident had not been worse, they drove on. As they were entering the forest area on a raised section of road, three young rhinos climbed onto the road in front of them. The jeep stopped hurriedly, but this time the animals seemed uninterested and disappeared into the forest. Just then, however, the mother of the three, who had been keeping an eye on her young, came crashing through the trees from their left. No time to shoot this time. The female rhino slammed into the side of the jeep and started to wrestle it off the road. Indian rhinos don't use their horns in a fight; instead they bite and this female's teeth were gouging deep into the side of the jeep.

The guide had laid down a rule for his guests at Kaziranga – 'No one is allowed to be scared.' But his guests were breaking the rule, praying the driver could get them out of there. With the engine screaming, at last the vehicle skidded free. Even then the rhino came after them and it was only 150 metres later that she gave up the chase.

A CLOSE SHAVE

Grammar past tenses review

6 Look at the grammar box. Match the tenses (1–4) with their uses (a–d). Then find other examples of the tenses in the article.

1 past continuous
2 past simple
3 past perfect simple
4 past perfect continuous

a to describe the main events in sequence, i.e. one after another
b to refer to an action that happened earlier i.e. not in the main sequence of events
c to describe a (background) event in progress around the time of the main event
d to describe an action in progress before or up to the main event(s) in the past

> **▶ PAST TENSES REVIEW**
>
> **Past continuous**
> *They were driving into the park to start filming, when their guide stopped the jeep.*
>
> **Past simple**
> *Winter, Chadwick and their guard got out to stretch their legs and watch.*
>
> **Past perfect simple**
> *Shaken, but relieved the incident had not been worse, they drove on.*
>
> **Past perfect continuous**
> *Winter and Chadwick had only been working there a few days when they had a very close shave.*
>
> For further information and practice, see page 86.

7 Complete the summary of Winter and Chadwick's story using the past tense of the verbs given. Use contracted forms where possible.

Steve Winter and Douglas Chadwick, who
¹ _____ (work) in Kaziranga National Park,
² _____ (have) three close encounters with rhinos all on the same day. Before entering the park, their guide ³ _____ (tell) them not to be afraid, so they ⁴ _____ (be / not) especially worried, but clearly the incidents ⁵ _____ (shock) them. They ⁶ _____ (know) that filming in the Park was dangerous work, but they ⁷ _____ (not / expect) to meet danger quite so soon or so frequently. But it ⁸ _____ (not / stop) them carrying on!

8 Pronunciation contracted negative forms

a ⏺ **1.10** Listen to the summary in Exercise 7 and circle the verbs where the speaker uses contracted forms. How many syllables does each contracted form contain?

b ⏺ **1.11** Work in pairs. Read these other phrases to each other. Say how many syllables each contracted negative form has. Listen and check.

1 I *haven't* been to India.
2 It *isn't* far.
3 You *aren't* allowed.
4 It *doesn't* matter.
5 I *hadn't* noticed.
6 They *weren't* late.
7 She *hasn't* called.
8 We *didn't* care.

9 Complete these reports of lucky escapes by putting each verb in the most appropriate past tense. Use contracted forms where possible.

THE NEAR MISS

I ¹ _____ (mountain-bike) with a friend in Wales and we ² _____ (just / finish) a long off-road climb out of the Dysynni Valley. It ³ _____ (rain) earlier but now the sun ⁴ _____ (shine) and we ⁵ _____ (feel) quite warm. Since the rest of the route was downhill on tarmac roads, I ⁶ _____ (take) off my bike helmet and ⁷ _____ (set) off. Suddenly the road ⁸ _____ (become) very steep and the bike ⁹ _____ (pick) up speed quickly. There was a turn ahead in the road and I knew I was going to crash. The bike ¹⁰ _____ (go) straight into a wall, but luckily I …

THE UNEXPECTED

Mr Charles Everson and his wife Linda ¹¹ _____ (drive) home from church one Sunday when a cow ¹² _____ (fall) from the sky and ¹³ _____ (land) on the bonnet of their van. The cow, which ¹⁴ _____ (escape) from a breeding farm, ¹⁵ _____ (graze) too close to the edge of a cliff next to the road and ¹⁶ _____ (slip) and plunged 200 feet. When the emergency services ¹⁷ _____ (arrive) at the scene they …

---

10 ⏺ **1.12** Complete the last sentence of each story. Then listen to the stories and check your answers to Exercise 9. Compare your endings with what you hear.

Speaking

11 Prepare a description of a time that you had a near miss or lucky escape. Choose one of the following themes. Use each tense at least once. Then tell your story to your partner. When you come near to the end, stop and ask your partner what they think happened next.

• escaping injury or physical accident
• a scary incident when something unexpected happened
• getting away with something you did wrong

2c Once upon a time ...

Reading

1 Work in pairs. What were your favourite stories as a child? Tell your partner what they were about and why you still remember them.

2 Look at these titles of fairy tales by the brothers Grimm. Discuss the questions.

> Cinderella   Little Red Riding Hood
> Sleeping Beauty   Snow White
> The Elves and the Shoemaker   The Frog Prince

1 Which of these fairy tales is depicted in the photo on page 27?
2 Which of them are well known in your country?
3 What is the name for them in your language? Is the name similar or very different?

3 Where did the stories in Exercise 2 come from originally and what did the brothers Grimm do to them? Read the article and find out.

4 Look back at the article and find significant (or surprising) facts about the following:

1 the popularity of the Grimms' fairy tales now
2 the popularity of the Grimms' fairy tales at the time
3 Germany at the time the brothers were writing
4 the stories of *Little Red Riding Hood* and *Snow White*
5 the attitude of parents to the stories

5 The writer uses various words and expressions associated with fairy tales. Find these words and expressions and match them with the definitions below.

1 a long time ago (para 1)
2 the opposite of *a hero* (para 1)
3 clever and knowledgeable (para 1)
4 distant countries (para 1)
5 the lesson to be learnt (para 5)
6 a woman (often bad) who does magic (para 6)
7 the opposite of *kind* (para 6)
8 for the rest of time (para 7)

Critical thinking close reading

6 What conclusions can you draw about the brothers Grimm from reading this article? According to the text, are these statements true (T) or false (F)? Or is there not enough information (N) to say if the statements are true or false?

1 They were very motivated young men.
2 The brothers had an academic interest in these stories.
3 Their aim was to write down stories that had previously been told orally.
4 They were interested in the stories themselves, not the social message behind them.
5 Wilhelm disliked the cruelty and violence in the stories.
6 In the end the stories reached the mass audience that the brothers had wished them to.

7 Work in pairs. Summarise the brothers Grimms' achievement, according to the writer.

Word focus *keep*

8 Work in pairs. Find three phrases with the word *keep* in the passage. Discuss what each one means. Then do the same with the phrases in these sentences.

1 Please **keep an eye on** the time. We mustn't leave any later than ten thirty.
2 Try to **keep your chin up**. I know you must be frustrated with the lack of progress, but I'm sure things will get better.
3 I wouldn't tell him your news just yet, if I were you. He's not very good at **keeping a secret**.
4 Technology is moving so fast these days. It's difficult to **keep track** of all the changes.
5 Sorry, I don't want to **keep** you. I just need to ask you a quick question.
6 I always think it's a good idea to **keep a diary** when you are travelling – to look back on later.

Writing and speaking

9 Think of a traditional story or fairy tale you know well. Make notes on the main elements of the story. Use a dictionary if necessary.

10 Work in pairs. Tell each other your story as you remember it, or tell the same story but in a modern setting. When you have each other's stories, change partner and tell your new partner the story you were told.

Once upon a time ...

Once upon a time there lived in Germany two brothers who loved a good story – one with magic and danger, royalty and villains. At school they met a wise man who led them to a treasure – a library of old books with tales more enchanting than any they had ever heard. Inspired, the brothers began collecting their own stories, listening to the folktales people told them. Soon they produced their own treasure – a book of fairy tales that would charm millions in faraway lands for generations to come.

The brothers Grimm, Jacob and Wilhelm, named their story collection *Children's and Household Tales* and published it in Germany in 1812. The collection has been translated into more than 160 languages, from Inupiat in the Arctic to Swahili in Africa. As a world publishing phenomenon it competes with the Bible. The stories and their characters continue to feature in virtually every media: theatre, opera, comic books, movies, paintings, rock music, advertising, fashion. The Japanese have built two theme parks devoted to the tales. In the United States the Grimms' collection helped launch Disney as a media giant.

Such fame would have shocked the humble Grimms. During their lifetimes the collection sold few copies in Germany. The early editions were not even aimed at children. They had no illustrations, and scholarly footnotes took up almost as much space as the tales themselves. Jacob and Wilhelm Grimm viewed themselves as patriotic students of folklore. They began their work at a time when Germany had been occupied by the French under Napoleon. The new rulers suppressed local culture. As young scholars, the brothers Grimm began work on the fairy tale collection in order to save the endangered oral storytelling tradition of Germany.

Long before the Grimms' time, storytelling thrived in inns, barns and the homes of peasant women. During winter nights, as they sat spinning wool, women kept each other company and entertained themselves with tales of adventure, romance and magic. Altogether, 40 such storytellers delivered tales to the Grimms, many of them coming to their house in Kassel. One of them, 'Marie', was credited with narrating many of the most famous tales: *Little Red Riding Hood*, *Snow White* and *Sleeping Beauty*. But these were not from the German oral tradition. Marie had had French nannies who retold stories to her that they themselves had read in a collection written by Charles Perrault in 1697, *Tales of My Mother Goose*.

Although the brothers implied that they were just keeping records of tales, Wilhelm continued to polish and reshape the stories up to the final edition of 1857. In an effort to make them more acceptable to children and their parents, he stressed the moral of each tale, and emphasised gender roles. According to the Grimms, the collection served as 'a manual of manners.' To this day, parents read them to their children because they approve of the lessons in the stories: keep your promises, don't talk to strangers, work hard, obey your parents.

Yet despite all Wilhelm's additions, the core of these stories was left untouched, in all their medieval coarseness. The cruel treatment of children (the children Hansel and Gretel are put in a cage by a witch and then fattened ready for eating), the violent punishments handed out to the stories' villains (in the original Snow White the evil stepmother is forced to dance in red-hot iron shoes until she falls down dead), are too much for some parents.

So what accounts for their popularity? Some have suggested it is because the characters are always striving for happiness. But the truth probably lies in their origin. Grimms tales were born out of a storytelling tradition without boundaries of age or culture. The brothers' skill was to translate these into a universal style of writing that seems to mirror whatever moods or interests we bring to our reading of them. And so it was that the Grimms' fairy tales lived happily ever after.

coarseness (n) /ˈkɔː.snəs/ being rough and down-to-earth; a lack of sophistication or refinement
folklore (n) /ˈfəʊkˌlɔːr/ the traditional songs, stories, proverbs, legends of a society
nanny (n) /ˈnæni/ a woman paid to look after young children
spin (v) /spɪn/ to make natural fibre (like wool) into thread

2d What a disaster!

Real life reacting to stories

1 Work in pairs. What kind of things do you find often go wrong day-to-day: computers, transport, things in the house, forgetting things?

2 🔊 **1.13** Look at these extracts from six personal accounts of things that went wrong. Discuss what you think happened next. Then listen and check.

1 The bus broke down on the motorway, so we were all left stranded until help could arrive.
2 My trousers got caught on the door handle and as I walked away they tore.
3 I bent the key trying to force it into the door lock and when I tried to straighten the key it snapped.
4 The lift got stuck between floors 25 storeys up and two of the occupants were completely panic-stricken.
5 The tyres on my bicycle were badly worn and when I hit a bump in the road one of them burst.
6 My computer froze without any reason while I was working.

3 🔊 **1.13** Look at the responses below. Can you remember which ones were used in each of the conversations in Exercise 2? Tell your partner. Then listen again and check your answers.

> ▶ **REACTING TO STORIES**
>
> **Sympathising when something bad has happened**
> Oh, that's awful.
> How embarrassing!
> What a disaster!
> Oh, that's really awkward.
> Poor you!
> What a nightmare!
> Really? That's odd.
> Really? How strange!
>
> **Commenting on a good outcome to a bad situation**
> Phew!
> That must have been a relief.
> That was clever.
> That was good thinking.
> That was lucky.
> That was a stroke of luck.
>
> **Talking about similar experiences**
> I can sympathise with that.
> Yeah, I think I would have done the same thing.
> Yeah, a similar thing happened to me once.
> Yeah, I once had the same experience …

4 Pronunciation linking and assimilation

a 🔊 **1.14** Listen to these short responses. Notice how the underlined sounds are either linked as in *been a* or assimilated as in *what did*, where the *t* of *what* disappears and is replaced by the *d* of *did*. Repeat each phrase.

That must have been͜ a relief.

So what͜ did you do?

b 🔊 **1.15** Work in pairs. Underline the sounds in these sentences that you think are linked or assimilated. Then listen and check. Practise saying the sentences.

Linked	Assimilated
1 What a nightmare!	5 That was good thinking.
2 Oh, that's awful. Poor you!	6 A similar thing happened to me.
3 How embarrassing!	
4 Really? That's odd.	

5 Work in groups. Choose one of the following topics each and prepare to tell a short story about something that happened to you. Those listening to the story should react.

- a time you were lost or stranded
- something embarrassing that happened to you
- a minor accident you had
- a computer problem
- a situation when someone you were with panicked
- a situation where something broke or got stuck

2e A real-life drama

Writing a story

1 Read the opening paragraph from a story about two men walking in the Amazon rain forest in Peru. Answer the questions.

1 What happened to Rowan?
2 How are the two characters in the story feeling?

2 Work in pairs. Identify the events and actions in the story. Put them in chronological order.

'I can't move,' cried Rowan, 'my foot's caught in something – it's really painful.' Chris knew that Rowan was struggling. He had been moaning all day about his sore feet and they had only covered a kilometre in the last half an hour. Chris was tired too from trudging through the thick jungle, but was keen to get back to the camp before it got dark. They weren't carrying many supplies with them and neither had eaten anything for at least three hours. 'It's probably just a thorn bush or something,' he said encouragingly, walking back slowly to see what the problem was. 'Reach down and try to free your foot.' But as he got nearer, he could see that it wasn't a bush that had caught Rowan but a metal animal trap which had clamped itself firmly to his right ankle.

3 Why does the writer choose to start the story at the point when Rowan cries out?

4 Writing skill using descriptive words

a Look at the highlighted expressions in the story. Which describe movement and which a way of speaking? Discuss the exact meaning of each expression.

b Look at the words in bold in these sentences. Try to work out their meaning from the context. Then check in a dictionary to see if you were right.

Speaking

1 'Help', she **screamed**, 'that man, running away. He's just stolen my wallet.'
2 They continued on their way, but Jake could tell that Jess was unhappy, because she kept **muttering** under her breath.
3 He **mumbled** something about it being unfair, but I couldn't catch his exact words.
4 'Ok. Let's try your way then', she **said wearily**. She had lost the energy to argue.
5 'I'll go first,' he **said bravely**, but she could see that he was scared.

Moving

6 We **edged** our way along the narrow path, conscious of the steep drop to our left.
7 When he heard the car arrive, he **leapt** to his feet and ran to the door.
8 She **stumbled** on a rock and almost fell, but then regained her balance.
9 We **walked briskly** for the next hour but then reverted to a more usual pace.
10 She **turned apprehensively** towards the door, wondering whether she should enter.

c Do you know any other verbs that describe a particular way of speaking or moving? Tell the class.

5 Write the ending of the story (at least five sentences). Try to use some descriptive verbs and adverbs, but don't overuse them!

6 Exchange your ending with your partner. Use these questions to check your partner's story.

• Have they used the different past tenses correctly?
• Have they included some descriptive verbs and adverbs?

7 Then read other students' stories. Decide which ending you like best.

2f History of film

Before you watch

1 Work in groups. Look at the photo and discuss the questions.

1 What do you think the man in the photo is doing?
2 When do you think the photo was taken?
3 Why do you think the photo is made up of several images?

2 You are going to watch a video about the history of film. Tick the things and people you think you will see in the video.

> actors arriving at an awards ceremony
> the Arctic   Charlie Chaplin
> a documentary filmmaker   an earthquake
> an old film projector   an Oscar statue
> a scene from an animated film
> a scene from a melodrama

While you watch

3 Watch the video and check your answers from Exercise 2. Which other early actor is mentioned in the video?

4 Watch the first part of the video (to 01.36). Number the events in the order they happened.

a The projector was developed.
b People watched films in arcades.
c Hollywood became the centre of the studio system.
d Melodramas became popular.
e Actors became part of a new American aristocracy.
f Edison and Dickson invented the kinetoscope.

5 Watch the second part of the video (01.37 to the end). Answer the questions.

1 What has film allowed us to do outside of Hollywood?

2 Name four events that the video shows being covered by early newsmen.

3 Name two unusual activities you see as examples of how documentary filmmakers have used the camera in new ways.

4 How have studio blockbusters influenced documentaries?

6 Watch the video again. Complete the phrases with the missing time expressions.

1 _____ , film has captured the imagination of audiences all over the world.
2 _____ , inventors realised they could create the illusion of motion by presenting a quick succession of pictures.
3 _____ , projection allowed large audiences to view the spectacle at the local cinema or nickelodeon.
4 _____ , the emerging film studio system was centred in Hollywood, California.
5 _____ , newsmen carried cameras looking for real spectacles and history in the making.
6 _____ , documentary filmmakers have learned to borrow from the studio blockbusters.

After you watch

7 Roleplay an interview with an actor or actress

Work in pairs.

Student A: Imagine you are a famous Hollywood actor or actress. Choose who you want to be. Read the information below and make notes.

Student B: You are going to interview a famous Hollywood actor or actress. Read the information below and prepare questions.

- background
- career to date (films and other work)
- how Hollywood has changed over the years

Act out the interview, then change roles and act out the interview again. Student B should choose a different actor or actress.

8 Work in groups and discuss these questions.

1 What kind of films do you prefer watching?
2 Do you enjoy watching documentaries? Why? / Why not?
3 How important is the film industry in your country?

> **arcade** (n) /ɑːˈkeɪd/ a passage with a roof and shops on both sides
> **entrancing** (adj) /ɪnˈtrɑːnsɪŋ/ fascinating
> **flickering** (adj) /ˈflɪkərɪŋ/ quick-moving and not very clear
> **landmark** (n) /ˈlændmɑːk/ an important historical moment
> **loop** (n) /luːp/ a circle
> **melodrama** (n) /ˈmelədrɑːmə/ an old style of drama that has exaggerated emotion and action
> **nickelodeon** (n) /nɪkəlˈəʊdjən/ an old type of cinema
> **peep** (v) /piːp/ look at something with difficulty
> **projection** (n) /prəˈdʒekʃən/ showing film on a screen
> **tinseltown** (n) /ˈtɪnsəltaʊn/ another name for Hollywood
> **train** (v) /treɪn/ point a camera lens at something
> **vaudeville** (n) /ˈvɔːdəvɪl/ a type of variety show

UNIT 2 REVIEW

Grammar

1 Complete the story below about a narrow escape told by wildlife photographer Neil Brompton. Put each verb into the correct tense: present perfect simple, past simple, past continuous, past perfect simple or past perfect continuous.

I [1] _____ (film) lions a lot – ever since I was 25 years old – and I [2] _____ (never / have) serious problems with them. Strangely, I [3] _____ (feel) most at danger when lions [4] _____ (want) to play. I remember an expedition a few years ago in Tanzania. I [5] _____ (sit) in my tent reading just after sunset. One of our guides [6] _____ (call) out 'Lion!' That [7] _____ (not / be) particularly unusual, so I [8] _____ (not / take) much notice. But when the guide [9] _____ (call) out again I looked out and saw that two lions [10] _____ (slowly / approach) our camp.
We [11] _____ (park) our car some distance away and it was too far to reach. So I [12] _____ (run) back to the tent and quickly [13] _____ (zip) it up. I could hear a lot of noise coming from the kitchen, so I [14] _____ (assume) the guides [15] _____ (go) back there to make a noise to scare the lions off. I [16] _____ (wait) ten minutes and when the noise [17] _____ (die) down a bit, I [18] _____ (look) out again. The two guides [19] _____ (lock) themselves in the car. The lions themselves were gone but where they [20] _____ (play) in the kitchen, there was an incredible mess of pots and pans and spilled food.

2 Work in pairs. Answer these questions.

1 Where did Neil hide from the lions?
2 What did Neil think the guides had done to save the situation?
3 What had actually happened?

I CAN	
talk about past experience (present perfect and past simple)	
use narrative tenses to tell a story or give an account of events	

Vocabulary

3 Choose the correct words.

1 A documentary should be *biased / impartial* and factually *accurate / authentic*.
2 The *author / publisher* of a book must make sure the *characters / cast* are believable.
3 I'm reading a thriller. The *script / plot* is very *gripping / touching*.
4 The film gives the *audience / cast* a very realistic *scene / portrayal* of life in nineteenth-century England.
5 The film was a *best-seller / blockbuster* based on a science fiction book with some very *thought-provoking / sympathetic* ideas.

4 Work in pairs. Describe a film of a book you have read. Was it a successful adaptation? How faithful was it to the book?

I CAN	
describe films and books	
talk about the different elements of a film or book	

Real life

5 Match the piece of news (1–6) with a response (a–f).

1 My pen leaked and ink went all over my jacket and my shirt, but it came out in the wash.
2 The garden was OK because we had asked a neighbour to water it while we were away.
3 When I got home at midnight all the lights in the house were on, but no one was there.
4 I went all the way to London to get my new passport, only to find the office is closed on Mondays.
5 He asked me for my honest opinion, so I gave it.
6 I picked up the phone and started reading the messages and then I realised it was my boss's phone.

a Poor you!
b Yes, I think I would have done the same thing.
c Really? That's odd.
d That must have been a relief.
e How embarrassing!
f That was good thinking.

6 Work in pairs. Tell each other about something bad (embarrassing, annoying, a narrow escape, etc.) which happened to you recently.

I CAN	
react to stories in a natural way	

Speaking

7 Work in small groups. Use the first and last lines below to make your own fairy tale. When you are ready each person should tell the story to a member of another group.

" There were once two neighbours, one very lazy and the other very hard-working …

… And so it was that these two, who had been enemies for so long, became the greatest of friends. "

Unit 3 Science and technology

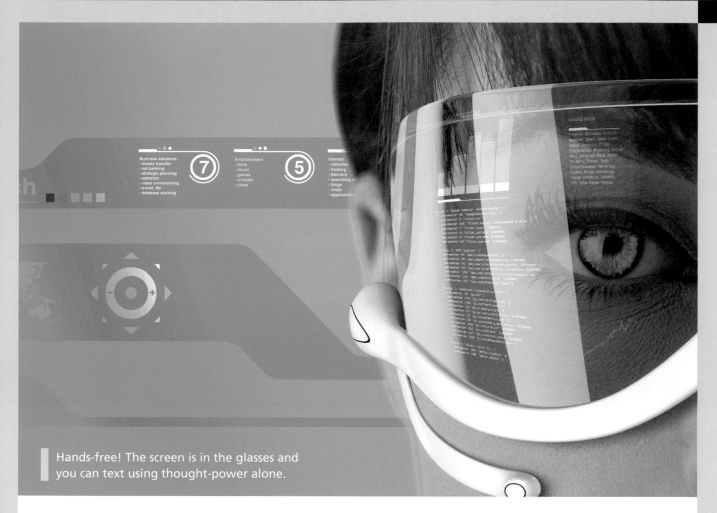

Hands-free! The screen is in the glasses and you can text using thought-power alone.

FEATURES

1 How much do you depend on technology in your day-to-day life and work? How affected are you if you lose your phone or if your computer crashes?

2 Work in pairs. Look at the photo and read the caption. Now look at the words below. In which of the areas is the technological breakthrough in the photo? In which area do you think the main breakthrough of the next 50 years will come?

> artificial intelligence   communications   energy use
> medicine   space exploration   transport

3 🔊 1.16 You are going to listen to three people making predictions about the future. Read their predictions. What justification do you think they will make for their prediction? Listen and check.

1 I expect that most of my generation will live to be around 100 years old.
2 I think in future people will be interacting with intelligent machines even more than they do now.
3 I don't think global warming is going to be the problem that everyone says it is.

4 Which of the predictions do you think will come true? Tell your partner.

Is technology the answer?

Kolkata's streets crammed with vendors, pedestrians and taxis.

Speaking

1 Work in groups. Look at the photo. Which of these following problems does it illustrate?

> congestion   epidemic
> overpopulation   pollution
> poverty   starvation

2 Which of these problems could have a technological solution?

Listening

3 🔊 **1.17** Read the opinions (1–3). Then listen to the presentation about overpopulation. Match the opinion with the people (a–c).

1   Whenever the population is too big, a disaster happens and reduces it.
2   Many people will die because there is not enough food for the growing population.
3   Science and technology will find a solution to the problem of overpopulation.

a   the speaker
b   Thomas Malthus
c   Paul Ehrlich

4 🔊 **1.17** Listen again. Are the sentences true (T) or false (F)?

1   The speaker has some ideas for action which can immediately solve the problem of overpopulation.
2   Paul Ehrlich thought that we should control the number of babies being born.
3   There will be seven billion people in the world by the middle of the century.
4   Nanotechnology has saved the world from mass starvation.
5   There is not enough space on the Earth for nine billion people.
6   The growth in the 'global middle class' will put big pressure on resources.
7   According to the speaker, people are basically lazy. They will only act when they have to.

5 What is the meaning of each underlined prefix in these words from the passage? Match the prefix (1–6) to the meaning (a–f).

1   <u>bio</u>fuels   a   very small
2   <u>nano</u>technology   b   very big
3   <u>mega</u>cities   c   extremely
4   <u>micro</u>phone   d   of life or living things
5   <u>semi</u>-retired   e   half
6   <u>ultra</u>-cautious   f $\times 10^{-9}$

> ▶ **WORDBUILDING prefixes**
>
> There are many prefixes in English taken from Latin and Greek, each of which have a particular meaning.
> *micro*phone, *mega*city
>
> For further information and practice, see Workbook page 123.

6 Do you share the speaker's faith in science and technology? Why? / Why not?

7 Pronunciation /r/ and /t/ in American English

a 🔊 1.18 The speaker of the passage is American. Listen to these words from the passage. What can you say about how she pronounces the letter *r*? And the letter *t*?

answer	better	birth	eating	first
heart	megacities	part	rate	world

b 🔊 1.19 Now listen to these phrases said by an American speaker. Write in the missing words. How do you think a British speaker would pronounce /r/ and /t/ in these phrases?

1 _____ metres
2 an _____ site
3 a _____ bar
4 a _____ letter
5 a _____ birthday
6 a _____ beater

c 🔊 1.20 Listen and check.

Grammar future forms review

> ### ▶ FUTURE FORMS REVIEW
>
> **will**
> One moment, I'll just adjust my microphone.
> It will be a bad thing for the planet if all those people start eating meat and driving big cars.
> The population will probably peak at around 9 billion by the middle of the century.
> **going to**
> I'm not going to speak for too long.
> Those of you who have come here looking for answers are going to be disappointed.
> **about to**
> Science is about to step in again with nanotechnology solutions.
> **Present continuous**
> I'm speaking to a government committee tomorrow.
> **Present simple**
> Oh, by the way, one more thing: the necessity train arrives in half an hour.
>
> For further information and practice, see page 87.

8 Look at the grammar box. Match the verb forms (1–5) with their uses (a–i). Some verb forms have more than one use.

1 *will*
2 *going to*
3 *about to*
4 present continuous
5 present simple

a a scheduled or timetabled event
b a future event in an *if* or *when* clause
c a prediction
d a confident prediction based on present information
e a decision made at the time of speaking
f an intention or previously made decision
g a formal arrangement
h a simple statement of fact
i an event in the immediate future

9 Underline the correct future forms in this presentation. Sometimes there is more than one possibility.

I think ¹ *we wait / we'll wait* a few moments until everyone ² *arrives / will arrive* … OK, ³ *I am beginning / I'll begin* now. Hello everyone and thank you for coming to hear my presentation about appropriate technology. I am ⁴ *about to / going to* speak for about 30 minutes and then I ⁵ *will take / am taking* your questions. If there ⁶ *is / is going to be* anything that you don't understand, please ask me then rather than during the presentation. My colleague, Liesel Babel, ⁷ *talks / is talking* this afternoon in the green seminar room, if people would like to learn more about appropriate technology. I think her session ⁸ *starts / is starting* at two o'clock. She ⁹ *is speaking / will speak* about her experience in the field, working on various development projects in Africa. OK ¹⁰ *I am going to show / I'll show* you a short film now, so could someone at the back please turn the lights down?

10 🔊 1.21 Complete the radio news headlines about overpopulation using an appropriate future form. Then listen and check.

1 World leaders _____ (meet) in Geneva tomorrow to discuss the issue of overpopulation.
2 In the next few weeks, the government _____ (introduce) a fee for each child that couples have after their first two children.
3 Scientists say that space colonies _____ (be) the only solution for overpopulation in the medium term.
4 Doctors have said that in future they _____ (not / spend) so much effort keeping the old alive.
5 The government _____ (launch) a new education programme later today to encourage women to have fewer children.
6 People _____ (have to) change their lifestyles if they _____ (want) the world's resources to support the growing population in the coming years.

11 Work in pairs. Underline all the time expressions in the sentences in Exercise 10. Then put them in order of the nearest to the most distant future. Compare your answers with another pair.

Speaking

12 Work in groups. Decide which of the ideas in Exercise 10, or one of your own, are the best course of action for dealing with overpopulation. Then explain your plan and the reasons for it to the rest of the class.

3b Revealed world

Speaking

1 Work in pairs. What information (news, travel advice, maps, a grammar rule, etc.) do you get through printed media and what through digital media?

> ▶ **WORDBUILDING compound nouns (noun + noun)**
>
> We can use two nouns together to mean one thing.
> *information overload, computer graphics*
>
> For further information and practice, see Workbook page 123.

R E V E A L E D

W O R L D By Tim Folger

Reading

2 Work in pairs. Look at the picture and the labels. Which information would you find useful or interesting if you were a visitor in Washington D.C.? What other information might you want?

3 Read the article about augmented reality and complete the table.

Other terms for augmented reality:	1	*AR*
	2	
Examples of augmented reality already in use:	3	
The kind of information we will be able to access:	4	*restaurant menus and prices*
	5	
Devices we will use to see the augmented reality world:	6	
	7	
Future applications for augmented reality technology:	8	*3-D repair instructions*
	9	

The regular world presented to us by our five senses – you could call it reality 1.0 – is not always the most user-friendly of places. We get lost in unfamiliar cities; we meet people whose language we don't understand. So why not try the improved version: augmented reality (AR) or reality 2.0? AR technology superimposes computer-generated images on the real world, via a mobile phone camera or special video glasses.

Early forms of AR are already here. With the right downloads, smart phones can deliver information about nearby ATMs and restaurants and other points of interest. But that's just the beginning. A few years from now the quantity of information available will have increased enormously. You will not only see that there's a Chinese restaurant on the next block, you will be able to see the menu and prices, read reviews of it and even find out how busy it is at the time.

This is where the next revolution in computing will take place: not in ever-more sophisticated games that exist in a virtual reality world, but rather in the interface between the real world and the information brought to us via the Internet. Imagine bubbles floating before your eyes, filled with cool information about anything and everything that you see in front of you. Information overload? Perhaps not.

Let's jump ahead to ten years from now. A person trying to fix their car won't be looking at a repair manual online or a book with illustrations; they will be wearing a device that projects animated 3-D computer graphics onto the equipment under repair, labelling parts and giving step-by-step guidance. Such technology is already being used by trainee mechanics in the US marines.

The window onto the AR world can be a smart phone or special video glasses that look like wraparound sunglasses. But in ten years' time these will have been replaced by contact lenses etched with tiny LEDs, which display text and images at a readable distance in front of the eye. So a deaf person wearing these inconspicuous lenses will be able to see a real-time transcript of what people are saying as they speak.

The question is: while we are all absorbed in our new augmented reality worlds, how will we be interacting with each other?

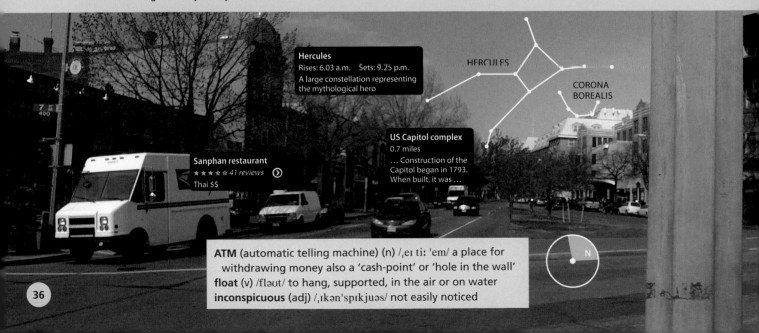

Hercules
Rises: 6.03 a.m.   Sets: 9.25 p.m.
A large constellation representing the mythological hero

HERCULES

CORONA BOREALIS

Sanphan restaurant
★★★★☆ *41 reviews* ⊙
Thai $$

US Capitol complex
0.7 miles
… Construction of the Capitol began in 1793.
When built, it was …

ATM (automatic telling machine) (n) /ˌeɪ tiː ˈem/ a place for withdrawing money also a 'cash-point' or 'hole in the wall'
float (v) /fləʊt/ to hang, supported, in the air or on water
inconspicuous (adj) /ˌɪkənˈspɪkjuəs/ not easily noticed

4 Discuss the questions. Then tell the class what you think.

1 Which of the AR applications described in the article do you think will be really useful?
2 Can you think of any other possible applications?
3 What do you think is the answer to the author's final question?

Grammar future continuous and future perfect simple

5 Look at the sentences (a–e) from the article and the verbs in bold. Answer the questions.

1 Which sentences describe an action in progress at a certain time in the future?
2 Which sentences describe an action completed before a certain point of time in the future?

a A few years from now the quantity of information available **will have increased** enormously.
b Ten years from now a person trying to fix their car **won't be looking** at a repair manual.
c They **will be wearing** a device that projects animated 3-D computer graphics onto the equipment under repair.
d In ten years time this device **will have been replaced** by contact lenses etched with LEDs.
e But in our new augmented reality worlds, how **will we be interacting** with each other?

▶ **FUTURE CONTINUOUS and FUTURE PERFECT SIMPLE**

Future continuous
We will be using …
We won't (will not) be using …
Will we be using …?
Future perfect simple
We will have used …
We won't (will not) have used …
Will we have used …?

For further information and practice, see page 88.

---

6 Look at the grammar box. Complete predictions (1–10) for mobile technology made by various industry experts by putting the verb in the future continuous or future perfect simple.
Ten years from now …

1 … very few people in the developed world _____ (use) credit cards because mobile phone payment _____ (replace) them.
2 … it is predicted that people _____ (sit) in front of traditional computers much less than they do now.
3 … data security _____ (become) a huge issue because mobile devices will store so much personal information.
4 … advertisers _____ (put) their adverts on mobile devices rather than on traditional media like TV, magazines, etc.
5 … we _____ (get) accustomed to advertisements which target us directly with personalised messages.
6 … body sensors connected to our mobile devices _____ (provide) us with real-time information about our health.
7 … the problem of short battery life in phones _____ (disappear) because phones and mobile devices _____ (use) more sophisticated power sources, like kinetic energy.
8 … mobile phones _____ (become) very sophisticated, so that as well as being your diary, address book and music player, you _____ (also / use) them as your secretary, accountant and lawyer.
9 … everyone _____ (use) universal translators in their mobile phones, which will make language learning less necessary.
10 … it is unlikely that we _____ (find) a way to use technology to know exactly where people are, because legally it is so difficult.

Speaking

7 Work in groups. Discuss the predictions for mobile technology in Exercise 6 and decide which ones you think will come true and which not. Then make two more predictions of your own.

Peregrine Expresso
195 feet
Free Wi-Fi

3c One size doesn't fit all

Reading

1 What does the term 'one size fits all' mean when used to describe a product? What products could it be applied to?

2 Read the article once quickly. Are the facts about appropriate technology true (T) or false (F)?

1 It's simple technology.
2 It's used in developing countries.
3 It improves people's lives.

3 Find a phrase in the article that defines what 'appropriate technology' means these days. What does the author say about this?

4 Work in pairs. Discuss what each of these devices is. Read the article again. What does the author use each as an example of?

a central heating system	a water purifier
a device for shelling corn	an efficient cooking
a sewing machine	stove
a solar-powered lamp	

5 Look at these phrases in bold from the article. Then choose the correct definition of the sentence.

1 in a way that **empowered** them (para 1)
   gave them more *energy / control*
2 **intermediate** technology solutions (para 2)
   temporary / not too complicated solutions
3 **has its place** in the developed world (para 3)
   can also *be useful / be found* in
4 a way to **harness** the energy (para 4)
   a way to *convert / make use of* the energy
5 they **valued** the time (para 5)
   they *appreciated / calculated* the time
6 **gas-guzzling** cars (para 6)
   cars that consume *a lot of petrol / little petrol*

Critical thinking balancing arguments

6 What are the potential risks and benefits associated with appropriate technology? Find the arguments in the article and make notes.

7 Work in pairs. Compare your answers. Is the author in favour of appropriate technology or not?

Vocabulary useful devices

8 Look at the expressions in bold in definitions 1–7. Complete the definitions with these adjectives.

appropriate	easy	efficient	long-term	old
renewable	useful			

1 It's a very **neat** solution: both clever and
   appropriate .
2 It's a **time-consuming process**. We need to find a solution that's more _____ .
3 We don't just want a **quick fix**; we want a _____-_____ solution.
4 It's a **handy gadget**, much more _____ than an average penknife.
5 It's not **cutting-edge technology**, but often the _____ ways are the best.
6 It's essentially a **labour-saving device**; it makes cutting up wood very _____ .
7 It's an **environmentally-friendly product** because it's made from _____ materials.

9 Work in pairs. Tell your partner about your favourite device or gadget in the home. Use one of the expressions in Exercise 8.

Speaking

10 Work in pairs. Complete the sentences (1–8) using these phrases. Discuss what you think each product is.

6 hours	6 people	light and a little heat
only £1.90	only 2 kilos	
put up in a few minutes		solar power
strong nylon		

Product 1
1 It can hold up to …
2 It's made of …
3 It can be …
4 It weighs …

Product 2
5 It runs on …
6 It lasts up to …
7 It costs …
8 It provides …

11 Work in groups. You are going to take part in a competition: 'Best appropriate technology product of the year'. Your group will have to present one of the products shown below. Look at the instructions on page 81.

one size doesn't fit all

Even if the term 'appropriate technology' is a relatively new one, the concept certainly isn't. In the 1930s Mahatma Gandhi claimed that the advanced technology used by western industrialised nations did not represent the right route to progress for his homeland, India. His favourite machines were the sewing machine, a device invented 'out of love', he said, and the bicycle, a means of transport that he used all his life. He wanted the poor villagers of India to use technology in a way that empowered them and helped them to become self-reliant.

This was also the philosophy promoted by E.F. Schumacher in his famous book *Small is Beautiful*, published in the 1970s, which called for 'intermediate technology' solutions. Do not start with technology and see what it can do for people, he argued. Instead, 'find out what people are doing and then help them to do it better'. According to Schumacher, it did not matter whether the technological answers to people's needs were simple or sophisticated. What was important was that solutions were long-term, practical and above all firmly in the hands of the people who used them.

More recently the term 'appropriate technology' has come to mean not just technology which is suited to the needs and capabilities of the user, but technology that takes particular account of environmental, ethical and cultural considerations. That is clearly a much more difficult thing to achieve. Often it is found in rural communities in developing or less industrialised countries. For example, solar-powered lamps that bring light to areas with no electricity and water purifiers that work simply by the action of sucking through a straw. But the principle of appropriate technology does not only apply to developing countries. It also has its place in the developed world.

For example, a Swedish state-owned company, Jernhuset, has found a way to harness the energy produced by the 250,000 bodies rushing through Stockholm's central train station each day. The body heat is absorbed by the building's ventilation system, then used to warm up water that is pumped through pipes over to the new office building nearby. It's old technology – a system of pipes, water and pumps – but used in a new way. It is expected to bring down central heating costs in the building by up to twenty per cent.

Wherever it is deployed, there is no guarantee, however, that so-called 'appropriate technology' will in fact be appropriate. After some visiting engineers observed how labour-intensive and slow it was for the women of a Guatemalan village to shell corn by hand, they designed a simple mechanical device to do the job more quickly. The new device certainly saved time, but after a few weeks the women returned to the old manual method. Why? Because they valued the time they spent hand-shelling: it enabled them to chat and exchange news with each other.

In another case, in Malawi, a local entrepreneur was encouraged to manufacture super-efficient wood-burning stoves under licence to sell to local villagers. Burning wood in a traditional open fire, which is a common method of cooking food in the developing world, is responsible for 10–20% of all global CO_2 emissions, so this seemed to be an excellent scheme. However the local entrepreneur was so successful that he went out and bought himself a whole fleet of gas-guzzling cars. 'We haven't worked out the CO_2 implications of that yet,' said a spokesman from the organisation that promoted the scheme.

3d Computer problems

Real life asking for and offering technical help

1 Work in pairs. Ask and answer the questions.

1 How are your computer skills?
2 Do you feel confident that you can use the following applications proficiently?

- a search engine (e.g. Google)
- spreadsheets (e.g. Excel)
- a presentation slide show (e.g. PowerPoint)
- photo editing (e.g. Photoshop)
- word processing (e.g. Microsoft Word)

2 Where do you turn for help if you can't do something on the computer? Do people turn to you for help?

3 🔊 1.22 Listen to a conversation about a computer problem. What is Ben trying to do? What two possible solutions does Sophie propose?

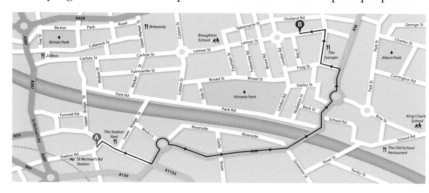

4 🔊 1.22 Listen again and complete sentences 1–10.

▶ ASKING FOR AND OFFERING TECHNICAL HELP	
Person in need of help	**Helper**
Can you give me a hand? I'm having trouble ¹ _____ .	
	OK. What do you want to do exactly?
I'm trying to ² _____ .	
	You could just ³ _____ .
The trouble is ⁴ _____ .	
	Let me have a look.
What shall I do then?	
	There are two possibilities. You can either ⁵ _____ or …
What does that involve?	
	I'll show you. Just ⁶ _____ . That should do the trick.
I see, but ⁷ _____ . What else do you suggest?	
	Have you tried ⁸ _____ ? If you do a search, you might ⁹ _____ .
OK I'll give that a try.	
	Feel free to ¹⁰ _____ .

5 Pronunciation stress in two-syllable verbs

a 🔊 1.23 Work in pairs. Listen to these phrases and note how the stress in the two-syllable verbs falls on the second syllable. Then practise saying them with your partner.

What do you su<u>gg</u>est?
What does that in<u>volve</u>?
It won't a<u>llow</u> me to copy it.
First se<u>lect</u> the picture, …
What are you trying to ach<u>ieve</u>?
What solution do you pro<u>pose</u>?
Did you a<u>ttach</u> the document?

b Think of two more two-syllable verbs. Put them into a phrase or sentence. Then tell another pair your words.

6 Choose one of the tasks below or think of a technical problem that you have had. Then roleplay a conversation similar to the one in Exercise 4. Use the box to help you. Begin like this:

> *Can you help me? I'm trying to edit this photo.*

> *I'll try. What do you want to do exactly?*

- editing a photo (of a person to leave only the head and shoulders)
- sorting a list of names (members of a club you are the secretary of) alphabetically from A–Z
- adding your comments to someone else's document (a report written by a colleague)
- making your presentation slides more interesting (they are just plain text at the moment)
- searching the Internet to get the right information (e.g. up to date news about smart technology)

3e A technical problem

Writing short email requests

1 Match the emails (1–4) with the correct reply (A–D) below. Answer the questions.

  1 What is the relationship between the correspondents in each case?
  2 What help is offered in response to each request?

2 Writing skill being polite

a How polite you are depends on your relationship to your correspondent and on what you are asking for. Underline the phrases used to make polite requests in emails 1–4 and the polite forms used to apologise in emails A–D.

b Now answer the questions.

  1 What word is used often for requests in the more formal relationships?
  2 What is the difference between *can you …* and *could you … ?*
  3 Is *would you mind -ing* more or less direct than *could you please?*
  4 What is a more formal way of saying *I'm sorry?*
  5 What auxiliary verb is used to mean *please?*

3 Word focus *out of*

a Work in pairs. Underline the expressions with *out of* in the emails and discuss what you think they mean. Then compare your answers with another pair.

1 Three months ago I bought one of your X3000 digital cameras from a shop in Oxford, which has since gone out of business. The camera is fine but I cannot find the user manual. Could you please tell me where I can find one? I've looked on the Internet, but without success. Thank you.

2 I bought a printer at your store only five weeks ago and the pages are coming out very faint. I am very disappointed and would like to return it and get a new one. Please can you advise me how to go about this?

3 Thanks a lot for the advice with the car, Jim. I changed the air filter and it's going much better now. Just out of interest, do you happen to know what kind of evo-chip I'd need to improve its performance? If so, do drop me a line to let me know.

4 Would you mind popping over and having a look at my bike some time? It's making a strange noise. I'd be really grateful. Please don't go out of your way though. Anytime in the next week is fine.

b Complete these other expressions with *out of* using the words given.

> blue   date   hands   luck   order   time

  1 I've done all I can to get them to change their decision. It's out of my _____ now.
  2 She is still in shock after losing her job; the news came out of the _____ .
  3 I'm afraid that printer is out of _____ – you'll have to use the one in the next office.
  4 This information is out of _____ – it's got last year's figures on it, not this year's.
  5 I'm sorry we are out of _____ . Let's carry on the discussion tomorrow.
  6 You're out of _____ there, I'm afraid. We sold the last one an hour ago.

4 Look at the following situation and write a short email requesting help.

You bought two cartridges for your printer online, but when they arrive you notice that the best before date on them has already passed. Write and ask for replacements to be sent.

5 Exchange emails with your partner. Use these questions to check your partner's email. Then write a reply.

  • Is the situation and the action demanded clear?
  • Is the email in the right register (formal or informal) and polite in its request?

A Sorry, I'd love to help, but I'm going on holiday tomorrow for three weeks. Why not take it to Cycle Surgery on the High Street? They're not expensive and they know their stuff.

B I am sorry, but an exchange is out of the question. It is too long after the original purchase date. However, from what you say, my guess is that it is just out of ink. Please check the ink cartridges. If that does not work, contact our technical team for further advice.

C I'm afraid I'm a bit out of my depth there. Try looking at the discussions boards for your particular model on the Internet. I'm sure someone'll know.

D I regret to say that we only supply user manuals with the equipment at the time of purchase. However, you can download one by following the link below.

3f Augmented reality

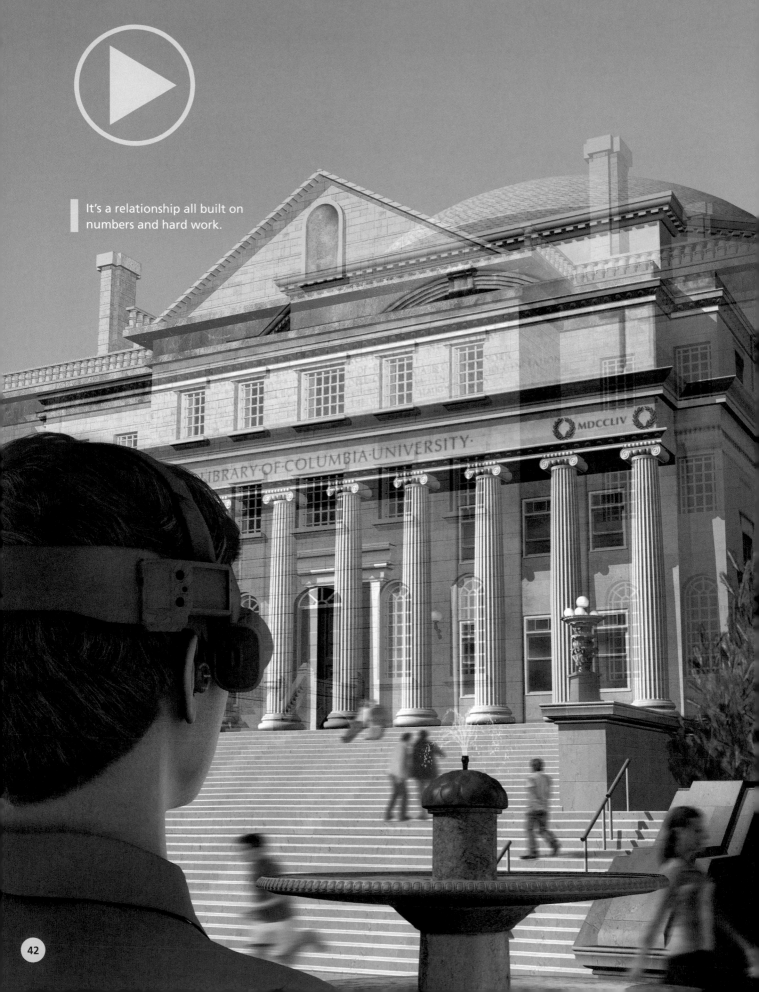

It's a relationship all built on numbers and hard work.

Before you watch

1 Work in groups. Look at the picture and discuss the questions.

   1 What do you know about augmented reality?
   2 Where do you think the man in the picture is?
   3 What is he wearing? Why?
   4 What do you think the caption means?

2 How do you think a headset like this could be used? Work in pairs and write down three things you think you could use it for.

While you watch

3 Watch the video and check your ideas from Exercise 2. Which three groups of people does the video say could benefit from this technology?

4 Watch the video again and correct these sentences.

   1 Professor Feiner is working with a group of biology students.

   2 The team wants to develop a virtual world that is separate from the physical world.

   3 The virtual world can provide extra information about what you feel.

   4 A global positioning system allows the team to use the equipment in the laboratory.

   5 The system wouldn't be very useful for people to find their way around places they don't know well.

   6 Visitors to the campus can use the system to find the university restaurant.

   7 Professor Feiner developed the technology because he has a bad sense of smell.

5 Watch the video again and answer the questions.

   1 What is the Columbia University programme trying to do?

   2 How could these people use this technology?
     a firefighters
     b pilots
     c tourists

   3 What do you think a 'situated documentary' is?

   4 What would visitors to the campus 'see' as well as the library?

After you watch

6 Roleplay an interview with Professor Feiner

Work in pairs.

Student A: Imagine you are a journalist from the Columbia University newspaper. Look at the information below and prepare a list of questions to ask Professor Feiner.

Student B: Imagine you are Professor Feiner. You are going to be interviewed for the Columbia University newspaper. Look at the information below and think about what you are going to say to the journalist.

- when you started the project
- how many students work with you
- what the technology could be used for
- what you have to do in the laboratory
- why you decided to do research on augmented reality
- how you think the technology could be taken further in the future

Act out the interview, then change roles and act out the interview again.

7 Work in pairs and discuss these questions.

   1 Have you ever seen or used any of the following devices?

     - simulators for learning to drive
     - night vision glasses for seeing in the dark
     - billboard advertisements that speak to pedestrians
     - Wii ™ games
     - T-shirts with moving images

   2 How useful do you think they are?
   3 What are the advantages and disadvantages of augmented reality technology?

asylum (n) /əˈsaɪləm/ a kind of hospital for people with mental illnesses
blueprints (n) /ˈbluːprɪnts/ plans
cockpit (n) /ˈkɒkpɪt/ place in an aeroplane where the pilot sits
handheld (adj) /ˈhændheld/ carried in the hand
obscure (v) /əbˈskjʊə/ hide
overlay (v) /əʊvəˈleɪ/ show on top of
prototype (n) /ˈprəʊtətaɪp/ an experimental working model
superimpose (v) /suːpərɪmˈpəʊz/ put one image on top of another
surroundings (n) /səˈraʊndɪŋz/ the area around something or someone

Grammar

1 Work in pairs. Can you remember at least three of the global problems mentioned in the unit?

2 Look at the photo. What global problems could these windmills be the answer to?

3 Read the text and answer the questions.

1 What is the problem the author mentions?
2 What should be our target if we want to solve the problem?
3 How can we achieve this target?
4 Why are windmills not a solution?

4 Choose the correct option.

Of all the problems facing the world, finding a technological solution to the problem of CO_2 emissions is perhaps the biggest. If we [1] *won't reduce / don't reduce* our emissions to almost zero, global temperatures [2] *will continue / are continuing* to rise. At the current rate, temperatures [3] *will be increasing / will have increased* by three or four degrees by 2050. CO_2 emissions [4] *will come / are about to come* down if one of three things [5] *happens / will happen*. Firstly, if we change our lifestyles and stop using electricity; secondly, if the gadgets we use don't need energy; or thirdly, if we find a way to generate electricity that doesn't produce CO_2. Well, it is clear that people [6] *are not stopping / are not going to stop* using electricity. If anything, in 30 years' time, they [7] *will be using / will have used* more. Perhaps in the future gadgets [8] *will consume / will be consuming* less energy, but certainly not zero energy. That leaves only one possibility. Scientists [9] *are having / will have* to find a way to generate large amounts of CO_2-free electricity. Wind and solar are only intermittent energy sources. What miracle invention [10] *will be generating / will have generated* our electricity in 2050? No one knows, but the miracle will need to happen soon.

I CAN	
talk about future events, intentions and arrangements using a variety of future forms	☐
make predictions using the future continuous and future perfect simple	☐

Vocabulary

5 Read the definitions. Complete the words. The first letter has been given for you.

1 too much information = information o_____
2 a big advance in science = a technological b_____
3 technology suited to its context = a_____ technology
4 a clever answer to a problem = a n_____ solution
5 a useful device = a h_____ gadget
6 a fast, easy solution to a problem = a quick f_____

6 Work in small groups and answer these questions.

1 Which of these problems do you think we will find technological solutions to? Why?

epidemics	overpopulation	pollution	starvation

2 In what area will new technology most change people's lives in the next 50 years?

I CAN	
talk about global problems and solutions	☐
talk about new technology: devices and gadgets	☐

Real life

7 Match each statement or question (1–5) with the correct response (a–e).

1 Can you give me a hand?
2 What do you want to do exactly?
3 If you restart the computer, that should do the trick.
4 What else do you suggest?
5 The trouble is the computer won't allow me to copy it.

a Have you tried looking for another type of map?
b Thanks. I'll give that a try.
c Sure. I'll be with you in a second.
d Let me have a look.
e I'm trying to paste this map into a document.

8 Work in pairs. Act out a conversation asking for help with a computer problem.

I CAN	
ask for and give technical help	☐
talk about computing tasks	☐

Speaking

9 Work in pairs. Tell each other your predictions for your life (education, job, where you live, travel, relationships, transport, etc.). Use the future continuous and future perfect simple with transport:

- a year from now
- three years from now
- ten years from now

10 Change partners and tell each other your original partner's predictions.

Unit 4 Art and creativity

A juggler in Scotland performs at dusk.
Photograph by Emanuele Picchirallo

FEATURES

1 Work in pairs. Match the type of artist or performer with what and where they perform. How many combinations can you make?

Example:

a dance company + a performance + a theatre

Who: a band, a comedian, a dance company, a circus act, a drama company, an orchestra, an artist

What: a gig, a show, an exhibition, a classical concert, a play, a musical, a performance

Where: a concert hall, a live music venue, a theatre, a gallery, a club, the street

2 Look at the photo and caption. Which words from Exercise 1 can describe what is happening? Have you seen anything like this in your country?

3 🔊 1.24 Listen to a conversation about two people who do artistic things in their free time. Answer the questions.

1 What does each person do as a day job?
2 What is each person's creative outlet?

4 Have you ever been surprised to find out how someone you know expresses themselves creatively? Tell your partner.

All about Melbourne

Listening

1 Work in pairs. Ask and answer the questions.

1 What art forms are popular in your city or country: theatre, dance, music, cinema, art (painting, sculpture, etc.)?
2 Which of the arts have you practised yourself?
3 Which of the arts do you particularly like to follow?
4 Can you describe an exhibition or performance that you've enjoyed recently?

2 Discuss what type of activities and opportunities Australia offers visitors and tourists.

3 🔘 **1.25** Listen to an extract from *The Travel Show*, a weekly radio programme, about Melbourne and answer the questions.

1 What is the essential difference between Melbourne and Sydney?
2 What does Melbourne offer visitors?
3 What does it offer local people? What do they enjoy in their free time?

4 🔘 **1.25** Listen again and say if the statements about Melbourne are true (T) or false (F).

1 Melbourne has great weather and many places of natural beauty.
2 It is known as the architectural capital of Australia.
3 The arts are enjoyed by a small number of art lovers.
4 The summer is a good time for festivals in Melbourne.
5 Melbourne's Formula One motor race and tennis tournament are world famous.
6 Not many visitors know about the local sports.

5 Would you like to visit Melbourne after hearing this guide? What would you do there?

Grammar expressions of quantity

6 Turn to the audioscript on page 96. Find the examples of the items below. Make a note of which expressions have *of* after them and which don't. Then compare your list with your partner.

- 6 expressions in the script that mean 'many or much'
- 3 expressions that mean 'not many or much'
- 3 expressions that mean 'some'

▶ **EXPRESSIONS OF QUANTITY**

+ plural countable noun
(not) many, (a) few, a (small) number of, several
+ uncountable noun
(not) much, (a) little, a bit of, an (large) amount of
+ plural countable or uncountable noun
*a lot of, lots of, plenty of, loads of, lack of,
(almost) no, (not/hardly) any, some, enough*

For further information and practice, see page 89.

7 Look at the grammar box. Then read the pairs of sentences and answer the questions.

1 Which expression means 'some' and which means 'only a small number of'?
  a **Few** people will be familiar with the sports the Melburnians follow.
  b Melbourne may have **a few** grey days.

2 Can you use the same expression in both sentences?
  a In fact there are **hardly any** forms of artistic expression that are not represented.
  b In fact there are **almost no** forms of artistic expression that are not represented.

3 Which expression is used more often in affirmative sentences?
  a **Lots of** people around the world know the Australian Formula One Grand Prix.
  b But there **aren't many** people who know Australian Rules football.

4 Which expression is used with countable nouns?
  a Australian Rules football and cricket enjoy **an enormous amount of** support.
  b There are **a huge number of** smaller art spaces and venues.

5 Which expression is used in negative sentences?
  a There is **a lot of** information on what to do in Melbourne on the website.
  b There **isn't much** information about where to eat on the website.

8 Choose the correct option to complete each sentence.

1 A visit to the opera can cost *much / a lot of* money.
2 A reasonable *number / amount* of the winter festivals are free.
3 There is almost *no / any* rain in Melbourne at Christmas time.
4 There are *few / a few* tickets for the Australian Open Tennis available at the gate for those who haven't booked in advance.
5 We saw *several / some* interesting street art at the Sweet Streets festival.
6 *Almost / Hardly* anyone attended the afternoon performance.
7 Visitors show *a little / little* interest in AR football.
8 There aren't as *many / much* differences between Melbourne and Sydney as people say.

9 Pronunciation weak form *of*

a 💿 1.26 Listen and note how *of* is pronounced in these phrases.

a bit of relaxation time	a lot of information
a huge amount of support	lots of people
a huge number of galleries	
a lack of natural attractions	

b Work in pairs. Practise saying these phrases where *of* is a weak form.

as a matter of fact	just the two of us
first of all	most of the time
in spite of that	of course
instead of me	that's kind of you

10 Work in pairs. Look at the charts on page 81 showing the results of a survey on Australians' participation in the arts. Complete the sentences describing what they show. Use one word in each space.

1 Overall quite a __lot__ of Australians take an interest in the arts, but only a _____ participate creatively.
2 It seems that _____ of Australians read literature and a surprising _____ of them also write creatively.
3 There is certainly _____ lack of interest in the visual arts, with half of the population being involved in some way.
4 _____ Australians attend concerts or musicals and _____ anyone said they did not listen to music at all.
5 The main reason for not participating is not having _____ time. But the _____ of money it costs to be involved and a _____ of opportunities are also important factors.

Speaking

11 Work in groups. Research your classmates' participation in the arts and then report your findings. Follow these steps:

• Each group must research ONE of the following: visual arts and crafts, theatre and dance, reading and writing, music.
• Make a list of four or five questions to find out how people participate (creatively or receptively) and reasons for non-participation.
• Circulate around the class asking and answering questions.
• Come back together, pool your results and make conclusions, using expressions of quantity.
• Present your findings to the class.

TALK ABOUT ▶ PARTICIPATION IN THE ARTS   ▶ AN ART COMPETITION ▶ MUSIC AND VALUES ▶ LIKES AND DISLIKES
WRITE ▶ AN ONLINE REVIEW

47

4b Reverse graffiti

Listening

1 🔊 **1.27** Look at the statements about art. Do you agree with any of them? Listen to an artist's opinion and write down what he says about each one.

1 Art should be pleasing to the viewer.
2 Art should involve effort on the part of the artist.
3 Art should involve technical skill.
4 Art should have a social message or make a political point.

2 🔊 **1.27** Listen again. What are the roles of an artist and a viewer according to the speaker?

3 Work in pairs. Discuss what each of these types of artwork is.

> graffiti   installation   landscape   sculpture   sketch

> ▶ **WORDBUILDING suffixes**
>
> Some noun suffixes have no clear meaning (-*ment*, -*tion*, etc.). Others like -*scape* have a particular meaning.
> *cityscape, landscape, seascape, moonscape*
>
> For further information and practice, see Workbook page 131.

REVERSE GRAFFITI

When is cleaning walls a crime? When you're doing it to create art, obviously. A number of street artists around the world have started expressing themselves through a practice known as reverse graffiti. Inspired by the 'clean me' messages that you see written on the back of some trucks, they find dirty surfaces and inscribe them with images or messages using cleaning brushes or pressure hoses. Either way, it's the same principle: the image is made by cleaning away the dirt.

Each artist has their own individual style but all artists share a common aim: to draw attention to the pollution in our cities. The UK's Paul Curtis, better known as Moose, operates around Leeds and London and has been commissioned by a number of companies to make reverse graffiti advertisements.

Brazilian artist, Alexandre Orion, turned one of São Paulo's transport tunnels into an amazing mural in 2006 by scraping away the dirt. Made up of a series of white skulls, the mural reminds drivers of the effect their pollution is having on the planet. 'Every motorist sits in the comfort of their car, but they don't give any consideration to the price their comfort has for the environment and consequently for themselves,' says Orion.

The anti-pollution message of the reverse graffiti artists confuses city authorities since the main argument against graffiti is that it spoils the appearance of both types of property: public and private. This was what Leeds City Council said about Moose's work: 'Leeds residents want to live in clean and attractive neighbourhoods. We view this kind of advertising as environmental damage and will take strong action against any advertisers carrying out such campaigns.' It seems that no action was taken against the advertisers – no fines nor any other punishment – but Moose himself was ordered to 'clean up his act'. How was he supposed to do this: by making all property he had cleaned dirty again?

As for the Brazilian artist's work, the authorities were annoyed but could find nothing to charge him with. They had no other option but to clean the tunnel – but only the parts Alexandre had already cleaned. The artist merely continued his campaign on the other side. The city officials then decided to take drastic action. They not only cleaned the whole tunnel but also every tunnel in São Paulo.

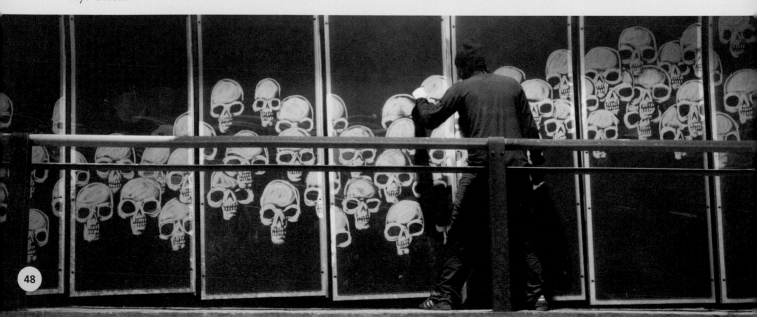

Reading

4 What do you think about graffiti in cities? Do you think it improves or spoils the appearance of the urban landscape?

5 What do you think *reverse graffiti* is? Read the article and check.

6 Use the information in the article to complete these sentences. Use one word per space.

1 Reverse graffiti works by cleaning away the _____ on walls.
2 The aim of the reverse graffiti artists is to highlight the problem of _____ .
3 Some reverse graffiti artists are paid to make images that act as _____ .
4 Orion made his message for _____ as they passed through a transport tunnel in São Paulo.
5 The local authorities in Leeds were _____ by this new type of graffiti.
6 In São Paulo the response of the authorities was to _____ every tunnel.

7 Work in pairs. Discuss the questions.

1 Do you like this kind of graffiti?
2 If you were a city authority, how would you deal with *reverse graffiti* in your city?

Grammar determiners

8 Work in pairs. Look at the highlighted words in the article and decide if the nouns that come after each are singular, plural or uncountable.

> ▶ **DETERMINERS**
>
> *each, every, either, the whole* + singular noun
> *all, both* + plural noun
> *any, no* + singular or plural noun
> *all, any, no* + uncountable noun
>
> For further information and practice, see page 89.

9 Look at the grammar box. Answer the questions.

1 Which determiner emphasises the individual?
  a **Every** artist has their own individual style.
  b **Each** artist has their own individual style.
  c **All** artists have their own individual style.

2 Which determiner(s) talk about two things?
  a **Every** way: it's the same principle.
  b **Either** way: it's the same principle.
  c **Both** ways: it's the same principle.

3 Which sentence(s) about the action taken against advertisers are negative?
  a They took **no** action against them.
  b They didn't take **any** action against them.
  c Did they take **any** action against them?

10 Choose the correct option. Sometimes there is more than one possibility.

'*Every / All / Each* child is an artist. The problem is how to remain an artist once he grows up.' *Pablo Picasso, artist*

'*Every / All / Each* art is an imitation of nature.' *Seneca, philosopher and writer*

'Drawing is the honesty of the art. There is *any / no* possibility of cheating. It is either good or bad.' *Salvador Dali, artist*

'As an artist you want it *both / either / every* ways. You want it to have an immediate impact, and you want it to have deep meanings as well.' *Damien Hirst, artist*

'Some days I produce something, other days nothing. *Each / Every / Either* way, I feel it's time spent well.' *Anonymous, artist*

'Science and art belong to *all / the whole / every* world, and before them vanish the barriers of nationality.' *Goethe, writer*

'Let *each / every / all* man exercise the art he knows.' *Aristophanes, dramatist*

'Do not fear mistakes; there aren't *no / any*.' *Miles Davis, musician*

11 Discuss the quotations. How do they fit with the definitions of art that you discussed earlier?

12 Complete the rules for the Turner Art Prize, held in Britain each year, with a determiner.

1 _____ candidates are chosen for an exhibition they have given in the last year.
2 Candidates are nominated by the public or by the Turner Prize jury. _____ way, the jury has the final say in the four who are shortlisted.
3 The aim of the prize is to celebrate _____ innovation and young talent.
4 _____ candidate is invited to display examples of their work at the Turner show.
5 _____ artist over 50 years can enter.
6 The artists can use _____ medium they like; painting, sculpture, film, etc.
7 The winner receives £25,000. _____ other shortlisted candidates get £5,000.

Speaking

13 Your city would like to commission an artwork that would a) improve the appearance of an area in the city centre; b) be fun; and c) attract visitors. Work in small groups and:

• discuss what kind of thing you would like to have and who you would like to make it
• make a list of criteria or rules for the competition

14 Exchange your rules with another group. Then submit an idea for an artwork to them for evaluation.

TALK ABOUT ▶ PARTICIPATION IN THE ARTS ▶ AN ART COMPETITION ▶ MUSIC AND VALUES ▶ LIKES AND DISLIKES
WRITE ▶ AN ONLINE REVIEW

49

4c Hip-hop planet

Reading

1 Work in pairs. Look at the different music genres in the box. Discuss the questions.

1 How often do you listen to each type of music?
2 When you listen, do you pay much attention to the lyrics?
3 Do you identify strongly with this type of music?

> blues   classical   country
> hip-hop   jazz   pop   reggae
> rock   soul   traditional / folk

2 Discuss what themes or attitudes you associate with hip-hop and rap music. Who do you think listens to this music? Then read the article and compare your answers with what the author says.

3 Read the article again quickly. Answer the questions.

1 What was the theme of the first rap song the author heard?
2 Apart from music, what are the other artistic expressions of hip-hop culture?
3 What do the DJs do to create hip-hop's individual sound?
4 What is the appeal of hip-hop to middle-class children?
5 Why does Assane say that rap belongs to his country?
6 What does the author not like about hip-hop music?

4 Explain these phrases from the article.

1 It sounded like a broken record (para 1)
2 the way you step over a crack in the pavement (para 2)
3 life on the other side of the tracks (para 4)
4 its macho pose (para 6)
5 the empty moral cupboard that we have left for our children (para 7)

Critical thinking analysing contrasts

5 This article is all about what hip-hop is and isn't. Find and underline sentences that tell you:

1 a what the author thought of rap music 26 years ago
  b what he thinks now
2 a the environment in which rap music originated
  b where it thrives now
3 a the message conveyed by the early rappers
  b the message conveyed by successful hip-hop artists now
4 a that hip-hop culture can seem selfish
  b that this selfishness in young people is not their fault

6 Work in pairs. Compare your answers and discuss if you feel more positively about hip-hop after reading this article. Now write a short summary of the values of hip-hop culture, according to the author.

Word focus *cool*

7 *Cool* has three basic meanings in English: 1) not warm; 2) stylish and fashionable; 3) calm. Which meaning does it have in the article (para 5) and in sentences 1–6?

1 I don't know what I've done to offend Liz. She was really **cool with** me when I spoke to her earlier.
2 It's not **cool** to arrive early to a party like that.
3 James **lost his cool** completely when his boss told him he had to work at the weekend as well.
4 That's a really **cool** jacket. Where did you get it?
5 I think she did very well to **keep her cool** with that customer. I would have got very angry with them.
6 Wait for the frying pan to **cool down** before you add more oil.

Speaking

8 Work in pairs. Look at the lyrics below from a country song and a rock song. What themes and attitudes to life can you identify in each genre?

Country song	*Rock song*
When you ain't got a friend to lean on	Ooh, be true to yourself
There are folks you can depend on	Don't let anyone put you down
Home, that's where you turn to	If you feel you're getting tied
Family won't turn their back on you	Then ride right on out of town
Yeah, it's all right there in your own backyard	Don't be nobody's slave
They'll be waitin' when times are hard	Live your life – that's what I say

9 Look at the genres in Exercise 1 and discuss the questions.

1 What values does each genre project?
2 Do you have to believe these values to like the music?

I first heard rap at a party in Harlem in 1980. It sounded like a broken record. It was a version of an old hit record called *Good Times*, the same four bars looped over and over. And on top of this loop, a kid chanted a rhyme about how he was the best disc jockey in the world. It was called *Rapper's Delight*. I thought it was the most ridiculous thing I'd ever heard.

For the next 26 years, I avoided rap music the way you step over a crack in the pavement. I heard it booming out of cars and alleyways from Paris to Abidjan, but I never listened. In doing so, I missed the most important cultural event in my lifetime. No American music has exploded across the world with such force since swing jazz in the 1930s. This defiant culture of song, graffiti and dance, collectively known as hip-hop, has permeated almost every society.

HIP-HOP PLANET
BY JAMES MCBRIDE

Hip-hop began in the mid-1970s, in an almost bankrupt New York City. The bored kids of the South Bronx and Harlem came up with a new entertainment. This is how it worked: one guy, the DJ, played records on two turntables. Another guy – or girl – served as master of ceremonies, or MC. The DJs learnt to move the record back and forth under the needle to create a *scratch*, or to drop the needle on the record and play a *break* over and over to keep people dancing. The MCs rapped over the music to keep the party going. One MC sought to out-chat the other. Dance styles were created. Graffiti artists also emphasised the *I* because the music was all about identity: I am the best.

Initially hip-hop artists produced socially-conscious songs that described life on the other side of the tracks, where people are denied the same opportunities as the rich. The lyrics of Grandmaster Flash's 1982 hit *The Message* are a perfect example.

They describe a child who is born and grows up in the ghetto, hating the world for his situation and all the things that he cannot have.

These days most commercial rappers in America brag about their lives of crime and the things that fame and money have brought them, among which women seem to be just another material possession. For those from poor backgrounds the life of a successful rapper has become an aspiration, for richer suburban kids it is a symbol of something cool.

In poor urban communities around the globe, rap music is a universal expression of outrage at the injustice of the distribution of wealth. Its macho pose has been borrowed from commercial hip-hop in the US, but for most the music represents an old dream: a better life. 'We want money to help our parents,' Assane, a nineteen-year-old budding DJ from Dakar in Senegal tells me. 'We watch our mothers boil water to cook and have nothing to put in the pot. Rap doesn't belong to American culture,' he says. 'It belongs here. It has always existed here, because of our pain and our hardships and our suffering.'

That is why, after 26 years, I have come to embrace this music I tried so hard to ignore. Much of hip-hop, particularly the commercial side, I hate. Yet I love the good of it. Even if some of it embraces violence, hip-hop is a music that exposes the empty moral cupboard that we have left for our children. They can hear it and understand it. The question is: can we?

brag (v) /bræg/ speak proudly about your achievements
defiant (adj) /dɪˈfaɪənt/ challenging or opposing another's authority
looped (adj) /luːpt/ repeated without a break
out-chat (v) /ˌaʊt ˈtʃæt/ chat longer or better than another

4d Personal tastes

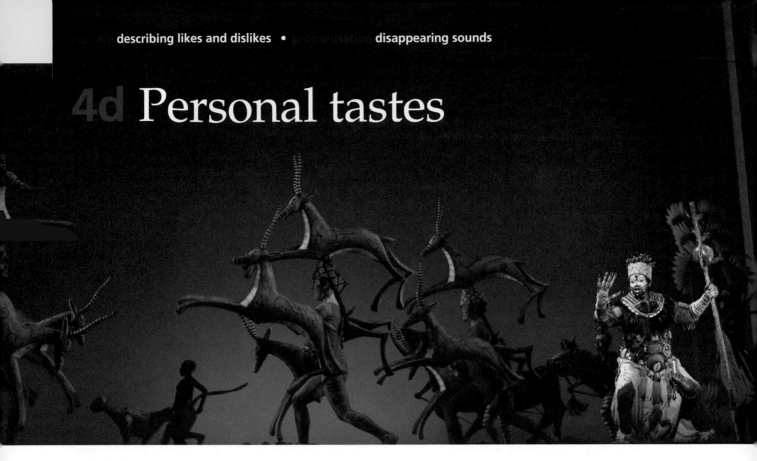

Real life describing likes and dislikes

1 Do you like musicals? Which ones have you seen? Did you see them live or on film? Tell your partner.

2 🎵 **1.28** Listen to a conversation in which Tom and his friend Jake talk about the musical, *The Lion King*. For each item below put a tick next to it if one of them likes it and a cross if one of them dislikes it.

cost of tickets for	the music in musicals ☐
musicals ☐	the visual effects ☐
Disney comic characters ☐	this production of
Elton John ☐	*The Lion King* ☐
musicals in general ☐	

3 🎵 **1.28** Look at the box. Tell your partner which of the phrases Tom and Jake used to express each like and dislike. Then listen again and check.

▶ DESCRIBING LIKES AND DISLIKES	
Likes	**Dislikes**
I love …	I can't bear …
I'm a big fan of …	I'm not generally a fan of …
I'm really into …	I'm not very keen on …
It is very inspiring	… doesn't really do
It sounds right up my street.	anything for me.
I have a lot of time for …	I never feel particularly
I could watch / read / listen	inspired by …
to … all day.	It doesn't really sound like
	my kind of thing.
	gets on my nerves
	I get a bit tired of …

4 Pronunciation disappearing sounds

a 🎵 **1.29** Listen to these words from the conversation. Underline the disappearing sound, the part of the word that is not pronounced.

different   everyone   generally

b 🎵 **1.30** Underline the disappearing sound in each of these words and then say them aloud. Listen and check if you were right.

beautifully   chocolate   comfortable
interesting   medicine   ordinary   secretary

5 Work in pairs. Look at these sentences and say which words most naturally go in each space.

1 I'm not _____ keen on romantic comedies.
2 I get _____ tired of reality TV shows.
3 I never feel _____ inspired by science fiction books.
4 I'm not _____ a fan of musicals.
5 Jazz music doesn't _____ do anything for me.
6 I'm afraid opera gets on my nerves _____ .

6 Now work in groups. Each person think of a musical, play, film, concert, TV programme or exhibition they have enjoyed recently. Describe your choice to the group and compare and discuss your likes and dislikes. Use the box to help you.

4e You've got to see this

Writing an online review

1 Read the online review of an exhibition by a recent visitor to London. Would you follow their recommendation? Why? / Why not?

2 Answer the questions. Then compare your answers in pairs.

1   How are the following themes organised in the review? Put them in order (1–5).
  • the author's recommendation
  • an introduction
  • the content of the exhibition
  • the occasion of the visit
  • the details of where and when it is on

2   What information about the event does she include?

3   Would you describe the tone of the review as personal or impersonal?

3 Writing skill personalising your writing

Work in pairs. Look at the following features of personal and impersonal writing. Then find examples of the personal forms in the review.

Personal tone
  • use pronouns
  • use active verbs
  • use contracted forms
  • use phrasal verbs
  • add personal details
  • use conversational linking phrases
    (e.g. *what's more*)
  • share your feelings

Impersonal tone
  • use pronouns
  • use passive verbs
  • use uncontracted forms
  • use formal verbs
  • avoid personal information
  • use formal linking phrases
    (e.g. *furthermore*)
  • be objective in your judgements

http://www.travelreviews.com

I find that it's always worth checking out the parks when you visit a foreign city: as well as providing a welcome break, they can contain some very interesting surprises. Last week, absolutely exhausted from visiting two museums and too tired even to think about shopping anymore, my boyfriend and I took a walk in Kensington Gardens. I was so glad we did, because otherwise we'd have missed Anish Kapoor's mirror sculptures.

There are four of them and rather than look out of place as so many modern sculptures can do, they really complemented their surroundings.

The sky mirror, as its name suggests, is placed at an angle to reflect the changing sky. Another, Red Mirror, is also directed at the sky, so that you see the sky's reflection, but this time with a red tint. The one I liked best was the C-curve, a convex mirror that makes you see everything upside down. It was so funny to watch dogs and children approach it, trying to work out what they were looking at.

The secret of this exhibition's success is that it makes you appreciate what is already a really delightful park even more. It will be on until 30th March and, if you are in London, I'd definitely recommend taking the time to go and see it for yourself. And by the way, it's free!

4 Write a brief personalised review of something you have seen and enjoyed for a *What's on* website. Then exchange your review with another person in the class.

5 Read your partner's review. Check the points below. Then feedback to the reviewer.

  • Does the review make you want to go and see this event?
  • Does the review include all the items described in Exercise 2 in their correct order?
  • Does it feel like a friendly and personal recommendation?
  • What features has the writer used from Exercise 3 to give this impression?

4f Urban art

Before you watch

1 Work in groups. Look at the photo and discuss the questions.

1 Where are the people?
2 What is unusual about the exhibition?
3 What do you know about graffiti?

2 Apart from graffiti, what other kinds of urban art can you think of? What kinds of art do you think you are going to see in this video?

While you watch

3 Watch the video and check your answers from Exercise 2.

4 Watch the video again and put these things in the order you first see them.

a a painting of a Japanese woman
b a train
c an art gallery
d a CD cover
e a shopping trolley
f paint cans
g a trumpet

5 Complete the table with the correct information (a–h).

Nick Posada	Jafar Barron

a He is a trumpeter.
b He is a graffiti artist.
c He grew up in a neighbourhood north of Philadelphia.
d He has a record deal.
e He grew up in Washington D.C.
f His parents are jazz musicians.
g His first exhibition was in Georgetown.
h He plays in clubs where he grew up.

6 Answer the questions.

1 In what ways is urban art about innovation? Give three examples.

2 Why is Nick Posada disappointed when he visits the wall of fame?

3 What does Nick think real graffiti artists know?

4 Why does Chris Murray like graffiti art?

5 What is Jafar Barron's music a mix of?

6 What does Jafar think are his influences?

7 Watch the last part of the video again (03.20 to 03.36). Use these words and phrases to complete what Don Kimes says about urban art.

authentic   boundaries   come from
emerge   envelope   one more step
to the edge

It's about sort of taking what it is that you
¹ _____ , what you ² _____ from,
what's ³ _____ for you and pushing it
⁴ _____ of its ⁵ _____ , to the edge
of its ⁶ _____ , its limits and taking
⁷ _____ .

After you watch

8 Roleplay interviewing an urban artist

Work in pairs.

Student A: Imagine you are an urban artist. Choose a medium (visual or sound). Invent information about the following:

- your life (for example, where you grew up, what your parents do, where you live now)
- your art (for example, what you do, why you do it, what your inspiration is)
- your aspirations (for example, what you would like to happen, where you see your work in five years' time)

Student B: Imagine you are a local journalist. Interview the urban artist about his or her life, art and aspirations.

Act out the interview, then change roles and act out the conversation again. Student B should choose a different medium.

9 Work in groups and discuss these questions.

1 What type of art do you like?
2 Does the type of art you like differ from art in your parents' generation? In what ways?
3 Is innovation in art a good thing?

authentic (adj) /ɔːˈθentɪk/ genuine, real
caution (v) /ˈkɔːʃən/ warn someone about a problem or danger
collector (n) /kəˈlektə/ a person who buys art
exposure (n) /ɪksˈpəʊʒə/ giving someone a particular experience
highlight (v) /ˈhaɪlaɪt/ draw people's attention to something
innovative (adj) /ˈɪnəveɪtɪv/ new and original
inventive (adj) /ɪnˈventɪv/ creative
uninhibited (adj) /ʌnɪnˈhɪbɪtɪd/ saying and doing anything you want
vilify (v) /ˈvɪlɪfaɪ/ say bad things about someone or something

Grammar

1 Work in pairs. What arts festivals are famous in your country? What happens at them?

2 Read the article. What is the Edinburgh Fringe Festival famous for?

3 Choose the correct option to complete the article. Sometimes more than one option is correct.

The Edinburgh Fringe Festival is the world's largest arts festival. It takes place ¹ *all / every / each* year in August and for the ² *all / every / whole* month the city is taken over by actors, street performers, comedians, artists, musicians, etc. There is ³ *some / little / enough* variety to please everyone. The festival attracts a huge ⁴ *number / amount / lack* of visitors from all over the world. There are over 2,000 different shows and during the festival up to two million tickets are sold. The tickets don't cost ⁵ *a lot / much / plenty* – £10 or £15 typically – but since most people try to see ⁶ *a lot / many / plenty* of shows over three or four days, the costs can add up.
⁷ *Few / Little / A few* artists just come to perform for the fun of it, but in ⁸ *many / enough / plenty* cases they are young performers hoping that this will be their chance to be noticed by the critics and producers. The Edinburgh Fringe Festival is perhaps best known for its comedy and has launched the careers of ⁹ *some / several / any* notable British comedians, including John Cleese of *Fawlty Towers* fame. But the festival is ¹⁰ *no / any / not any* respecter of reputations. ¹¹ *All / Both / Either* unknown and well-known artists compete for attention and ¹² *all / each / every* have an equal chance of success or failure.

I CAN	
use expressions of quantity	
use determiners	

Vocabulary

4 Put these words into three categories: music, art and theatre (four words per category).

a band   a gig   a musical   a play   a show
a sketch   an installation   drama company
folk   landscape   lyrics   sculpture

5 Work in small groups. Answer the questions.

1 Do you have a favourite work of art? What art or copies of art (e.g. prints, posters) do you have at home? Describe them and why you chose them.
2 What was the most memorable concert you ever saw?
3 How often do you go to the theatre? What is the best thing you have seen there?

I CAN	
describe different art forms, performers and venues	
talk about different kinds of art	

Real life

6 Put these phrases (a–f) into two groups: like and dislike.

a I can't bear …
b I'm not very keen on …
c … don't really do anything for me.
d I'm a big fan of …
e … get on my nerves.
f I have a lot of time for …

7 Work in groups. Use the phrases in Exercise 6 to tell each other about the kind of TV programmes that you like and dislike.

I CAN	
describe my own personal tastes in music, art, film and theatre	

Speaking

8 Work in groups. Tell each other about the arts in your city or country:

- how many people do what
- how expensive each activity is (e.g. there's no charge for visiting museums)
- how the government views the arts

Unit 5 Development

A minimalist beach chalet under construction on the Persian Gulf.
Photograph by George Steinmetz

FEATURES

1 Work in pairs. Look at the photo and the six types of development in the box. What kind of development is represented here?

> economic   personal   product   social   sustainable   urban

2 🔘 **1.31** Match the examples of development below with the types of development in Exercise 1. Then listen to the three speakers and say which one each is talking about.

> a new housing project   a new university
> a new railway line   a zero energy house
> a new smart phone   learning a language

3 🔘 **1.31** Listen again. What advantages does each speaker mention? Compare your answers with your partner.

4 Describe examples of two types of development from your own experience. Were they positive developments?

> *I went on a public speaking course. I don't really need it for my work, but I just thought it would be good for my own personal development. It was a really interesting experience: it made me feel much more confident.*

5a From reality to fantasy

Reading

1 Work in pairs. The photo was taken in Dubai. Discuss the questions.

1 Where was it taken from?
2 What can you see below?
3 What do you know about Dubai? For example, where it is, its famous landmarks, who goes there?

2 Read the article and answer the questions.

1 What was Dubai like 50 years ago and how has it changed?
2 According to the author, what are the attractions for visitors and residents?
3 What do other countries feel about this change?

3 Would you like to visit Dubai? Why? / Why not?

FROM REALITY TO FANTASY

There once was a sheikh with big dreams. His land was a sleepy village occupied by pearl divers, fishermen and traders who docked their boats along a small creek through the town. It was here that Sheikh Rashid bin Saeed al Maktoum imagined creating a gateway to the world. It was a dream he could not afford to realise. So in 1959 he asked a neighbour to lend him many millions of dollars. He made the creek wider, built roads, schools and homes. With his young son, Mohammed, by his side, he walked along the empty waterfront and painted his dream with words. And some years later, it was as he had said. He built it, and they came.

Then it was his son's turn to carry on developing his father's vision. Sheikh Mohammed bin Rashid al Maktoum transformed Dubai into an air-conditioned fantasy world of 1.5 million people. No project seemed to be too ambitious for him. He built the world's tallest high-rise building, the 828 metre Burj Khalifa, the world's biggest shopping mall and the world's largest motorway intersection. He helped Little Dubai become the shopping capital of the Middle East. In the last five years, it has attracted more tourists than India. Its most famous landmark, the Palm Jumeirah, an artificial island built in the shape of a palm tree, provides holiday villas for the rich and famous.

But the financial crisis in 2008 made people think again and Dubai failed to sell many of its new luxury apartments. Up to then property in Dubai had been increasing in value and it had been easy to get people to invest. These days, investors risk losing money.

The rest of the world looks on with a mixture of wonder and suspicion. Is this a capitalist model that people want to copy or do they feel that Dubai has decided to abandon its true heritage and become instead the Las Vegas of the Middle East?

creek (n) /kriːk/ a small stream that flows into a river (often they dry up in summer)
dock (v) /dɒk/ to 'park' a boat in a harbour or at a sea port
pearl (n) /pɜːl/ a round white jewel found in the sea (in oyster shells)

58

Grammar verb + infinitive or *-ing*

4 Complete the sentences from the article.

1 Sheikh Rashid imagined _____ a gateway to the world.
2 It was a dream Sheikh Rashid could not afford _____ .
3 In 1959 he asked _____ him some money.
4 He helped _____ the shopping capital of the world.

5 Read the article again quickly and find:

1 two more verbs followed by the *-ing* form
2 four more verbs followed by *to* + infinitive
3 one more verb followed by somebody + *to* + infinitive
4 one more verb followed by the infinitive without *to*

▶ VERB + INFINITIVE	VERB + *-ING*
Verb + *to* + infinitive *He couldn't afford to build a new harbour.* **Verb + someone + *to* + infinitive** *He asked a friend to lend him some money.* **Verb + someone + infinitive** *He helped Dubai become a great city.*	**Verb + *-ing*** *He imagined building an amazing city.*
For further information and practice, see page 90.	

6 Look at the grammar box. Then put the verbs in the right form.

1 The population of Dubai grew from half a million in 1990 to 1.5 million in 2008 and has kept on _____ (grow) to this day.
2 Sheikh al Maktoum decided _____ (make) Dubai the region's most important financial centre.
3 Attracting foreign banks and companies involved _____ (reduce) taxes for companies and individuals.
4 The expansion of the airport allowed _____ (Dubai / become) the fourth busiest international airport in the world.
5 If you enjoy _____ (shop), Dubai has over 70 shopping malls to choose from.
6 By planting 10,000 trees each year for the past four years, the city planners have managed _____ (create) many green spaces.
7 The banking crisis made _____ (construction / slow) down.
8 But it seems that Dubai can't help _____ (build) more property and tourist attractions.

Listening and vocabulary

7 Work in pairs. Make urban features by combining words in A and B.

> **A** green high-rise leisure luxury motorway pedestrianised shopping waterfront

> **B** apartment building centre development intersection mall spaces zone

8 🔊 **1.32** Listen to someone describing a redevelopment that took place in their own city in the 1960s. Answer the questions.

1 What was redeveloped and why?
2 Was it successful?

9 🔊 **1.32** Work in pairs. Complete the sentences with the missing verbs. Then listen again and check your answers.

1 In the 1960s the local authority decided to _____ the area as a shopping district.
2 This involved _____ all the houses and making way for huge car parks.
3 Even the residents seemed to accept that the area had to be _____ .
4 If you proposed _____ houses into shops on such a big scale today, I don't think you would be allowed to do it.
5 The result was that they _____ the character of the city centre.
6 Now 50 years later the local authority wants to _____ it into a mixed area again.

10 Replace the underlined words in the questions (1–6) with words from Exercise 9 that mean the same thing.

1 Have any old factories been <u>turned into</u> flats or houses?
2 Is there an area of the town that has been <u>changed completely</u> in your lifetime?
3 Is there an area of the town that has been <u>damaged</u> by new development?
4 Do you have a transport system that needs to be <u>brought up to date</u>?
5 What buildings were you sorry to see <u>knocked down</u>?
6 Is there a run-down area of the city that you would like to see <u>rebuilt</u>? How?

Speaking

11 Work in pairs. Ask and answer the questions in Exercise 10 for your own town or city centre.

TALK ABOUT ▶ CHANGES IN YOUR TOWN ▶ A HAPPY SOCIETY ▶ SENSITIVE DEVELOPMENT ▶ REACHING A DECISION
WRITE ▶ AN OPINION ESSAY

59

5b The Kerala model

Listening

1 Look at the two photos taken in the Indian state of Kerala. Which of these adjectives could you use to describe each place shown?

> exotic   fertile   gorgeous   hectic
> prosperous   remarkable   tranquil

2 🔊 **1.33** Listen to an interview with a journalist who has recently been in Kerala. What is surprising about the level of social development in Kerala?

3 🔊 **1.33** Listen again. Are the sentences true (T) or false (F)?

1 The journalist went to Kerala to write an article.
2 The state of Kerala has a lot of people in a small area.
3 One of the signs of Kerala's social development is people's high level of education.
4 Women have a superior social position to men.
5 People in Trivandrum are too busy to be involved in politics.
6 One of the secrets of Kerala's success is the open-minded attitude of its people.

4 Convert these definitions to adjectives. Check your answers in the audioscript on page 97.

Having …
1 a good rate of literacy = _literate_
2 a good standard of living = ...-

3 ....
4 a good education = ...-
4 good health = ...
5 a high level of culture = ...
6 strong interest in politics = ...

7 tolerance of differences = ...

> ▶ **WORDBUILDING adverb + adjective**
>
> Adverbs and adjectives can be combined to describe people and things.
> *politically engaged, highly cultured*
>
> For further information and practice, see Workbook page 139.

5 Work in pairs. Answer the questions.

1 What do you think is the main reason for Kerala's success as a society?
2 Could this kind of society work anywhere?

6 Pronunciation: rhyming words

a 🔊 **1.34** Work in pairs. Words that rhyme end with the same sound. Match the words from the listening (1–9) with the word that rhymes (a–i). Listen and check. Then practise saying them.

1 state   a faced
2 poor   b plane
3 low   c opt
4 head   d though
5 course   e weight
6 main   f force
7 stopped   g fun
8 none   h law
9 waste   i said

b Look at these words. Can you think of a word that rhymes with each but has a different spelling?

> break   foot   height   signed   walk   word

Grammar: verbs with *-ing* and *to* + infinitive

7 Match each verb in bold to the correct meaning (a or b).

1 Have you **tried visiting** India?
2 I'm **trying to show** how remarkable Kerala is.
   a attempting something
   b experimenting with something

3 I was intending to **go on to tour** other parts.
4 The students **went on protesting** for four days.
   a continuing an action
   b a change of situation

5 It was **meant to be** a holiday.
6 Usually that would **mean** people **having** a fairly poor quality of life.
   a describing intentions
   b describing what is involved

7 I don't **regret changing** my plans.
8 No land is wasted, which I **regret to say** is not always the case in some developing countries.
   a apologising for what you are about to say
   b saying you are sorry about a past event

9 I **remember going** there in the 1990s.
10 Please **remember to send** me a copy.
   a describing memories
   b talking about things that need to be done

11 We **stopped to visit** an Indian journalist I know.
12 Keralites never **stop debating**.
   a ending something
   b the reason for stopping

▶ VERBS WITH *-ING* AND *TO* + INFINITIVE

Verbs with two meanings
remember, go on, stop, mean, try, regret + *-ing* and *to* + infinitive

Verbs with no change in meaning
prefer, continue, hate, like, love, start + *-ing* and *to* + infinitive

For further information and practice, see page 91.

---

8 Look at the grammar box. Then choose the correct form in these other sentences.

1 No one knows how long Kerala will be able to go on *to maintain / maintaining* this model society.
2 This is the journalist's impression of Kerala. You would have to try *to live / living* there yourself to see if it was the reality.
3 I regret *to tell / telling* you that getting there by plane is quite expensive.
4 If you stopped *to see / seeing* some other places in India on the way, it would make it more worthwhile.
5 But that would also mean *to plan / planning* your trip more carefully.
6 The other man remembers *to visit / visiting* beautiful beaches and lagoons.

9 Complete this interview with a sociologist about the Kerala model of society. Use the correct form of the verbs in brackets.

Interview

WHAT INTERESTED YOU IN KERALA IN THE FIRST PLACE?

Well, I remember [1] _____ (read) an interesting article about it about fifteen years ago and I meant [2] _____ (visit) and see for myself, but I only managed to do that last year.

AND WHAT DID YOU FIND? WAS IT THE PERFECT MODEL THAT MANY PEOPLE HAVE SAID IT IS?

I think what they have achieved is amazing. The government implemented a number of measures to try [3] _____ (improve) people's quality of life and on the whole these have succeeded.

FOR EXAMPLE?

The most important is land reforms. In the 1960s they stopped [4] _____ (allow) landlords to charge rent to tenant farmers. This meant [5] _____ (give) the land back to the people, mostly peasants, who worked on it.

SO POOR PEOPLE BENEFITTED?

Certainly. At the same time, the government also started [6] _____ (invest) heavily in the education systems, so poor people not only became better off, they also became better educated.

AND WHAT ARE THE NEGATIVE EFFECTS OF ALL THIS? THERE MUST BE SOME.

No system is perfect, I regret [7] _____ (say). The problem in Kerala is that the economy is still largely based on agriculture. And someone who leaves school with a good education probably doesn't want to go on [8] _____ (work) in the fields. So even though they prefer [9] _____ (live) in Kerala, they often move to another more industrially developed state in India or even abroad to get a decent job.

Speaking

10 Work in pairs. Ask and answer the questions on page 81 to find out how happy your society is. Then compare your answer with another pair. Were people's answers very different? If so, why?

5c Sustainable development?

Reading

1 Work in pairs. Look at the photo on page 63 of the Mekong River in Laos before a hydroelectric dam project. How do you think the dam affected the lives of the people living near the river?

2 Read the article quickly and check your answers from Exercise 1. In what other ways did the dam affect peoples' lives?

3 Read the article again more carefully and answer the questions.

1 Who helped to finance the project?
2 Why was this surprising?
3 How much electricity will it generate?
4 Who will use the electricity?
5 How many local people are affected?
6 What will happen to the local people?
7 Who says life is better for local people after the dam?
8 Why do environmentalists think life for local people could be worse?

4 Find words in the article to complete these statements.

1 The dam flooded a big area and created a huge _____ . (para 1)
2 The World Bank would like the project to be a _____ that everyone can admire. (para 2)
3 The people from the flooded area should have better _____ in future. (para 5)
4 Because their farmland has disappeared, locals will have to find new ways to _____ a _____ . (para 5)
5 The people now have _____ that they didn't have before, like electricity, sanitation and clean water. (para 8)
6 Changing the environment so dramatically has a big effect on the local _____ and _____ . (para 10)

Vocabulary *re*-verbs

5 Underline all the words in the article beginning with *re-*. Then circle the verbs that mean 'to do something again'. Form the nouns from these words.

> ▶ **WORDBUILDING prefix *re*- with verbs and nouns**
>
> verb: *redevelop*
> noun: *redevelopment*
>
> For further information and practice, see Workbook page 139.

Critical thinking fact or opinion

6 Work in pairs. This article contains a mixture of facts and opinions about the benefits of the Nam Theun 2 hydropower project. List the facts and opinions about the projects:

- economic benefits
- effects on local people
- effects on the environment

7 Look back at the article. What told you when an opinion was being given rather than a fact? Tell your partner.

8 Compare your answers with another pair. Do you think that the dam has brought more benefits than disadvantages to Laos?

Word focus *pick*

9 Work in pairs. Find three phrases in the article using the word *pick* and discuss what they mean. Then do the same for the phrases in bold below.

1 I think it's easy to **pick holes** in the World Bank plan, but at least they are trying to do the right thing.
2 Can I **pick your brains** for a moment? I'm writing something about Laos and I'm not sure my facts are right.
3 Sales of electricity to Thailand were slow at first but they**'re picking up** now.
4 He feels that he **is being picked on**. The choice of location wasn't only his; it was the responsibility of the whole team.
5 I asked him to **pick me up** from the airport because taxis into the centre are so expensive.
6 We have a range of services – from basic banking to business advice. You can **pick and choose** which you want.

Speaking

10 Work in pairs. What is the impact on people and the environment in the following development projects? How do you deal with this sensitively? Discuss and make lists.

- helping a city damaged by a hurricane
- building a high-speed railway line between two cities
- moving people from a poor and depressed area in a city to a new town

Kai Kensavaong will never again walk along the muddy lanes of Sop On, the village in southern Laos where she was born. Her old home now lies at the bottom of a reservoir of brown water created to feed a hydroelectric power plant, the first to be funded by the World Bank for over twenty years. 'I'll never forget that place,' says the 41-year-old villager. 'It was my home. I picked my first bamboo stalks there.'

The World Bank stopped financing hydroelectric dam projects in developing countries twenty years ago because of criticism that such projects were harming local communities and the environment. But Nam Theun 2 – a 39-metre high dam on the Mekong River that generates over 1,000 megawatts of electricity – is the showpiece for the bank's new policy of supporting sustainable hydropower projects. For Laos it is part of a longer-term strategy to revitalise the economy and become the battery of South-East Asia.

The bank says that lessons have been learnt from the projects of the sixties and seventies when people were forced to resettle and whole areas of forest or agricultural land were flooded. When it comes to clean sources of energy, the bank thinks hydropower is the pick of the bunch, offering the best solution in a world where 1.5 billion people have no access to electricity.

In 2010 the dam brought $5.6 million in sales of electricity and it is estimated that during the next 25 years Nam Theun 2 will generate around $2 billion in revenue to Laos, one of Asia's poorest countries, since most of the electricity will be exported to its power-hungry neighbour, Thailand. The government has promised that this money will be spent on reducing poverty and both renewing and improving the country's infrastructure.

Seventeen villages in the flooded area have now been rebuilt and the 6,200 people – mostly farmers – who lived in them have been retrained to make a living from the reservoir.

The power company has promised to double their living standards within five years. According to the World Bank, 87 per cent of those resettled believe life is much better than before as they now have electricity, sanitation, clean water, new roads and greater access to schools and health care.

'In the old village things just weren't convenient,' said Tiea, 25, one of the relocated villagers. 'It wasn't a pretty place, the houses weren't very nice and we didn't have power. In the new village we have electricity, we can see better.'

But the old criticisms have not gone away. Environmental and human rights groups warn that the dam will have a negative impact on water quality and fish and that the local people who were relocated after the area was flooded may not be able to support themselves economically in future.

'People are happy with these new amenities, but the real problem is how to restore sustainable livelihoods for communities who used to rely on the natural resources – forests, fish and grazing lands for their animals – now that they've lost these,' says Ikuko Matsumoto, programme director for the environmental group, International Rivers.

As well as the 6,200 villagers already rehoused, activists also point out that there are over 110,000 people in riverside villages downstream from the dam whose lives will have to change because of the new river ecosystem. They claim that these people will have to deal with issues like flooding, decline of the fish population and poor water quality. How quickly they will pick up new skills is uncertain.

But the World Bank says it is responsive to these problems. A 4,100-square kilometre protected area has been established around the dam to safeguard flora and fauna. It admits though that rebuilding the lives of the villagers is not a short-term process and everyone is trying to learn and readjust as they go along.

SUSTAINABLE
DEVELOPMENT?

5d Evaluating a project

Real life reaching decisions

1 Work in pairs. What kind of development would most improve your town? Choose three items and number them (1–3) in order of importance.

> a new arts centre (theatre, music, film, fine art)
> a new leisure centre
> a new shopping mall
> better local shops
> better public transport
> fewer cars (pedestrianised zones, cycle tracks)
> more (affordable) housing
> more green spaces

2 🔊 **1.35** The National Development Bank gives loans to local businesses and public authorities for projects that will improve towns and help the local economy. Listen to a meeting of some bank employees who are discussing a project they have funded and complete the notes.

1 Amount of loan	The bank lent the local authority £_____ .
2 Purpose of loan	To help redevelop a _____ in the city.
3 Aims of project	To give local residents a nicer park and some _____ facilities.
4 Progress so far	They have cleaned the area up, planted _____ , laid new _____ . They have also built the _____ and the children's _____ .
5 Other work	They have built a _____ and bought a sculpture for £_____ .
6 Needs	A new loan of £250,000 to complete the _____ courts and _____ golf course.

3 🔊 **1.35** Listen again. What do the bank employees decide to do about the new loan? Do they all agree?

4 🔊 **1.35** Complete the sentences in the box with the phrases the speakers use to give their opinions and to agree and disagree. Then listen and check.

> **▶ REACHING DECISIONS**
>
> What do you think we should do?
> What's your view?
> If you ¹_____ , that's completely wrong.
> Personally, I think that's absurd.
> I don't think we ²_____ give them another penny.
> I find it amazing / ridiculous that he said that.
> I think we should / we ought to give them the benefit of the doubt.
> ³_____ be too hasty. / We shouldn't be too hasty.
> We need ⁴_____ whether they are in the spirit of the original aims of the project.
> That really ⁵_____ the opinion of the local residents.
> The ⁶_____ see it, it's probably a good thing.
> I'd ⁷_____ with that.
> That's right.
> I agree.
> Is everyone OK / happy with that?
> Exactly.
> Are we all ⁸_____ that?
> That ⁹_____ to me.

Speaking

5 Work in pairs. Read the report on page 81 about another project which the bank is financing and consider these points.

- name of project
- date started
- original aims
- action taken and money spent
- results (positive and negative)
- next steps and money needed

Then decide together if you think the bank should lend more money for this project. Discuss your decision with another pair and try to come to an agreement with them.

TALK ABOUT ▶ CHANGES IN YOUR TOWN ▶ A HAPPY SOCIETY ▶ SENSITIVE DEVELOPMENT ▶ REACHING A DECISION
WRITE ▶ AN OPINION ESSAY

5e Big cities, big problems

Writing an opinion essay

1 Work in pairs. Why do you think people want to live in big cities? Make a list of the reasons. Do you think their lives are better there?

2 The chart shows the percentage of the world's population living in cities. What problems do you think this creates?

3 Look at the title of the opinion essay and then read the answer. What is the opinion of the writer?

% of world population living in cities

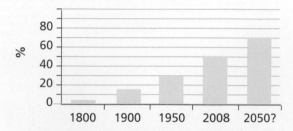

> *Our cities have become too big. The problems they create outweigh the benefits.* **Discuss.**

In 1800 only two per cent of the world's population lived in cities. Over the last twenty years more and more people have moved to cities looking for work and a better life. *As a result*, more than half the world's population now live in cities and that number is expected to grow. Cities are monuments to the amazing organising abilities of human beings. However, in some cases, they also have many social, economic and environmental problems. The question is: do the problems they create outweigh their benefits?

Cities exist because they are more convenient places to live. Jobs, schools, hospitals are all close to people's homes. There is a wide choice of people to socialise with and good possibilities for entertainment and leisure.

On the other hand, there also seems to be more crime, more poverty and more pollution and often there problems are found in a particular area of a town, making them seem even worse. But this is not so surprising, if you think about it. The same problems exist in the countryside or in smaller towns, but they are not so concentrated. *Because of this*, they are noticed less.

As long as the population of cities does not grow more quickly than the services available for it, cities can solve a lot of our problems. They stop the population spreading into areas of the countryside. *In addition*, they provide jobs and a more interesting life. The problem with cities is not how big they are, but how well managed they are.

4 Does this opinion essay follow the standard format?

Introduction → Arguments for → Arguments against → Conclusion

5 The introduction can take different forms. Which of these does the writer choose?

- giving a dramatic example of the problem
- telling a story about the problem from the writer's own experience
- giving some statistics that illustrate the seriousness of the problem
- quoting what someone famous has said about this problem

6 Writing skill linking words

a Look at the linking phrases below. Then underline other examples of each type in the essay. Compare your answers with your partner.

Adding an argument	Introducing a contrasting fact	Explaining the consequences
Furthermore, As well as this,	Then again,	Consequently,

b Choose an appropriate linking phrase to complete the sentences.

1 Certain cities in the world have become especially popular. _____, we have seen the emergence of what are called megacities: cities with over ten million inhabitants.
2 A lot of people find a better standard of living in big cities. _____, you can also find very poor people living in them.
3 _____ being very convenient for the residents, cities are also very convenient for business.

7 Write an opinion essay about the statement below. Then compare your answer with your partner. Did you use the same arguments?

In our modern urban lifestyles, we have lost our sense of community. We need to return to a simpler way of life. Discuss.

8 Read your partner's essay and check the following:

- Do you find the arguments convincing?
- Is it organised in clear paragraphs?
- Does it follow the format suggested in Exercise 4?
- Does it use one of the introduction techniques suggested in Exercise 5?

5f Aquarium on Wheels

The programme really means a lot to me because I want to major in marine biology.

Before you watch

1 Work in groups. Look at the title of this video and the photo and discuss the questions.

1 Why do you think the video is called 'Aquarium on Wheels'?
2 Do you think aquariums can teach children about more than just fish in the sea?
3 What might the programme teach young people?

2 Work in pairs. Tick the things you think you will see in the video.

> a boy dressed as a monkey a computer
> a crocodile   a diver   a fish tank   a frog
> a necklace   seashells   a tiger   a toy snake

While you watch

3 Watch the video and check your answers from Exercise 2.

4 Watch the first part of the video (to 02.17). Choose the correct option to complete the sentences.

1 The students in the video are:
   a employees of the Aquarium on Wheels programme.
   b visitors to the National Aquarium.
2 The students want to help their audience to understand:
   a recycling.   b conservation.
3 The students perform a play about:
   a snakes.   b monkeys.
4 The children laugh because the actor says that:
   a fighting is going to make his hair look untidy.
   b he doesn't have any leaves to eat.
5 Aquarium administrators want to give students:
   a training in marine biology.
   b lessons for life.

5 Watch the second part of the video (02.18 to the end). Answer the questions.

1 What kind of skills do the students need?

2 What do these students want to do that other people in their family haven't done?

3 What does DejaNé Jones say is the most important thing the programme has taught her?

4 What did the students learn from performing the play?

5 What does George Faulk want to be?

6 Why is the programme personally important for Martha Schaum?

After you watch

6 Roleplay an interview with Martha Schaum

Work in pairs.

Student A: Imagine you work for a local newspaper. Use the information below to prepare questions to ask Martha Schaum about the Aquarium on Wheels programme.

Student B: Imagine you are Martha Schaum. A reporter from a local newspaper is going to interview you about the Aquarium on Wheels programme. Look at the information below and think about what you are going to say to the reporter.

- the overall objectives of the Aquarium on Wheels programme
- who is involved with the programme
- what the student employees have been doing this year
- what the programme gives the student employees
- what Martha gets out of the programme personally

Act out the interview, then change roles and act out the interview again.

7 At the end of the video, the narrator says: 'The Aquarium on Wheels programme is having a powerful impact on more than just the rain forests.' What does he mean? Why do you think the programme is so successful?

8 Work in groups and discuss these questions.

1 What kind of education about the environment do young children in your country receive? Is it effective?
2 The overall goal of the Aquarium on Wheels programme is to entertain and educate. Do you think these two aims are compatible? Can you think of examples that meet both aims successfully?

---

advantageous (adj) /ˌædvənˈteɪdʒəs/ having a good effect
camouflage (n) /ˈkæməflɑːʒ/ something an animal uses to make it difficult to see
major (v) /ˈmeɪdʒə/ take a university degree in
mess up (v) /mes ˈʌp/ make something look untidy
overall (adj) /ˌəʊvəˈrɔːl/ general
poison dart (n) /ˈpɔɪzn ˈdɑːt/ a small arrow covered with poison at one end which is fired from a long tube by blowing

UNIT 5 REVIEW

Grammar

1 Work in pairs. What is the main industry in your town or city? How has this affected the character of the city?

2 Read the interview with a resident of Berlin. Answer the questions.

   1 What is the main new industry of Berlin?
   2 How does this resident feel about it?

3 Complete the interview with the correct form of the verb: -ing, to + infinitive or infinitive without to.

I = Interviewer; R = Resident

I: So, are you enjoying [1] _____ (live) here again after a fifteen-year absence? Has Berlin changed a lot since you were last here?

R: Of course. There has been a huge amount of development. They have kept on [2] _____ (build) and [3] _____ (redevelop) since the early nineties. And in many ways that is great for the city, but I regret [4] _____ (say) that its character has changed … and not for the better.

I: What do you mean by that?

R: Well, there are so many tourists here now – people say as many as nine million a year. It's as if the city authorities have decided [5] _____ (turn) Berlin into a tourist park.

I: But surely tourists are a good thing? If they stopped [6] _____ (come), the city would lose a lot of jobs and income. I heard that tourism will help [7] _____ (create) 50,000 new jobs here in the next few years.

R: I'm not anti-tourist. I understand that tourism means [8] _____ (earn) useful income, but a lot of this money goes straight to private companies. I think the city should ask tourists and tourism companies [9] _____ (pay) a tax for visiting Berlin. Then this money could be invested in real jobs for Berliners.

I CAN	
use verbs which take the gerund and infinitive after them	☐
use verbs which take both the gerund and infinitive after them, but with different meanings	☐

Vocabulary

4 Match the words (1–6) with their meaning (a–f).

1	convert	a	bring up to date
2	spoil	b	change completely
3	modernise	c	rebuild
4	demolish	d	damage
5	transform	e	turn into
6	redevelop	f	knock down

5 Work in pairs. Use a different verb in each space to complete these statements.

   1 Green spaces can really _____ a built-up part of a city.
   2 In the 1970s and 1980s there was a fashion for _____ older buildings in city centres and replacing them with high-rise buildings.
   3 It's a good idea to _____ the city centre into a pedestrianised zone.
   4 People complain that the character of many famous cities like London, New York and Paris has been _____ . By _____ them with luxury apartments and expensive shops, developers have forced out ordinary working people.

6 Discuss with your partner if any of the items in Exercise 5 are features of your city. Do you agree with the statements? Why? / Why not?

I CAN	
talk about the different features of a city	☐
describe changes in a city	☐

Real life

7 Work in pairs. Put a verb in each space to complete these sentences expressing opinions.

   1 What do you _____ of the idea to restore the city centre to how it was 200 years ago?
   2 I _____ it amazing that no one has thought of doing it before.
   3 If you _____ me, it's not a good idea.
   4 No, that doesn't _____ right to me either. You have to look forwards not backwards.
   5 The way I _____ it, if it's good for the local economy, then it's a good thing.
   6 I think it _____ on whether local people actually want it to be restored.
   7 Yes, I'd _____ along with that.

8 Work in small groups. Decide if it is better to restore old buildings or to knock them down and start again.

I CAN	
reach a decision by expressing opinions and agreeing or disagreeing	☐

Speaking

9 Work in pairs. Tell each other about a large development project you know about (transport, regeneration of an area, new town, sports or leisure complex, etc.). Cover these points:

- the benefits that the development brings / will bring
- whether it is sustainable or not
- who supports the project; who opposes it
- your opinion

Unit 6 Alternative travel

The Hotel de Glace, Quebec, Canada; the only ice hotel in North America.
Photograph by Ralph Lee Hopkins

FEATURES

70 Staycations

People who holiday at home

72 Voluntourism

Working holidays around the world

74 Unusual places to stay

Hotels with a difference

78 East Timor

A video about tourism in one of the world's richest diving areas

1 Look at the photo. What do you think there is to do in this hotel? Would you like to stay here? Why? / Why not?

2 **1.36** Listen to someone describing her stay there. What did she like about her stay? What didn't she like as much?

3 Work in pairs. Choose the correct option. Then ask each other the questions.

1 How much *holiday / days off* do you get from work each year?
2 Do you like to stay in hotels or do you prefer *self-catering / self-service* accommodation?
3 When you book into a hotel, do you usually ask for a room with a *sight / view*?
4 Do you generally take a lot of *suitcase / luggage* when you travel or do you prefer to travel light?
5 What is your favourite kind of *scenery / countryside*: the coast, forest, mountains or desert?
6 Do you generally enjoy the *travel / journey* as much as actually getting there?
7 Which *aeroplane / airline* do you prefer to fly with?
8 When you last went on holiday, how long did it *take / last* to get to your destination?

6a Staycations

Speaking

1 Work in pairs. How well do you know your own capital city and its attractions? Ask each other these questions to find out.

   1 Can you name five important tourist attractions in your capital city?
   2 How many of these have you visited?
   3 Have you ever been on a bus tour or walking tour of the city?
   4 Have you ever been to a famous street market in the city?
   5 How often do you visit the city's main museums or galleries?
   6 Do you know the name of a good, reasonably-priced hotel in the city?

2 Are there parts of your local area that you haven't ever visited or feel that you don't know? Would you consider taking a holiday there? Why? / Why not?

Reading

3 Read the blog. Are the sentences true (T) or false (F)?

   1 Staycationers always sleep at home.
   2 Staycationers go out and do different activities during their staycation.
   3 Staycations have all the stresses of normal travel.
   4 Staycations simulate traditional holidays.

4 Now use the information in the blog to complete the statements.

   1 People first started having staycations because of …
   2 Staycations are good for the local economy because …
   3 Some people think that visiting local attractions isn't as exciting as …
   4 Without leaving New York, Karen Ash was able to have a …

STAYCATIONS

You probably don't like the term 'staycation'. Me neither. But you mustn't be put off. As a concept, it is quite attractive. Perhaps you've already had one, but weren't aware that's what it was called. Staycations don't just mean staying in doing things around the house or just relaxing at home. They involve getting out more by taking day trips from your home to see local sights. If you don't want to stay at home, you can holiday locally – for example, camping at a local campsite.

Staycations originally became popular after the financial crisis of 2008, when people were looking for ways to cut back on their spending. Apart from the savings, let's not ignore the other benefits: you don't have any of the problems associated with travel, such as packing, long drives, delays at airports and so on; and you bring money to the local economy, by eating out, for example. The only people who hope this kind of holiday won't catch on are the holiday companies themselves.

Some staycationers who base themselves at home like to follow a set of rules, such as setting a start and end date, planning their activities ahead of time and avoiding routine. You don't have to do these things, but it helps to create the feel of a traditional vacation. Others, aware that an extra barbecue and a visit to the local zoo may not match the thrill of foreign travel, take it a step further. A recent example was Karen Ash, whose story appeared in the *Wall Street Journal*.

A resident of New York, Karen Ash decided not to go to Japan, as she had originally planned, but instead took a weeklong Japanese vacation in her own city. This included buying postcards and souvenirs at a Japanese market, admiring bonsai plants, eating ramen (and even speaking Japanese when ordering), all without leaving New York. Her itinerary also involved joining in at a traditional Japanese tea ceremony, attending a taiko drumming concert and watching Japanese soap operas on DVD. I don't think many people would want to take this much trouble to create their staycation, but you get the idea!

Vocabulary phrasal verbs with *in* and *out*

5 Work in pairs. Find two phrasal verbs in the article with *in* and two with *out*. Discuss what they mean.

6 Complete the sentences using *in* and *out*.

1 I'd like to try _____ that new restaurant in the centre of town. I've heard it's excellent.
2 Shall we eat _____ tonight? We've got loads of food.
3 Can you drop _____ at the supermarket on your way home and pick up some milk?
4 All I seem to do is work and sleep these days. I need to get _____ more.
5 My daughter stayed _____ until 3 a.m. last night. I was really worried.
6 Can you just fill _____ this form with your name, address and passport number?

> ▶ **WORDBUILDING phrasal verbs with *in* and *out***
>
> Some verbs can be used with both *in* and *out*. Sometimes they give opposite meanings and sometimes they give different meanings. Other verbs may only be used with either *in* or *out*.
> eat in, eat out; drop in, drop out; join in, ~~join out~~
>
> For further information and practice, see Workbook page 147.

7 Ask each other the following questions.

1 Do you feel you get out enough? If not, what would you like to do more of?
2 How often do you eat out?
3 What do you usually do in the evenings, if you are staying in?
4 If you saw some people in the park playing volleyball, would you watch or join in?
5 How late were you allowed to stay out when you were fifteen years old?
6 Do you like to try out new types of food?

Grammar *not*

8 Underline these examples in the article and comment on the position of *not* in each case:

1 a negative infinitive (para 4)
2 a negative sentence using *want* (para 1)
3 the negative form of *must* (para 1)
4 the opposite of *must* (para 3)
5 a negative sentence using *hope* (para 2)
6 a negative sentence using *think* (para 4)
7 a negative sentence using *let* (para 2)

> ▶ **NOT**
>
> **Negative infinitive**
> *It's cheaper not to go abroad.*
> *They advised us not to stay at that hotel.*
>
> **want**
> *I didn't want to stay in …* *~~I wanted not to stay in …~~*
>
> **mustn't and don't have to**
> *You mustn't book a holiday without comparing prices first.*
> *You don't have to spend a lot of money to enjoy your holiday.* *~~You mustn't spend a lot of money …~~*
>
> **hope and think**
> *I hope it doesn't rain.* *~~I don't hope it rains.~~*
> *I don't think that's right.* *~~I think that's not right.~~*
>
> **let's**
> *Let's stay at home this year. Let's not go abroad.*
>
> For further information and practice, see page 91.

9 Look at the grammar box. Then make each sentence express the opposite idea using negatives.

1 Let's spend a lot of money on a foreign holiday.
2 I want to stay in a big modern hotel.
3 I think staycations can replace foreign holidays.
4 I hope the accommodation is all booked up.
5 I told them to wait until the last moment before booking their holiday.
6 We must go swimming – if you want to, that is.

10 Look at these tips from a travel magazine. Choose the correct option.

Let's [1] *don't forget / not forget* that the main reason for choosing a staycation is to save money. So you really [2] *mustn't spend / don't have to spend* the same amount as you would have if you had gone abroad. For example, if you [3] *don't want to spend / want not to spend* a lot on eating out, just take a picnic with you when you go on a day trip. It [4] *mustn't be / doesn't have to be* a cheap picnic – you can still treat yourself to a few luxuries.

Try [5] *to not choose / not to choose* only activities that cost money. One idea is to plan a two or three day walk and take a tent with you. If you [6] *don't think you'll enjoy / think you won't enjoy* camping, then look up some youth hostels you could stay in instead.

The most important thing is to be adventurous. The fun of any holiday is discovering new places and there is no reason why a staycation should be any different. I [7] *hope it isn't / don't hope it's* a disappointment!

Speaking

11 Work in small groups. Plan a five-day staycation in your own area or the area you are studying in. Try to give the staycation a theme, as in the article, e.g. a sporting theme, or a foreign theme. Make a short itinerary of at least five activities.

12 Work with another group. Compare your staycation ideas. Have a class vote on which staycation sounds the most fun and practical.

6b Voluntourism

Listening

1 Work in pairs. What do you think the English saying below means? Do you have a similar saying in your language? Do you think it's true?

" A change is as good as a rest. "

2 🔊 **1.37** Voluntourism is when people travel to a foreign location to work for free. Look at the photo. What sort of volunteering do you think people do here? Listen to the interview and check if you were right.

3 Which of the statements best summarises Katie Samuel's opinion of what a good volunteer vacation should be?

a   a working holiday where you learn practical and useful skills
b   a cultural experience where both the visitor and the host benefit
c   an enjoyable way to help others less fortunate than yourself

4 🔊 **1.37** Listen again and complete these sentences with one word per space. Then discuss what each expression means.

1   You probably thought that sort of vacation was for eighteen year olds on **their** _____ **year**.
2   For most of us, who only get **a few weeks** _____ **a year**, wouldn't they prefer a more relaxing option?
3   This should be **a** _____ **travel experience**, not just **a work** _____ .
4   In return the locals take them for _____ **walks**, which are like mini-safaris.
5   They have to pay for their flight, **their** _____ **expenses** and something to cover the organisation costs.
6   The CRTP helps to restore **cultural** _____ **sites** around the world.

5 Work in groups. Discuss the questions. Then tell the class.

1   What do you think of this type of vacation?
2   Is it right that people have to pay to be a volunteer?
3   What other ways can you think of to get close to local people on a vacation?

Grammar **negative and tag questions**

6 There are various ways of phrasing a question. Look at these examples (1–4) from the interview and match each one to the answer the speaker wants (a–c).

1   Have you ever thought of doing a bit of building work during your holidays?
2   You probably thought that sort of vacation was for eighteen-year-olds, didn't you?
3   Wouldn't most people prefer a more relaxing option?
4   It's not really a holiday as we know it, is it?

a   Doesn't expect a particular answer (*yes* or *no*)
b   Wants the answer to be *yes*
c   Wants the answer to be *no*

7 Work in pairs. Find four more examples of questions that expect a particular answer in the audioscript on page 97.

> ▶ **NEGATIVE and TAG QUESTIONS**
>
> **Open questions (no confirmation of opinion demanded)**
> *Do you like visiting new places?*
> *Yes, now and again.*
>
> **Negative questions**
> *Don't you like visiting new places?*
> *No, not at all.*
>
> **Tag questions**
> *You like visiting new places, don't you?*
> *Yes, I love it.*
> *You don't like visiting new places, do you?*
> *No, you're right. I don't.*
>
> For further information and practice, see page 92.

8 Look at the grammar box. Convert these open questions into negative or tag questions that fit the answer given.

1 Do you like the idea of volunteer vacations? (tag question)

_____?

Yes, that's right ... very much

2 Do you think it's an interesting idea? (negative question)

_____?

No, I don't.

3 Have you been on a volunteer vacation? (tag question)

_____?

Yes, two years ago.

4 Did it seem strange to pay money in order to work? (negative question)

_____?

No, not really.

5 Will you be going again this year? (tag question)

_____?

No. We're having a staycation this year.

9 Pronunciation intonation in questions

a 🔊 **1.38** Look at the grammar box. Listen to the sentences and answer the questions.

1 Does the speaker's intonation rise or fall at the end of an open question?
2 Does the speaker's intonation rise or fall at the end of a negative question?
3 Does the speaker's intonation rise or fall at the end of each tag question?

b 🔊 **1.39** Work in pairs. Practise saying the sentences in Exercise 8 with the correct intonation. Then listen and check your pronunciation.

10 🔊 **1.40** The Great Continental Divide is a cycling and hiking trail that crosses North America from Mexico to Canada. Read this telephone conversation between Mike (M), a volunteer, and Jeff (J), from the Great Continental Divide Alliance. Convert the sentences in bold into either negative or tag questions. Then listen and check your answers.

M: Hi, I'm interested in helping out on the Great Continental Divide this summer. My friend did four days last summer. [1] _____ **(I / can / work / for / just a few days)**

J: Absolutely. Anything from two days to two months.

M: That's great. I have about a week in June. How much does it cost to take part?

J: It's free.

M: Sorry? [2] _____ **(I / have to / pay / for / my accommodation)**

J: No, it's completely free. You just have to register by filling out a form and sending it to us.

M: [3] _____ **(I / can / do / that / online)**

J: Sure, you can. It's on our website. [4] _____ **(you / have / visited / our website)**

M: Yes, I've had a quick look. And where on the trail can I work?

J: New Mexico, Montana, Wyoming …

M: [5] _____ **(you / have / something / in Colorado)** That's where I live.

J: Yes, we do. We have spaces in Winfield and a few in Mount Elbert.

M: [6] _____ **(and / you / give / training / first)**

J: It's on the job training, unless it's very specific. We're looking for a chef at the moment. [7] _____ **(you / want / to be / a chef)**

M: No. I just want to help build some trails …

Speaking

11 Ask negative or tag questions to try to persuade others of your opinions about these aspects of travel. Speak to as many people as possible.

- beach holidays
- experiencing local culture
- travelling alone
- trying out local food
- volunteer vacations
- working abroad

TALK ABOUT ▶ PLANNING A STAYCATION ▶ **TRAVEL** ▶ AN UNUSUAL HOTEL ▶ GETTING AROUND
WRITE ▶ A LETTER OF COMPLAINT

73

6c Unusual places to stay

Reading

1 Work in pairs. Make a list of what you look for in a place to stay on holiday (comfort, a beautiful setting, modern facilities, etc.). Then compare your list with another pair.

2 Read the extract from a travel magazine's guide to unusual places. Answer the questions.

1 Which seem like comfortable places to stay?
2 Which seem to have the most disadvantages?

3 Read the article again. Choose the correct option to complete the sentences.

1 Karosta's own description of its hotel:
   a is surprising. b is not truthful.
2 The writer thinks the cost of a night in prison:
   a is too high. b is about right.
3 For a long time after the gold rush Virginia City:
   a was uninhabited.
   b was a rich town.
4 The cabins at the Nevada City Hotel are:
   a all newly built.
   b a mix of old and new.
5 The caves of Sassi di Matera have always been:
   a lived in. b used to store things.
6 The new owners have tried to keep the original:
   a furniture. b feel of the caves.
7 In a lot of art hotels the art is not:
   a very good. b very prominent.
8 The different rooms at the Propeller Island City Lodge are decorated:
   a in a dramatic way.
   b in a similar way.

4 All these words describe parts of a building. Find them in the article and discuss their meaning with your partner. Use a dictionary if necessary.

| balcony   balustrade   corridor |
| earth roofs   saloon   vaulted ceilings |

5 Which of these places would you prefer to stay in? What are your reasons? Tell your partner.

Critical thinking claims and justifications

6 Each of these hotels claims to offer an authentic experience. For each hotel say what the experience is, which facts support this claim, and which facts, if any, don't support it.

Hotel	Claims to be ...	Supporting facts	Contradictory facts

7 Work in pairs. Discuss the questions.

1 Does it matter that some of the claims the hotels make are not always justified?
2 Does it make you less likely to trust them?
3 Does it make you less likely to stay there?

Word focus *mind*

8 Work in pairs. In each paragraph there is an expression with the word *mind*. Discuss if it is a noun or a verb, and what it means. Then work out what these other expressions with *mind* mean.

1 I am **in two minds** about whether to stay at a hotel or drive back home that night.
2 **Mind** how you go in the city. It can get dangerous there at night.
3 If you **change your mind** about coming with me, let me know before Friday.
4 I'm sure you can think of a solution if you **put your mind to it**.
5 Sorry I haven't got back to you about the weekend. I've had a lot **on my mind** lately.
6 Sorry, I know I've heard his name before but my **mind's gone blank**.

9 Write three sentences with different phrases with *mind*, but leave a blank where the phrase should be. Exchange sentences with another pair and fill in the blanks.

Speaking and writing

10 Work in small groups. Create your own idea for an unusual place to stay. Discuss:

- where the hotel is
- how your hotel is different
- whether it should be luxurious or basic
- what facilities you can offer that fit with the theme

11 Write a short description of it. Then present your idea to the class. Vote for which one sounds the most interesting.

Unusual places to stay

PRISON HOTELS Built in 1905, Karosta naval jail in Latvia was originally home to mutinous Russian sailors. In the 1970s it housed political prisoners. According to their website this is 'an opportunity to stay overnight on real prisoners' benches and mattresses'. In direct contrast to most hotel publicity, the website goes on to describe Karosta proudly as 'unfriendly, unheated and uncomfortable'. They are not lying. This is more a reality jail experience than a hotel. 'Reception' is a dark corridor where a former prison guard explains the rules to you (no luggage except a toothbrush, no attempts to escape), and then fires his gun in the air to show you he is serious. After a meal of bread and sweet Russian tea, 'guests' are given five minutes to wash before making up their own bed from a wooden bench and thin mattress. Sound unpleasant? It is. Mind you, for $12 per night, what do you expect?

PERIOD HOTELS Would you like to experience life in America's Wild West 150 years ago? Virginia City in Montana, a former gold-rush town, was a ghost town until it began to be restored in the 1950s for tourism. Owned largely by the state government, the town operates now as a large open-air museum. Nearby is the Nevada City Hotel and cabins where you can hang up your Stetson hat and enjoy life as a cowboy. The rooms feature period Victorian furniture and downstairs the saloon has a true Wild West feel. The cabins look extremely rustic and basic from the outside – two even have their original earth roofs – but inside they have large double beds and private bathrooms. Bear in mind that if you book in the week, you might be disappointed because the city only comes to life at weekends, when actors walk around in period costumes, such as sheriffs, cowboys and gold prospectors.

CAVE HOTELS If you had more primitive accommodation in mind, why not try the caves of Sassi di Matera on the toe of Italy, which have been inhabited since the Bronze Age? During the Renaissance they developed into more sophisticated rooms with stone walls, vaulted ceilings and balustrades. But in recent history they are best known as the poor homes of the peasants who lived there with their animals until as late as 1952. Now, however, they have been renovated to provide hospitality in a historical setting. Although visitors to Le Grotte Della Civita must do without television or fridges, the rooms are comfortably furnished with antique furniture and period terracotta tiles. The owners wanted the caves to still feel as authentic as possible, so they have built the furniture into the walls of the caves and left in place the iron rings where peasants tied up their animals. Prices start at $300 per night.

ART HOTELS A modern art gallery is a place where you can lose yourself in an artist's vision of the world. A hotel is essentially a place where you can spend the night, in either more or less comfort according to your budget. As its advertising promises, Propeller Island City Lodge in Berlin manages to combine the two. Housed in a former apartment block, the hotel is a collection of individually designed rooms – the upside-down room, the all-orange room, the mirror-filled room – which are often so extreme that you have no choice except to get into the spirit of it. In some art hotels, you could forget the art and simply enjoy the comfort of your surroundings. That's not the case with Propeller Island. However, the rooms can be small and claustrophobic (although some have balconies) and often you have to share a bathroom with other guests. But if you don't mind that, it may be the next best thing to spending the night in a gallery.

6d Couch surfing

Real life getting around

1 Work in pairs. Take one minute to read this description of couch surfing. Then discuss how couch surfing works. Is it something you would do? Why? / Why not?

2 You are going to listen to a conversation between a couch surfer and a host. Look at the box. Who do you think says each expression?

3 🔊 **1.41** Listen to the conversation. Check your answers from Exercise 2.

4 🔊 **1.41** Listen again. Complete the expressions.

> ▶ **GETTING AROUND**
>
> I'm coming in by ¹ _____ .
> I wanted to pick you up, but ² _____ .
> That's ³ _____ , but I can make my own way.
> How do I get to ⁴ _____ ?
> You could just get ⁵ _____ .
> Alternatively, you can hop on ⁶ _____ .
> Look out for the ⁷ _____ on your right.
> It's only a twenty-minute ⁸ _____ .
> The easiest thing is to ⁹ _____ .
> I'll come out and ¹⁰ _____ .
> If I get held up, I'll ¹¹ _____ . But otherwise, expect a call around six thirty.

5 Pronunciation intonation in sentences with two clauses

a 🔊 **1.42** Listen to these two sentences with *but*. Notice how the speaker's intonation rises at the end of the first clause, indicating that they have not finished speaking.

I wanted to pick you up, but my car's at the garage that day.
You could just get a taxi, but it's about eleven kilometres from the centre.

b Practise saying these sentences using the same intonation.

1 I'll try to get home by six, but I can't promise I will.
2 Normally it's a ten-minute drive, but the road works have made it longer.
3 I can't make it today, but I'll pop over tomorrow.
4 It's kind of you to offer, but we can make our own way.
5 The bus is cheap, but the train is much quicker.

6 Work in pairs. Take turns to play the roles of couch surfer and host. As the guest, imagine you come from another country and are touring the host's country. Telephone your host and ask about the best way to get to his/her home from another city.

Originally the idea of a New Hampshire student who emailed 1,500 students at the University of Iceland asking if he could sleep the night on their couches, couch surfing is now an established worldwide practice. This is how it works. When you have made your travel plans, you contact people on the couch surfing network by email, to find out if they can offer you a bed for the night in the places you are going to visit. There's no fee. The only obligation on your part is to be able to offer a place to stay at your home when someone asks in the future. Apart from being free, the benefit is that you meet people with local knowledge. If you're lucky, some might even become long-term friends.

TALK ABOUT ▶ PLANNING A STAYCATION ▶ TRAVEL ▶ AN UNUSUAL HOTEL ▶ **GETTING AROUND**
WRITE ▶ A LETTER OF COMPLAINT

6e A disappointed customer

Writing a letter of complaint

1 Have you ever had a bad experience on holiday that caused you to complain? What happened and what was the outcome?

2 Read this complaint from a guest about a stay in a hotel and answer the questions.

1 Why is the customer unhappy?
2 What does she want the hotel to do about it?
3 Does her complaint seem justified?

---

44 Ascot Street
Oxford
OX4 1EP

Sweet Hotel Group
54 Pembroke Road
London
W8 6NX

Dear Sir / Madam

I am writing to express my dissatisfaction with my stay at the Victoria Arms Hotel on 12th April. I made a reservation through another website which was offering one night for two people with an evening meal and breakfast for £110. However, when we arrived at 5.30 p.m. we were informed that there was no table available in the restaurant and that we could either dine at 6.00 p.m. or find another restaurant in the town.

We had the strong impression that because it was a discounted offer, we did not receive the same level of hospitality as regular, full-paying guests. The situation was both embarrassing and inconvenient. After some discussion with the staff, we opted to dine in the restaurant, but much later than we wished – at 9.30 p.m. No one apologised for this.

Given the circumstances, compensation is not my principal concern. Rather, I would ask you to investigate the matter thoroughly to ensure this does not arise in future with other guests.

Yours faithfully

Ann Dunhill

---

3 Work in pairs. Formal letters follow certain conventions. Answer the questions.

1 What is the correct position for each address?
2 When do we write *Yours faithfully* and when do we write *Yours sincerely*?
3 Where is the reason for writing mentioned?
4 Where is the request to the recipient of the letter for action?

4 Writing skill formal language

a Find the formal words or phrases in the letter that say the following:

1 say I was unhappy   7 wanted
2 we were told   8 what worries me
3 a cheap deal   most
4 get   9 look into
5 after we talked to   10 make sure
6 chose to eat

b Convert the phrases in bold in these sentences into more formal language. Use the letter to help you.

1 We **want** to **tell you how unhappy we were** with the standard of the food on the cruise ship *Golden Dawn*.
  Example:
  We wish to express our dissatisfaction with the standard of the food on the cruise ship Golden Dawn.
2 I **told** the receptionist that I **had booked the room** for two nights, not one.
3 After **I'd talked to** the manager, she **said she was sorry** and promised to **look into** the problem with the shower. **But** no action was taken.
4 I would have expected that the safety of the guests **was what the staff were most worried about**.
5 Given the **trouble** this caused us, we expected **to get some money back**.
6 The manager said no other rooms were **free**, but if the opportunity **came up**, she'd move us.

5 Read the situation and then write a letter of complaint to the hotel.

You recently stayed at a small hotel in the centre of Oxford in the UK. During the night you were woken up by some noisy people trying to climb a wall into the hotel courtyard. You went down to reception to tell a member of the hotel staff but no one was there. You are angry and upset that no staff were on duty during the night.

6 Exchange letters and read your partner's letter. Use these questions to check their letter.

- Does it begin with the reason for writing?
- Does it end with what action is expected?
- Does it use rhetorical or other types of question to be persuasive?

6f East Timor

East Timor ... for the intrepid few, an emerging tourism destination with unspoiled natural beauty.

Before you watch

1 Work in groups. Look at the photo of East Timor and discuss the questions.

   1 What do you know about East Timor?
   2 Why do you think the caption says that East Timor is 'for the intrepid few'? What does this suggest about the country?

2 Only two of these scenes appear in the video you are going to watch. Tick the two scenes.

   a a person sunbathing on a tropical beach
   b builders renovating a damaged building
   c a group of people pulling in fishing nets from the sea
   d tourists having drinks in a hotel bar

While you watch

3 Watch the video and check your answers from Exercise 2.

4 Watch the first part of the video (to 00.45). Complete the conversation between a journalist (J) and Ann Turner (A).

J: Hi Ann, where do you work?
A: ¹ _____
J: Why did you first come to East Timor?
A: ² _____
J: And when did you decide that you wanted to stay?
A: ³ _____
J: What four things would you say impressed you most?
A: ⁴ _____
J: How many fish species are there?
A: ⁵ _____
J: Why is there such a huge diversity of fish species here?
A: ⁶ _____

5 Watch the second part of the video (00.46 to the end). Answer the questions.

   1 What is the main problem on East Timor?

   2 How long has East Timor been independent?

   3 What happened after people in East Timor voted for independence?

   4 What is the government worried about?

   5 What policies is the government working on?

   6 What should people who want to start a tourism business in East Timor do?

6 Watch the whole video again. Number the extracts in the order you hear them.

   a The subsequent recovery effort has been painfully slow.
   b Welcome to East Timor, one of the world's newest countries.
   c It faces an age-old predicament: how to make the most of its natural assets without destroying them.
   d East Timor is a former war zone.
   e We are still developing policies and regulations.

After you watch

7 Roleplay talking about a new project

Work in pairs.

Student A: Imagine you are an expatriate, living on East Timor. You want to build a small beach hotel. Look at the ideas below. Think about what you are going to say to a government official.

• what you hope to do
• how you will ensure the environment is protected
• how your hotel will benefit the local economy

Student B: Imagine you are an East Timor government official. Look at the information below. Think about what you are going to say to an expatriate business person.

• You are interested in attracting tourism to your country but you also want to protect the environment.
• Find out how the beach hotel project will do both.

Act out the conversation. Then change roles and act out the conversation again with a new business. Decide whether the business is a good idea or not.

8 Work in groups and discuss these questions.

   1 Which areas of your country attract tourists?
   2 How does tourism contribute to the economy of your country?
   3 What impact does it have on natural assets?
   4 Do you think the government does enough to protect the natural assets of your country?

asset (n) /ˈæset/ a valuable possession
emerging (adj) /ɪˈmɜːdʒɪŋ/ in the process of being formed
expatriate (n) /eksˈpætriət/ someone who lives in a foreign country
infrastructure (n) /ˈɪnfrəstrʌktʃə/ basic services that are necessary for a community to function
intrepid (adj) /ɪnˈtrepɪd/ brave, willing to take risks
meagre (adj) /ˈmiːgə/ small
militia (n) /məˈlɪʃə/ an armed group
rampage (v) /ræmˈpeɪdʒ/ behave in a wild and violent way
ruin (v) /ˈruːɪn/ destroy
unspoiled (adj) /ʌnˈspɔɪld/ in the natural state

Grammar

1 Work in pairs. Look at the photo. What kind of tourist attraction do you think this is?

2 Read the conversation and see if you were right.

3 What is Pauline's idea for her next holiday? Why has she decided this?

4 Complete the conversation using a phrase with *not* in each space.

M = Marina; P = Pauline

M: You're planning to go to Mexico for your holidays, ¹_____?

P: That was the plan, but I've ²_____ (decide / go) now. I thought to myself, 'You're always travelling to exotic places. Why ³_____ (find) out something about your own country for a change?'

M: That's interesting. That's called a *staycation*, ⁴_____? You'll certainly save a lot of money.

P: Well, I hope so. But I ⁵_____ (want / stay) at home. I'm going to travel around the north of France. Giverny, the garden where Monet painted his water lilies, is one place I'd really like to go. I ⁶_____ (hope / rain) a lot.

M: Where are you going to stay? Or have ⁷_____ (decide) yet?

P: I'll take a tent with me, but I ⁸_____ (think / I will use) it all the time. Let's ⁹_____ (be) too ambitious! I'll stay in guest houses sometimes.

M: Well, I think it sounds like a great idea. It means you ¹⁰_____ (must / worry) about visas and changing money and vaccinations and all that sort of thing.

I CAN	
use *not* correctly with *hope*, *think*, *want*, *let*, *must* and in the infinitive	
make negative questions and negative tag questions	

Vocabulary

5 Put in the correct preposition to complete these questions about holidays.

1 Do you prefer to cater for yourself or do you generally eat _____ when you're on holiday?
2 Do you like to try _____ new food when you're on holiday or do you prefer to play safe?
3 Do you generally join _____ with group activities and organised excursions or do you prefer to do things alone?
4 If you had two weeks _____ work, how far would you consider travelling on holiday?
5 Before you can enter the country, you have to fill _____ an immigration form.
6 Try not to stay _____ too late, we have an early start tomorrow.

6 Work in pairs. Ask each other the questions in Exercise 5.

I CAN	
use phrasal verbs with in and out	
talk about holidays and travel	

Real life

7 Work in pairs. Find the correct ending from list B for each phrase in list A.

A	B
I'm coming in	in traffic.
The easiest thing is to hop	my own way.
I'll pick you up	ride.
I'll call if I get held up	to your house?
Look out for the Hoover building	by train.
I can easily make	on a bus.
It's only a ten-minute	on your right.
How do I get	from the station.

8 Tell your partner how to get to a well-known meeting point in your town when they have arrived by public transport.

I CAN	
describe the best way to get to one place from another	
ask for directions and travel advice	

Speaking

9 Work in pairs. What do you look for when choosing where to go on holiday? Tell each other which of these things are more important to you and why:

• the comfort OR the experience
• the journey OR the destination itself
• familiarity with the place OR not knowing anything about it
• relaxation OR being active

UNIT 3c Exercise 11, page 38

Instructions

- Form a group of three or four people and ask the teacher which product you are going to present.
- Turn to page 82 and read the description of the product.
- Together prepare a brief presentation of the product: what it is, how it works, what it is appropriate for and why it is special.
- Choose one person to give the presentation (the others will have to answer questions). Think about the questions you may be asked.
- Give and listen to the presentations, asking and answering questions as you go.
- Take a class vote on which product you think is the best.

UNIT 4a Exercise 10, page 47

Participation by art form

Art form	Creative participation %	Receptive participation %	Total participation %
Visual Arts & Crafts	22	38	49
Theatre & Dance	7	40	42
Reading/ Creative Writing	16	84	84
Music	15	57	62

Participation in music

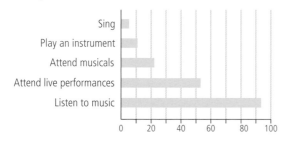

Reasons for non-participation

Reason	Non-participants %
It's difficult to find the time	54
I'm not really interested	43
It costs too much	41
There aren't enough opportunities close to where I live	28

UNIT 5d Exercise 5, page 64

Aston Homes for the Elderly

The National Development Bank agreed a loan of £9 million with the Aston Housing Association (AHA) in September 2009. The purpose of the loan was to convert eight residential houses into groups of self-contained apartments for elderly people in the community who did not want to go into nursing or care homes.

Work started in December 2009 and so far five of the houses have already been converted, creating 40 self-contained apartments. The AHA has sold 30 of these, raising £4.5 million. It has also made repayments to the bank correctly and on time.

However, there have been complaints from local residents that AHA has sold some of the flats to people who are not so elderly (one lady was in her late fifties) and that they have allowed people from outside the area to buy them. It seems that the price of the apartments is in fact too high for many local people.

The AHA now intends to convert a further two houses in the same area and is asking for a further loan of £2.2 million.

UNIT 5b Exercise 10, page 61

Questionnaire

1. HOW SATISFIED DO PEOPLE SEEM WITH THE AMOUNT OF MONEY THEY HAVE?

2. DO PEOPLE HAVE A GOOD BALANCE BETWEEN WORK AND FREE TIME?

3. HOW HAPPY ARE PEOPLE WITH THE EDUCATION THEY RECEIVE?

4. HOW CONFIDENT ARE PEOPLE IN YOUR COUNTRY'S HEALTH SYSTEM TO LOOK AFTER THEM?

5. WHAT KIND OF FOOD DO PEOPLE EAT? IS IT HEALTHY OR NOT?

6. HOW ENGAGED ARE PEOPLE POLITICALLY?

7. HOW OFTEN DO PEOPLE PARTICIPATE A LOT IN CULTURAL ACTIVITIES?

8. ARE PEOPLE TOLERANT OF THE DIFFERENT GROUPS IN SOCIETY?

UNIT 3c Exercise 11, page 38

Description 1

Portable Clay Cooler
Building upon an ancient food-storage technique, the pot-in-pot system uses evaporation from a layer of wet sand between two pots to help extend the life of farmers' goods. Tomatoes can last weeks instead of just days, meaning more fresh produce at the market and more income for farmers.

Developed by: Mohammed Bah Abba
Website: none available
Launch country: Nigeria

UNIT 3c Exercise 11, page 38

Description 3

Water Container
In poor rural areas, clean water is often miles away from the people who need it, leaving them vulnerable to diseases found in unclean water. The strong Q Drum holds thirteen gallons in a rolling container that makes it easy to transport safe, drinking water – a task that is usually done by women and children.

Developed by: P. J. and J. P. S. Hendrikse
Website: http://www.qdrum.co.za
Launch country: South Africa

UNIT 3c Exercise 11, page 38

Description 2

Sugarcane Charcoal
Burning wood and dung, the main fuel sources for many in the developing world, has contributed to deforestation and breathing problems among inhabitants. These briquettes made from crushed sugarcane stalks not only make use of a local resource, they also burn more cleanly and allow residents to start a charcoal business for less than $50.

Developed by: MIT D-Lab
Website: http://d-lab.mit.edu/resources
Launch country: Haiti

UNIT 3c Exercise 11, page 38

Description 4

Solar Wi-Fi Streetlight
The StarSight system consists of a series of pylons that use solar panels to power streetlamps, a Wi-Fi box for wireless Internet access, and if needed, closed-circuit TVs for security surveillance. The result is an integrated system of electricity and communication, plus better street lighting, which has been shown to help reduce crime.

Developed by: Kolam Partnership Ltd.
Website: http://www.starsightproject.com
Launch countries: Nigeria, South Africa, Turkey

UNIT 1
Present tenses review
Form
Present simple

Affirmative	Negative
I/you/we/they **live**	I/you/we/they **don't live** (don't = do not)
he/she/it **lives**	he/she/it **doesn't live** (doesn't = does not)

Interrogative	Short answer
do I/you/we/they **live**?	Yes, I/you/we/they **do**. No, I/you/we/they **don't**.
does he/she/it **live**?	Yes, he/she/it **does**. No, he/she/it **doesn't**.

Present continuous

Affirmative	Negative
I**'m living** ('m = am)	I**'m not** living ('m not = am not)
you**'re**/ we**'re**/they**'re living** ('re = are)	you/we/they **aren't living** (aren't = are not)
he**'s**/she**'s**/it**'s living** ('s = is)	he/she/it **isn't living** (isn't = is not)

Interrogative	Short answer
am I **living**?	Yes, I **am**. No, I**'m not**.
are you/we/they **living**?	Yes, you/we/they **are**. No, you/we/they **aren't**.
is he/she/it **living**?	Yes, he/she/it **is**. No, he/she/it **isn't**.

Present perfect simple

Affirmative	Negative
I**'ve**/you**'ve**/we**'ve**/they**'ve lived** ('ve = have)	I/you/we/they **haven't lived** (haven't = have not)
he**'s**/she**'s**/it**'s lived** ('s = has)	he/she/it **hasn't lived** (hasn't = has not)

Interrogative	Short answer
have I/you/we/they **lived**?	Yes, I/you/we/they **have**. No, I/you/we/they **haven't**.
has he/she/it **lived**?	Yes, he/she/it **has**. No, he/she/it **hasn't**.

Note the spelling rules for -ed endings:
work → work**ed**; play → play**ed**; die → di**ed**; lie → li**ed**; try → tri**ed**; study → stud**ied**; stop → sto**pped**
Some verbs have irregular past participles, for example:
do → done; find → found; have → had; make → made

Present perfect continuous

Affirmative	Negative
I**'ve**/you**'ve**/we**'ve**/they**'ve been living** ('ve = have)	I/you/we/they **haven't been living** (haven't = have not)
he**'s**/she**'s**/it**'s been living** ('s = has)	he/she/it **hasn't been living** (hasn't = has not)

Interrogative	Short answer
have I/you/we/they **been living**?	Yes, I/you/we/they **have**. No, I/you/we/they **haven't**.
has he/she/it **been living**?	Yes, he/she/it **has**. No, he/she/it **hasn't**.

Note the spelling rules for -ing endings:
work → working; play → playing; live → living; have → having; stop → stopping; run → running; die → dying; lie → lying

Use
Present simple
We use the present simple to talk about:
* facts or things which are generally true. *Orang-utans **eat** bark, fruit and leaves. The Earth **doesn't move** around the Moon. Where **do** polar bears **live**?*
* daily routines and habits. *I **work** in that factory every day. I always **have** a shower in the morning.*
* a permanent state or situation. *She **doesn't play** the piano. **Do** you **live** in Manchester?*

We often use adverbs of frequency (*always, usually, often, sometimes, rarely, never*) and expressions of frequency (*once a week, on Fridays, at the weekend, in the summer, every Saturday*) with the present simple to talk about how often we do something.
*We **always** play football on Saturday morning.*
*She **never** talks to strangers.*

Present continuous
We use the present continuous to talk about a situation in progress or things which are happening now or around now. With the present continuous we often use these time expressions: *at the moment, (right) now, this week, this summer.*
*The boys **are playing** tennis in the park.*
*Paul **isn't staying** in Paris long.*
***Are** you **doing** your report, Chris?*

Present perfect simple
We use the present perfect simple to talk about a recent action or situation which started at some time in the past. The situation may also continue into the present or have a result in the present.
*The dogs are happy because she **has** just **fed** them.*
*Michael can't come with us because he **hasn't renewed** his passport.*
***Have** you **visited** your grandparents lately?*

Present perfect continuous

We use the present perfect continuous to talk about an action or situation that was in progress in the recent past. The situation may also continue into the present or have a result in the present. We use the present perfect continuous, not the present perfect simple, to emphasise the duration of an action.

I've been working in this office for six months. (I'm still working in the office.)
They've been behaving like this since they arrived.
What *have you been doing* since I saw you last?
She *hasn't been working* hard enough lately!

We often use the present perfect simple and continuous with *since* and *for* to talk about how long a situation has continued. We use *since* with the point of time when the activity started, for example *since Monday, since ten o' clock, since January, since I was a boy*. We use *for* to talk about a period of time up to now, for example *for an hour, for two months, for a long time*.

We've been friends *since* we were twelve years old.
We've been playing at the club *since* 2010.
I've lived in this house *for* six months.
I've been going to Asia on holiday *for* eight years.

Practice

1 Choose the correct option.

Can you believe these other unlikely friendships between animals?

- A baby hippo [1] ___*has been living*___ with a giant tortoise since a devastating tsunami in 2004. They [2] ___ and [3] ___ together.
- One intrepid explorer says that his Eskimo dogs [4] ___ an extraordinary relationship with some polar bears. They [5] ___ together each year since 2008, when the dogs first travelled through the Arctic lands of Canada.
- Ellie, a dog, and Hattie, an elephant, [6] ___ the best of friends since they met in 2009.
- At a reserve in South Africa, a leopard cub and Tommy, a dog, often [7] ___ together several times a week. At the moment they [8] ___ in the same kennel.

People are amazed by these friendships. 'It's true to say that there has been an evolution in the animal kingdom recently,' says one animal expert.

1 a has been living b has lived c is living
2 a are eating b have eaten c eat
3 a are sleeping b have slept c sleep
4 a have been b have been getting c have got
5 a are playing b have played
   c have been playing
6 a become b are becoming c have become
7 a play b are playing c have played
8 a sleep b are sleeping c have slept

The passive
Form

We form the passive with the correct form of the verb *to be* + past participle.

Tense	Active	Passive
Present simple	makes/make	**is/are** made
Present continuous	is/are making	**is/are being** made
Present perfect simple	has/have made	**has/have been** made

Use

We use the passive voice when we want to focus on an action or the object of the action, rather than the person who is doing the action. The object of the active sentence becomes the subject of the passive sentence.

                    subject   object
Active: Parents are questioning the new values.
                      subject   object
Passive: The new values are being questioned by parents.

In a passive sentence, we can say who did the action (the agent) using *by*. We use *by* + agent when it is important to know who did the action. It isn't always necessary to use *by* + agent. We don't usually use the agent when it is obvious who has done the action, when we don't know, or when it isn't important or relevant.

The best products are selected **by the product manager**.
Guests are asked ~~by the hotel~~ *to sign the visitors' book.*

We also use the passive when the agent doesn't want to be known in order to avoid criticism.
I'm sorry, but the window has been broken ~~by me~~.

Practice

2 Rewrite the sentences in the passive form. Use *by* + agent where appropriate.

1 They are changing people's lives every day.
   People's lives are being changed every day.
2 We make new plans all the time.

3 The government is bringing in some new laws.

4 They have changed the whole system since I was a student.

5 Young people are forgetting the old way of life.

6 We haven't seen good manners for a very long time.

7 We are still respecting a lot of the old customs.

8 Are they respecting the way that people used to live?

UNIT 2

Past simple and present perfect simple

Form

Past simple

We add -ed to regular verbs to form the past simple.

Affirmative	Negative
I/you/he/she/it/we/they **worked**	I/you/he/she/it/we/they **didn't work** (didn't = did not)

Interrogative	Short answer
did I/you/he/she/it/we/they **work**?	Yes, I/you/he/she/it/we/they **did**. No, I/you/he/she/it/we/they **didn't**.

Note the spelling rules for other regular verbs:
- for verbs ending in -e, we add -d: *realise → realised*
- for verbs ending in -y, we change the -y to i and add -ed: *carry → carried*
- for verbs ending in vowel + consonant (not -w, -x or -y), we double the consonant: *plan → planned*

Some verbs have an irregular affirmative form in the past simple:
be → was/were; do → did; go → went; see → saw; write → wrote

Present perfect simple

We form the present perfect simple with the present simple of the verb *to have* + past participle.

See page 84: Present perfect simple

Use

Past simple

We use the past simple to talk about finished actions in the past when there is a clear link to a specific time in the past. We often use a time phrase (*yesterday, last week, five years ago*) with the past simple.
*He **finished** the film script two hours ago.*
*They **didn't go** to the cinema last night.*
***Did** you **meet** Alex at the meeting earlier?*

We use the past simple to talk about someone's life, when they are dead.
*Sharpe **fought** as a soldier in the army during the Napoleonic wars.*

Present perfect simple

We use the present perfect simple to talk about a recent action or situation which started at some time in the past. The situation may also continue into the present or have a result in the present. We use the present perfect simple when the experience is more important than the time and the time is not stated.
I've seen a lot of different films in the last five years.
She's visited a lot of interesting places in her life.
He hasn't seen the new Lord of the Rings film yet.

We also use the present perfect simple to talk about people's life experiences (when the person is still alive).
I've never been to New Zealand.
Have you ever been to the North Pole?

When we talk about a period of time that is not finished, we use the present perfect simple, even if the action itself is finished.
Have you talked to the producer this afternoon? (It is still afternoon.)

When the period of time is finished, we use the past simple.
Did you talk to the producer this afternoon? (It is the evening, the afternoon has finished.)

Practice

1 Choose the correct option.

1 I *saw / have seen* a very gripping film yesterday.
2 *Did you ever read / Have you ever read* an Agatha Christie story?
3 I *didn't like / haven't liked* the end of his new novel. It was too sentimental.
4 They *enjoyed / have enjoyed* watching the play last night.
5 Elena *didn't study / hasn't studied* literature for a long time.
6 The students *wrote / have written* some very original short stories on last year's creative writing course.
7 His parents *told / have told* him a lot of funny anecdotes from when he was a child.
8 When *did you find out / have you found out* about the stories of Borges?

Past tenses review

Form

Past simple

See page 86: Past simple

Past continuous

Interrogative	Short answer
was I/he/she/it **working** there?	Yes, I/he/she/it **was**. No, I/he/she/it **wasn't**.
were you/we/they **working** there?	Yes, you/we/they **were**. No, you/we/they **weren't**.

Past perfect simple

Affirmative	Negative
I'**d**/you'**d**/he'**d**/she'**d**/ it'**d**/we'**d**/they'**d worked** ('d = had)	I/you/he/she/it/we/they **hadn't worked** (hadn't = had not)

Interrogative	Short answer
had I/you/he/she/it/we/they **worked**?	Yes, I/you/he/she/it/we/they **had**. No, I/you/he/she/it/we/they **hadn't**.

Past perfect continuous

Affirmative	Negative
I'**d**/you'**d**/he'**d**/she'**d**/ it'**d**/we'**d**/they'**d been working** ('d = had)	I/you/he/she/it/we/they **hadn't been** working (hadn't = had not)

Interrogative	Short answer
had I/you/he/she/it/we/they **been working**?	Yes, I/you/he/she/it/we/they **had**. No, I/you/he/she/it/we/they **hadn't**.

Use

Past simple
We use the past simple to talk about the sequence of the main events of a story.
*Giles **got up** at six o'clock and **left** the location early.*

Past continuous
We use the past continuous to describe a background event which was in progress around the time of the main event. We often use the past continuous with the past simple.
*The sun **was coming up** as Paul arrived at the park.*

We don't usually use stative verbs in the past continuous.
*I **knew** the route well. (Not I ~~was knowing~~ the route well.)*

Past perfect simple
We use the past perfect simple to talk about something that happened before the main event, i.e. to talk about something that happened earlier.
*When Juliet saw the animals, she remembered what the trainer **had said** the day before.*

Past perfect continuous
We use the past perfect continuous to describe an action that was in progress before or up to the main event in the past.
*When Becky arrived, the other actors **had** already **been rehearsing** for two hours.*

We don't usually use stative verbs in the past perfect continuous.
*I **had known** him for ten years. (Not I ~~had been knowing~~ him for ten years.)*

Practice

2 Complete the text with the correct past tense form of the verbs.

Esther ¹ _____ (walk) in the park near her home. It ² _____ (be) a beautiful evening. The sun ³ _____ (shine) all day and now it ⁴ _____ (set) behind some tall trees by the river. Suddenly she ⁵ _____ (hear) a scream. She thought that it ⁶ _____ (come) from the direction of the river so she ⁷ _____ (run) there as fast as she could. When she ⁸ _____ (reach) the river she ⁹ _____ (see) a young boy in the water. He ¹⁰ _____ (slip) on the muddy bank and ¹¹ _____ (fall) head first into the water. Now he ¹² _____ (struggle) and unable to swim. Esther quickly ¹³ _____ (take) off her shoes and she ¹⁴ _____ (jump) in. She ¹⁵ _____ (catch) the boy by the arm and ¹⁶ _____ (drag) him out.

UNIT 3
Future forms review
Form
will

Affirmative	Negative
I/you/he/she/it/we/they**'ll** go ('ll = will)	I/you/he/she/it/we/they **won't** go (won't = will not)

Interrogative	Short answer
will I/you/he/she/it/we/they go?	Yes, I/you/he/she/it/we/they **will**. No, I/you/he/she/it/we/they **won't**

going to future

Affirmative	Negative
I**'m going to** visit	I**'m not going to** visit
you**'re**/we**'re**/they**'re going to** visit	you/we/they **aren't going to** visit
he**'s**/she**'s**/it**'s going to** visit	he/she/it **isn't going to** visit

Interrogative	Short answer
am I **going to** visit?	Yes, I **am**. No, I**'m not**.
are you/we/they **going to** visit?	Yes, you/we/they **are**. No, you/we/they **aren't**.
is he/she/it **going to** visit?	Yes, he/she/it **is**. No, he/she/it **isn't**.

about to

Affirmative	Negative
I**'m about to** start	I**'m not about to** start
you**'re**/we**'re**/they**'re about to** start	you/we/they **aren't about to** start
he**'s**/she**'s**/it**'s about to** start	he/she/it **isn't about to** start

Interrogative	Short answer
am I **about to** start?	Yes, I **am**. No, I**'m not**.
are you/we/they **about to** start?	Yes, you/we/they **are**. No, you/we/they **aren't**.
is he/she/it **about to** start?	Yes, he/she/it **is**. No, he/she/it **isn't**.

See page 84: Present continuous
See page 84: Present simple

Use

will
We use *will*:
- to talk about a prediction. *I expect he**'ll** be here in a minute.*
- to talk about a decision we have made at the time of speaking. *'I can't start my car.' 'Don't worry. I**'ll** give you a lift.'*
- in the main clause of a first conditional sentence. *If the population increases, there **won't be** enough food.*

going to future

We use *be + going to + infinitive*:

- to talk about a plan or intention for the future. This has been decided before the moment of speaking. *When I'm in Europe, I'm going to travel to France, Spain, Portugal and Italy.*
- to make a prediction about the future based on present information. *My team is playing very badly. They're going to lose this match.*

about to

We use *be + about to* to talk about an event in the immediate future.
I can't talk to you now – I'm about to go into a meeting.

We often use *just* in front of *about to*.
Tell me the details later – I'm just about to go into town.

Present continuous

We use the present continuous to talk about:

- an intention or previously made decision or arrangement. *They aren't coming to the theatre.*
- a formal arrangement. *They're having a meeting at ten o'clock.*

We often use the present continuous with a specific (or understood) time in the future.
I'm travelling to New York on Thursday evening.

We normally use the present continuous (not *going to*) with the verbs *go* and *come*.

Present simple

We use the present simple to talk about:

- a scheduled or timetabled event. *The concert starts at eight o'clock. What time does the train leave?*

Practice

1 Complete the conversation with the correct future tense of the verbs.

> A: The first talk [1] _____ (start) in five minutes.
> B: [2] _____ you _____ (go) to it?
> A: No, I think I [3] _____ (give) it a miss. It's not really a subject that interests me.
> B: Really? I think it [4] _____ (be) really interesting.
> A: No, it's OK. I [5] _____ (meet) a colleague anyway in half an hour to discuss the presentation we [6] _____ (give) this afternoon.
> B: Oh. When does that [7] _____ (start)?
> A: It [8] _____ (be) at 2.00 p.m. in the green room.
> B: Oh good. I [9] _____ (try) to come to that.
> A: You'd be very welcome. Anyway you'd better go. Your talk [10] _____ (be) to start …

Future continuous and future perfect simple

Form

Future continuous

We form the future continuous with *will be + -ing*.

Affirmative	Negative
I/you/he/she/it/we/they **will be doing**	I/you/he/she/it/we/they **won't be doing**

Interrogative	Short answer
will I/you/he/she/it/we/they **be doing**?	Yes, I/you/he/she/it/we/they **will**. No, I/you/he/she/it/we/they **won't**.

Future perfect simple

We form the future perfect simple with *will have + past participle*.

Affirmative	Negative
I/you/he/she/it/we/they **will have done**	I/you/he/she/it/we/they **won't have done**

Interrogative	Short answer
will I/you/he/she/it/we/they **have done**?	Yes, I/you/he/she/it/we/they **will**. No, I/you/he/she/it/we/they **won't**.

Use

Future continuous

We use the future continuous to talk about an action which you know or think will be in progress at a certain time or during a certain period of time, in the future.
In five years' time, everyone will be using HD phones. This time tomorrow I won't be sitting in this office. What will scientists be researching ten years from now?

Future perfect simple

We use the future perfect simple to talk about an action which is going to be completed at or before a certain point of time in the future.
In 50 years' time, people will have stopped using cash. He won't have finished installing the new system by the weekend. Will you have sent that email by five o'clock?

Practice

2 Choose the correct option.

1. Next year people (will be using) / will have used wind power for their electricity.
2. By next January the company *will be designing / will have designed* a smaller computer chip.
3. Scientists *will be making / will have made* some important breakthroughs by 2020.
4. It is predicted that scientists *will be discovering / will have discovered* a cure for cancer in the next ten years.
5. I expect that I *will be working / will have worked* in a laboratory next month.
6. I'm sure he *will be studying / will have studied* biology all his life.

UNIT 4

Expressions of quantity

Form

(not) many, (a) few, a (small/large) number of, several + plural countable noun
*There were **not many people** at the concert.*
*Ella has only been to **a few** classical **concerts**.*

(not) much, (a) little, a bit of, a (large/small) amount of + uncountable noun
*There isn't **much live music** at the festival.*
*You can see **a bit of sculpture** as part of the exhibition.*

a lot of, lots of, plenty of, loads of, (a) lack of, (almost) no, (not/hardly) any, some, enough + plural countable or uncountable noun
*You can buy **plenty of food and drink** at the show.*
*Because of the show, there were **hardly any cars** in town today.*

Use

We use quantifiers with countable or uncountable nouns to talk about quantity (how much or how many of something).

Large quantities

We use the following quantifiers to express large quantities.
With plural countable nouns: *a large number of, a huge number of*
With uncountable nouns: *a large amount of, an enormous amount of*
With plural countable and uncountable nouns: *some, a lot of, lots of, plenty of, loads of*
***An enormous number of** people are actively involved in the arts, many more than you would imagine.*
***Some** visitors return three or four times a year.*
*There were **a lot of/loads of** great bands at the festival.*
Note that *loads of* is less formal than *a lot of/lots of*.

Small quantities

We use the following quantifiers to express small quantities.
With plural countable nouns: *(not) many, (a) few, a (small) number of, several*
With uncountable nouns: *(not) much, (a) little, a bit of, a small amount of*
With plural countable and uncountable nouns: *some, a lack of, (almost) no, (not/hardly) any*
*In most towns, there are **a few** interesting places to visit.*
***Hardly any** artists become rich in their lifetime.*

We use *little/a little* and *few/a few* to talk about small quantities in affirmative statements. *A little* and *a few* have a positive meaning (= some, but not many). *Little* and *few* have a negative meaning (= only a small number of).
***A few** people watched his latest play.* (= some, but not many)
***Few** people watched his latest play.* (= only a small number)

*They arrived very late so they only saw **a little** of the show.* (= some, but not much)
*He ate **little** of the meal in the restaurant as he didn't like seafood.* (= only a small amount of)

We don't usually use *much* in affirmative statements. We normally use *a lot of/lots of*.
*They haven't got **much** knowledge of the local area.*
*We've got **a lot of** brochures about the area.*

Several usually means three or more things or people.
*There were **several** people in the audience.*

enough

We use *enough* to say we have the correct or sufficient quantity. We use *not enough* to say we have less than we want or need.
*There are **enough** members of the orchestra now.*
*There **aren't enough** artists signed up for the festival yet.*

We can use *a large amount, enough, plenty, several, not much, not many* without nouns when the meaning is clear.
*Do you have many theatres in your town? Yes, we have **several**. / No, there **aren't many**.*

Practice

1 Choose the correct option.

1 There aren't *much /* (*many*) */ a little* films on this week.
2 There is *a few / several / lots of* paint in the studio.
3 Is there *many / much / a few* interest in the exhibition?
4 There were *few / not much / a little* people at the gallery.
5 There aren't *much / many / some* art books on the shelf.
6 There is only *a little / lots of / plenty of* talent amongst these new actors.
7 There were *a little / not much / almost no* good paintings on show.
8 Are there *a bit of / enough / not much* bands playing at the festival?

Determiners

Form

each, every, either, the whole + singular noun
***Each visitor** to the gallery receives a plan of the exhibition.*
***Every exhibit** in the museum is catalogued.*
*People can buy **either** a day ticket or a season ticket.*

all, both + plural noun
***All** the shortlisted artists gained a lot of publicity.*
***Both** artists exhibited three pictures.*

any, no + singular or plural noun
*Have you seen **any** good films this month?*
*They received **no** complaints.*

all, any, no + uncountable noun

All literature has value.
Can we use any material we like?
No culture is superior to another.

Use

every, each, all

We use *every*, *each* and *all* to talk generally about people or things.
Every musician played well.
Each artist had some interesting work on display.
All the paintings were very good.
We use *each* and *every* to refer to the individuals or individual parts of a group. We use *all* to refer to the whole group.

We use *every* (+ singular noun) and *all, all the, all of the* (+ plural noun/uncountable noun) when the plural noun refers to **three** or more people or things.
Every person had the opportunity to be an artist for a day. (There were three or more people.)
All of the participants wrote a poem about nature. (There were three or more participants.)
We use *each* (+ singular noun) to talk about **two** or more people or things.
Each member of the group made some form of contribution. (There were two or more people.)

both, either

We use *both* and *either* to talk about **two** things or people. We use *both/both of the* (+ plural noun) to say the same thing about two people or things. We use *either* (+ singular noun) to say there are two possible options.
Both (of the) sculptors made three works of art for the exhibition.
They could choose to use either stone or clay.

We use *neither* to express a negative meaning.
Neither contestant made it to the final.

(not) any, no

We use *(not) any* or *no* to talk about a negative idea.
They didn't allow any graffiti on the walls at all.
There are no original ideas left in art.

We can use *(not) any* without a noun when the meaning is clear.
Have you got any tickets left? No, I'm sorry, there aren't any.

Practice

2 Complete the sentences using a suitable determiner. There may be more than one possible answer.

1 There were ten pianists in the competition, and they were <u>all</u> very good.
2 _____ member of the band plays a different instrument.
3 Gilbert and George work as a pair, but _____ men are artists in their own right.
4 They were both good players, and _____ of them could have won.
5 _____ performer was better than the others.
6 _____ student was asked to bring a sketch book to the gallery.

UNIT 5

Verb + infinitive or -ing

Form

Verb + infinitive	
verb + *to* + infinitive	*They **wanted to create** a luxury holiday resort.*
verb + *someone* + *to* + infinitive	*He **asked his father to lend** him the money for the deposit.*
verb + *someone* + infinitive (without *to*)	*She **helped her friend establish** a new theme park.*

Verb + -ing	
verb + -*ing*	*I **enjoy going** to shopping malls.*

Use

verb + to + infinitive

After certain verbs we use *to* + infinitive. This is often to talk about hopes, intentions and decisions.
He offered to draw the plans for the redevelopment.
They didn't want to work on the project any more.
Common verbs which are followed by *to* + infinitive include: *agree, appear, arrange, choose, decide, expect, hope, intend, manage, need, offer, plan, prepare, pretend, promise, refuse, seem, want, wish, would like.*

verb + someone + to + infinitive

Some verbs are followed by an object and *to* + infinitive.
He reminded his employees to arrive early.
They'd like the contractors to submit their proposal by the end of the week.
Common verbs which are followed by *someone* + *to* + infinitive include: *allow, ask, expect, force, help, invite, need, remind, teach, tell, want, would like.*

verb + someone + infinitive without to

Some verbs are followed by an object and the infinitive without *to*.
He watched his ex-partner become the richest businessman in the world.
She helped her daughter expand her business.
Common verbs which are followed by *someone* + infinitive without *to* are: *feel, hear, help, notice, see, watch.*

verb + -ing

We use verb + -*ing* after certain verbs.
I enjoy staying in luxury hotels.
The architect suggested adding some green space.
Common verbs which are followed by -*ing* are: *avoid, can't help, like, love, enjoy, prefer don't like, hate, can't stand, (not) mind, keep, miss, practise, risk, suggest.*

Practice

1 Choose the correct option.

1 I always enjoy (*going*)/ *to go* to work in developing countries.
2 He watched his country *growing* / *grow* richer every day.
3 They asked the IMF *lending* / *to lend* the government some money.
4 The President decided *to invest* / *investing* in property.
5 The ministers suggested *to start* / *starting* an investment bank.
6 The government refused *giving* / *to give* them planning permission.

Verb + *-ing* or *to* + infinitive

Form

verb + *-ing* and verb + *to* + infinitive (two different meanings)

He **remembered listening** to the programme.
They **remembered to listen** to the programme.

verb + *-ing* and verb + *to* + infinitive (no change in meaning)

He **continued travelling** around Asia in spite of not having any money.
He **continued to travel** around Asia in spite of not having any money.

Use

Some verbs can be followed by either *-ing* or *to* + infinitive but the meaning changes.
Jan **stopped talking** to journalists. = *Jan used to talk to journalists but now he has stopped.* (We talk about the action which has ended, i.e. he is no longer talking to journalists.)
Jan **stopped to talk** to a local resident. = *Jan stopped and then he talked to a local resident.* (This tells us the reason for stopping, i.e. to talk to a local resident.)
Common verbs which can be followed by *-ing* or *to* + infinitive with a change in meaning are: *forget, remember, go on, mean, regret, stop, try.*

Some verbs can be followed by either *-ing* or *to* + infinitive with very little or no change in meaning.
Lizze **likes reading** business economics books.
Lizzie **likes to read** business economics books.
Common verbs which can be followed by *-ing* or *to* + infinitive with little or no change in meaning are: *begin, continue, hate, love, prefer, start.*

Practice

2 Complete the sentences with the correct form of these verbs.

| ask | bring | borrow | ~~buy~~ | change | inform |

1 I forgot __*to buy*__ some milk when I was at the supermarket.
2 I don't remember _____ any money from Mike but he says I did.

3 We regret _____ you that your bank account has been closed.
4 I meant _____ them if the water was safe to drink or not.
5 Did you remember _____ the plans for the new development with you?
6 If we want the company to be profitable, it means _____ our prices.

UNIT 6

not

Form

Negative infinitive

We form the negative infinitive by putting *not* in front of the infinitive. Note that *not* goes before *to*.
*We decided **not to go** abroad on holiday this year.*

want, would like

To make a sentence negative with *want* or *would like*, we make the main verb negative.
*She **didn't want** to visit India.*
*They **wouldn't like** to work there.*

mustn't and don't have to

The negative form of *must* is *mustn't* and the negative form of *have to* is *don't/doesn't have* to.
*You **mustn't** travel without your passport.*
*If you are British, you **don't have to** get a visa to visit France.*

hope and think

The negative form of *hope* and *think* is different. When we form a negative sentence with *hope*, we make the following verb negative. When we form a negative sentence with *think*, we use *don't/doesn't think*.
*I **hope he isn't** late.*
*He **doesn't think** she should travel alone.*

let's

To form the negative of *let's*, we use *let's not*.
***Let's not** go on holiday in the UK this summer – I want to go somewhere warm!*

Use

Negative infinitive

We often use the negative infinitive to make suggestions and give advice or orders about what **not** to do.
*It would be better for you **not to meet** him tomorrow.*
*He advised me **not to fly** next week because of the strikes.*

want, would like

We use *don't/doesn't want* and *wouldn't like* to talk about a wish not to do something in the future.
*I **don't want** to go to the party tomorrow. (Not I ~~want not~~ to go to the party tomorrow.)*
*I **wouldn't like** to read that book again.*

mustn't and don't have to

We use *mustn't* to say that it is important not to do something.
*You **mustn't** forget to apply for your visa.* (= It's important that you don't forget.)

We use *don't/doesn't have to* to show that something is not important or essential.
*He **doesn't have to** get a new passport before he goes.* (= It's not essential.)

hope and think

*I **hope** my holiday **won't be** a disappointment.* (not I ~~don't hope~~ …)
*I **don't think** her accommodation **will be** very luxurious – it was very cheap!* (not I think her accommodation ~~won't be~~ luxurious …)

let's

We use *let's not* + infinitive when we want to make a negative suggestion.
*Let's see what time they arrive. **Let's not** go out now.*

Practice

1 Complete the sentences using *not* and the correct form of the verb. Use contractions where possible.

1 He told me ___not to spend___ (spend) too much money on holiday.
2 Sarah _____ (want) to go to the museum at the weekend.
3 Let's _____ (tell) Peter about it – it will upset him.
4 Mike asked me _____ (book) self-catering accommodation.
5 We _____ (think) the aeroplane will take off on time.
6 We decided _____ (stop) off in Paris on the way.

Negative and tag questions
Form
Open questions

We form open questions using an auxiliary verb (e.g. *do, have*) and invert the subject and verb.
Do you enjoy travelling by train?
Has he played tennis before?

Negative questions

We form negative questions using the negative form of the verb. We usually use the contracted form.
Don't you enjoy travelling by train?
Hasn't he played tennis before?

Tag questions

To form tag questions we use the auxiliary of the verb in the main sentence. When the main verb in the sentence is affirmative, the tag question is negative:
They were at the party, weren't they?
When the main verb in the sentence is negative, the tag question is affirmative:
He didn't stay late, did he?

When you write tag questions, put a comma between the main sentence and the tag.

Note that when the subject is a pronoun, we repeat the pronoun in the tag question. When the subject is a noun, we use an appropriate pronoun in the tag question.
*It's very interesting, isn't **it**?*
***Mike** travels to South Africa every year, doesn't **he**?*

Tense	Positive-negative	Negative-positive
to be (is, are, was, were)	*It's a long way, isn't it?* *I was there, wasn't I?*	*It isn't a long way, is it?* *I wasn't there, was I?*
Present simple (do/does)	*She works there, doesn't she?*	*She doesn't work there, does she?*
Present continuous (is, are)	*They're arriving soon, aren't they?*	*They aren't arriving soon, are they?*
Past simple (did)	*She went there yesterday, didn't she?*	*She didn't go there yesterday, did she?*
Past continuous (was, were)	*They weren't working yesterday, were they?*	*They were working yesterday, weren't they?*
Present perfect simple and present perfect continuous (has, have)	*You've been here before, haven't you?* *They've been studying late, haven't they?*	*You haven't been here before, have you?* *They haven't been studying late, have they?*
Past perfect simple (had)	*They'd met him before, hadn't they?*	*They hadn't met him before, had they?*
will	*You'll do it tomorrow, won't you?*	*You won't do it tomorrow, will you?*
Modals (must, should, can, would, etc.)	*I can go, can't I?* *He should know about the plans, shouldn't he?*	*I can't go, can I?* *He shouldn't know about the plans, should he?*

Use
Open questions

We use open questions when we don't know what the answer will be or when we don't expect a particular answer.
Are you going on holiday this year? (Possible answers: Yes, I am. No, I'm not. Well, maybe. I don't think so.)
Did he tell you where he was going? (Possible answers: Yes, he did. No, he didn't. I can't remember.)

Negative questions

We use negative questions to check some information or something you think is probably true. We answer negative questions with *yes/no* answers.
Don't you always visit your parents on Sunday? Yes, I do.
Wouldn't you prefer to stay in a hotel? No, I wouldn't.

We also use negative questions.
* to show surprise. *Don't you enjoy eating out?*
* to make a suggestion. *Don't you want to invite him too?*
* to request something, especially when we expect a negative answer. *Can't I have a different room?*

Tag questions
We use tag questions to ask for information, or to check and confirm information.
*We're meeting at two o'clock at the airport, **aren't we**?*
*That's the meeting point, **isn't it**?*

Practice

2 Complete the negative and tag questions.

1 _____Don't_____ you want to stay here? It's really comfortable.
2 India is a very diverse country, _____isn't it_____ ?
3 Sue didn't go mountain climbing last year, _____ ?
4 _____ you booked the flights yet? I thought I asked you to last week.
5 The group won't travel to Athens by train, _____ ?
6 Those old map books wouldn't be much use, _____ ?
7 _____ he pay for his accommodation before he arrived?
8 _____ she like to visit somewhere different for a change?

Unit 1

🔘 1.1

Speaker 1

It's a bit odd because I see him almost every day at work. He has a job in the marketing department on the 4th floor and my office is on the 5th floor and occasionally, just occasionally, we're asked to attend the same meetings. Umm … it's strange seeing someone you're so close to in a different context. We've been married for seven years, and colleagues for longer than that, but we try not to discuss work when we're at home with the rest of the family …

Speaker 2

We were such good mates at school and then we went travelling together, but we see each other very rarely now, because John lives in Birmingham with his wife and I still live in London. The funny thing is, it doesn't matter how little we see each other – we're still great friends. Actually, he never calls me – and every time I call him he says 'Oh, I've been meaning to call you for ages', but I don't mind …

Speaker 3

We get on very well as colleagues, but I never see him outside work. He's one of those people that can always make you laugh, which is really important in a stressful work environment. He's very good at his job too and I'm always asking for help for things.

🔘 1.2

It's known that animals often co-operate in their own social groups, helping each other to hunt or raise their young. Some highly intelligent animals, like elephants, go even further than this, and help other animals who are not in their own family group. But co-operation between animals of different species is unusual, so that's why the story of Suriya, the orang-utan, has attracted a lot of interest.

Suriya lives with his keepers at The Institute of Greatly Endangered and Rare Species in Myrtle Beach, South Carolina, which is a kind of sanctuary for rare animals. Recently this orang-utan has made an unlikely friend in a local hound dog. Now most dogs avoid apes, because they are scared of them basically, but these two have formed a strong bond. Each day the dog comes into the compound and searches out Suriya.

When he finds him, they carry on like long lost friends, wrestling and hugging and playing together. They've been doing this every day since they first met and their friendship has attracted the curiosity of millions of viewers on the *National Geographic Channel*. The founder of the institute, Dr Antle explains: 'It's clear they are having the time of their life. What is more striking is that Suriya has also understood that the hound dog is very hungry and so he regularly shares his monkey biscuits with him. Orang-utans are very generous creatures. If you give one a piece of candy, often they will break it in half and hand one piece back to you.'

So how does he explain the fact that their relationship has a lot of the characteristics of what we call 'friendship'? Antle says that the two animals are fulfilling a basic social need in each other that perhaps we don't normally associate with animals. 'It's a relationship with attributes of fun and interaction that they are not getting from anyone else'.

🔘 1.3

There are many children like Bella in China. They admire western brands. They have been spoiled a little perhaps by their parents. Often these children receive a better education than their parents. They are sent to private schools and are encouraged to go to university. In China everyone's hopes and aspirations are being raised by the new economy.

🔘 1.4

G = Greta; T = Tim

G: Tim, hello. Fancy bumping into you here. How are you?

T: Oh hi Greta. Yeah, I'm doing fine, thanks. Wow, what a surprise …

G: It's been ages. What have you been up to?

T: I know. It's been far too long. Umm … I've been working abroad for the last eighteen months.

G: Anywhere exciting?

T: Yes, in India, actually. I had a contract with the British Council, doing some teacher training.

G: Well, it obviously suits you: you're looking very tanned and relaxed.

T: Oh, thanks, it's been a lot of fun. And you? You're looking well too. How are things?

G: Oh you know, busy as ever. I've been completely snowed under with work the last few months, trying to get my online shoe shop business off the ground.

T: Is it going OK?

G: Well, you know. It has its ups and downs. But we're getting there.

T: And what about Amanda? Do you see much of her?

G: Yeah, we still get together now and then. She was asking after you the other day, actually.

T: Oh. Well I probably won't have time to look her up this time. I'm only back for a week. But do give her my regards.

G: I will.

T: And the next time I'm back, perhaps we can all meet and catch up.

G: Yeah, that'd be great. How long will you be gone for?

T: I've just got to do another two months over there. Then I'll be back in the UK for a while, I hope.

G: OK. Well give me a call when you're back. You've got my number, haven't you?

T: Yes, if it's still the same one.

G: Yeah, it is. I'll look forward to that. Is Sarah going out there with you?

T: She has been with me, but umm … she's staying back this time.

G: Oh. Well, say hello to her from me … er … Look, I don't mean to be rude, but I need to get back to work – but it was really nice to see you. Hope the trip goes well.

T: Thanks. Yeah I've got to rush too. Anyway, great to see you too, Greta. Take care … and see you soon. Good luck with the business.

Unit 2

🔘 1.6

A: Have you seen the film *Senna*?

B: No, I read a biography of him a few years back. I've heard the film's really good. What did you think?

A: I thought it was fantastic. It's a documentary essentially, but unlike most documentaries there's no narrator. It just tells the story of his life through archive footage. Actually, I'm not a huge fan of Formula One so I wasn't really expecting to enjoy it, but it's really gripping.

B: Oh, so it didn't really give any opinion on whether Senna really believed he was superior to every other driver or whether he acted unfairly sometimes …

A: No, not at all … it leaves you to make up your own mind about him completely. A lot of the film focusses on his driving career, from his early wins to his death in a crash in ummm 1994, I think it was. For much of it, he had this big rivalry with the French driver Alain Prost and they took each other off the track at critical times. But the film doesn't say who was right or wrong … although in the end you come down on Senna's side …

B: Well, you say it's objective, but of course the viewer's opinion can be manipulated by the director … just in the way he chooses to edit the film.

A: Yes, no, I suppose that's true … but it's not a sentimental film. Perhaps you feel sympathetic towards Senna, 'cos he seemed like a nice guy – ummm … he did a lot of charity work in his native Brazil – but it felt very fair and impartial …

B: Well, that's very different from the biography I read. The writer made his opinion very clear. He was very biased against Alain Prost and took every opportunity to tell you so.

A: Was it good otherwise?

B: Well, quite good but rather repetitive and not very well written. But there were a few good anecdotes in it. There are better biographies out there, I'm told.

🔘 1.7

P = Presenter; M = Mark Mowlam

P: Take a bestselling book, a great storyline and add a great cast, an experienced director and a large filming budget. And what do you get? A box office success, you would think. Think again. There's no guarantee that a book that has enjoyed great success will make a good film. Some film adaptations have worked, others have flopped. So what's the secret? That was the question I put earlier to film critic Mark Mowlam, who's followed the progress of many book-to-film adaptations in his time and has recently reported on the making of Tolkien's *The Hobbit*.

M: Well, the goal is really to make a good film that remains true to the spirit of the book. There are many examples of adaptations which have failed because they tried to remain too faithful to the plot and the characters of the book. Probably because at the time the producers worried that they'd alienate loyal readers if they departed too much from the original text. But in fact that's a mistake: what works well on the page doesn't necessarily work well on screen; you have to give the screenwriter freedom to create a script that flows, even if that means changing the original. So what we find is a lot of good films – *Sense and Sensibility*, *The Shining*, for example – that are completely unlike the original book. And readers are generally OK about this because they think of book and film as two separate works of art. But there are films that have managed to stay true to the book and still be good films. What they've done – a bit like in cooking, I suppose – is to put in all the book's good ingredients and then boil them down to a concentrated mixture that's packed with the flavour of the original work. Probably the best example of this is *The Lord of the Rings* trilogy by Peter Jackson. The central theme of the book – which is a struggle between the forces of good and evil – perhaps wasn't so difficult to portray, but J.R.R. Tolkien created a very original other world and reproducing that was a much more difficult task, because each reader has their own very distinct idea of what this world was like. I think Jackson did a fantastic job, using the spectacular scenery of New Zealand for the film's location. The other thing about the *The Lord of the Rings* is that it's a very substantial work – three books each containing over twenty long chapters – so Jackson had to leave some elements of the story out. To compensate for this, he took the most important scenes and then put all the emotional force behind these. The result is that it has become one of the most successful films of all time, a blockbuster that has grossed almost $3 billion.

1.10

Steve Winter and Douglas Chadwick, who were working in Kaziranga National Park, had three close encounters with rhinos all on the same day. Before entering the park, their guide had told them not to be afraid, so they weren't especially worried, but clearly the incidents shocked them. They knew that filming in the park was dangerous work, but they hadn't been expecting to meet danger quite so soon or so frequently. But it didn't stop them carrying on!

1.12

I was mountain-biking with a friend in Wales and we'd just finished a long off-road climb out of the Dysynni Valley. It had been raining earlier but now the sun was shining and we were feeling quite warm. Since the rest of the route was downhill on tarmac roads, I took off my bike helmet and set off. Suddenly the road became very steep and the bike picked up speed quickly. There was a turn ahead in the road and I knew I was going to crash. The bike went straight into a wall, but luckily I flew over it and landed in a field of long grass.

Mr Charles Everson and his wife Linda were driving home from church one Sunday when a cow fell from the sky and landed on the bonnet of their van. The cow, which had escaped from a breeding farm, had been grazing too close to the edge of a cliff next to the road and had slipped and plunged 200ft. When the emergency services arrived at the scene they found the cow dead and Mr and Mrs Everson in shock.

1.13

Conversation 1
A: The bus broke down on the motorway, so we were all left stranded until help could arrive.
B: What did you do?
A: Luckily another bus came within about 15 minutes and we all transferred to that one.
B: That must have been a relief.

Conversation 2
A: My trousers got caught on the door handle and as I walked away they tore.
B: Oh, that's awful.
A: Yes, I had to walk right across the restaurant back to our table with my hands over the hole.
B: How embarrassing!

Conversation 3
A: I bent the key trying to force it into the door lock and when I tried to straighten the key it snapped.
B: How did you get in?
A: I went to the neighbours', but they weren't at home. So I just had to wait 'til someone came home.
B: Yeah, a similar thing happened to me once.

Conversation 4
A: The lift got stuck between floors 25 storeys up and two of the occupants were completely panic-stricken.
B: What a nightmare!
A: It was. Then the lights in the lift went off and one of them started screaming.
B: Yeah I think I would have done the same thing.

Conversation 5
A: The tyres on my bicycle were badly worn and when I hit a bump in the road one of them burst.
B: Poor you!
A: Well, I came off and cut my hand. Thank goodness there were no cars behind me.
B: That was lucky.

Conversation 6
A: My computer froze without any reason while I was working.
B: Really? How strange!
A: Yeah, I thought I'd lost about four hours' work, but I when I rebooted the computer I searched for some of the key words in my document and I found a temporary file which had most of the document in it.
B: That was good thinking.

Unit 3

1.16

1
I expect that most of my generation will live to be around a hundred years old. There are already 12,000 people in the UK aged over a hundred and it's predicted that by the year 2060 that number will have risen to about one million.

2
I think people will be interacting with intelligent machines even more than they do now. I read this article about things called *chatbots* which are programs that can hold intelligent conversations with people in chat rooms on the Internet. These programmes already exist.

3
I don't think global warming is going to be the problem that everyone says it is. By the middle of this century I think humans will have discovered ways to control the weather. If you think about it, the benefits, commercial and otherwise, are so great – for agriculture, for stopping natural disasters and so on – that it's only a matter of time before someone works out a way.

1.17

Hello everyone … one moment, I'll just adjust my microphone … OK, that's better. I can see a lot of hopeful-looking faces out there. I'm speaking to a government committee tomorrow and I hope they look as bright-eyed as you do … Let me just say that I'm afraid that those of you who have come looking for immediate answers to overpopulation are going to be disappointed, but I hope I can at least give you some cause for optimism. I'm not going to speak for too long because I'd like to hear what you have to say, but let me tell you first how I see the situation …

In 1798 an English economist, Thomas Malthus, claimed that the population always grows faster than the food supply, until war, disease or famine arrive to reduce the number of people. A century and a half later in 1968, Paul Ehrlich wrote in his book *The Population Bomb* that medical science was keeping too many people alive and that we had failed to control the birth rate. He predicted that as a result hundreds of millions of people would soon starve to death.

But his bomb was a dud. Yes, medical science has extended life expectancy and the population carries on growing: around seven billion today and it will probably peak at around nine billion by 2050. But mass starvation? It hasn't happened. Why? Because science stepped in with better seeds and better pesticides to boost food production and it's about to step in again with nanotechnology, which will in turn help us to engineer safer and cheaper foods.

So what about overpopulation? Let me give you a fact: if in 2045 there are nine billion people in the world, the population density will still only be half that of France today. And no one complains about overcrowding there: France is the world's favourite holiday destination! Some of the new megacities of Asia might not be such pleasant places to live … but the problem is not just the number of people. The problem is how people consume resources.

By 2030 more than a billion people in the developing world will belong to the 'global middle class'. That's a good thing. But it will be a bad thing for the planet if those people start eating meat and driving big cars every day. Some, ultra-cautious, people say we should bring in wartime emergency measures to conserve resources. I don't think that's the answer, but then I'm a scientist at heart even if I'm semi-retired now. For me the answer lies in innovations like biofuels and other alternative energy sources …

I'll talk about these specific solutions in the second part of my talk but let's just go back to Malthus for a moment. People, he argued, are basically lazy. They won't do anything unless they are forced to by necessity. But what he didn't take into account is that faced with disaster people are not lazy. Mankind and science will rise to the challenge … that is my sincere belief … Oh, by the way, one more thing: the necessity train arrives in half an hour …

1.21

1 World leaders are meeting in Geneva tomorrow to discuss the issue of overpopulation.
2 In the next few weeks, the government is going to introduce a fee for each child that couples have after their first two children.
3 Scientists say that space colonies will be the only solution for overpopulation in the medium term.
4 Doctors have said that in future they are not going to spend so much effort keeping the old alive.
5 The government will launch a new education programme later today to encourage women to have fewer children.
6 People will have to change their lifestyles if they want the world's resources to support the growing population in the coming years.

1.22

B = Ben; S = Sophie
B: Can you give me a hand? I'm having trouble making this map.
S: Hang on. I'm just finishing a letter. I'll be with you in a second. … OK. What do you want to do exactly?
B: I'm just making some directions for some friends who are staying in our house next week. I'm trying to paste this map into a Word document.
S: Are you going to email it to them? Because if so, you could just email them the link to the map.

B: No, I'm going to print it out and give it to them when they get here, because we're going away … The trouble is it won't allow me to copy it.

S: Let me have a look. Oh, I see … Oh, it's a Google map; you can't select and copy them, I'm afraid.

B: Oh … what shall I do then?

S: Well, you've got two possibilities. You can either take a screen shot …

B: What's that?

S: Here I'll show you. Just press alt print screen like this, then open a new Word document and paste it in. That should do the trick.

B: Oh, I see, but it's come out very small. That's going to be too difficult for them to read. What else do you suggest?

S: Have you tried looking for a different map? If you do a search, you might find one that you can copy.

B: OK … I'll give that a try. Thanks …

S: Feel free to ask me again if that doesn't work.

Unit 4

🔊 1.24

A: People are never quite what you expect, are they? There's a teacher that I work with who's really quite a shy person … never expresses a strong view or imposes herself in a group. I worked with her for about a year before I found out that every weekend she becomes a street performer.

B: What kind of street performer?

A: Well, she turns out to be some kind of acrobat. She was brought up in a circus and she still gets together at weekends with friends and puts on shows of circus skills with them in public places, like a busy shopping street on a Saturday afternoon. She doesn't do it for money – just for fun. But it's not what you imagine her doing when you meet her …

B: That sounds a bit like my neighbour. He works for a firm of accountants, watches a lot of sport, but in his free time he writes poetry. I don't think many people have read it, because he's rather private, but he showed me a poem a while ago that he wrote when his little boy was sick in hospital and it was absolutely beautiful …

🔊 1.25

'Nature has done everything for Sydney, man nothing; man has done everything for Melbourne, nature nothing,' a visitor to Australia once noted. Herein lies the essential difference between Australia's two largest cities. Melbourne is Australia's second city, but it has plenty of first-class qualities, from a buzzing arts scene to its enormous range of restaurants. It may have a few grey days, and a muddy river instead of a beautiful harbour, but don't let that worry you. The lack of natural attractions has meant that Melbourne has had to create its own man-made pleasures … and in doing so it has become Australia's cultural capital. Theatre, music, street sculpture, fashion – in fact, there are hardly any forms of artistic expression which you can't find here – all thrive, alongside a cosmopolitan mix of cafés, restaurants and pubs.

What's great about Melbourne for the visitor is how accessible all these arts are. As well as traditional museums and galleries like the National Gallery of Victoria and concert halls, like Hamer Hall, there are an enormous number of smaller art spaces and venues which cater for every kind of taste. Art is not something for a small minority. In fact, for most inhabitants of Melbourne a weekly visit to the cinema or an art exhibition is a routine event. Several festivals take place during the winter months including the International Film Festival in July and the Fringe Festival in September which has loads of interesting (even if not always that good!) comedy, dance and theatre acts.

If the locals appreciate their art, they absolutely love their sport. Lots of people around the world will know the Australian Formula One Grand Prix and the Australian Open Tennis, which attracts over half a million spectators to Melbourne in a carnival atmosphere, but few people will be familiar with the sports Melburnians themselves follow. Australian rules football and cricket enjoy a huge amount of support and, if you have enough time, a visit to see either is well worth it just for the atmosphere. If you're looking to participate rather than just watch, why not try a bit of surfing or swimming? Cycling, jogging or a visit to one of Melbourne's many gyms are other possibilities. All this information is on our website at *thetravelshow.org* so do have a look if …

🔊 1.27

I = Interviewer; W = Will

I: OK, Will, I'm going to fire some statements at you about what various people say art should be and I want to know which of these you agree with. OK?

W: Er … OK … but I'm already a bit suspicious, because I don't actually think that 'should' has a lot to do with it. People have a very fixed idea about what art 'should' be – a certain kind of portrait or landscape very often … but, anyway, anyway, I'll play the game, so … let's hear what they say …

I: Good, here's the first one then … *Art should be something pleasing for the viewer.*

W: Mmm no, not necessarily – the artist's intention might be to make you feel uncomfortable, not to give you a warm feeling …

I: OK. What about this, then? … *Art should involve effort on the part of the artist.*

W: OK that's more interesting, but still the answer is 'not necessarily' – Monet did some of his paintings in five minutes.

I: Did he? I didn't know that. That's amazing … well, that ties in with the next one, perhaps. *Art should involve technical skill.*

W: Ummm … I can think of quite a lot of examples of successful art that wasn't technically difficult, but was just based on a clever idea.

I: OK … *Art should have a social message or make a political point.*

W: No, certainly not. Is the Mona Lisa political? I don't think so. Look, … an artist's role is simply to present an idea in a visual form. The viewer's role is to give that effort their time and attention and then they can say either 'Yes, I really like that', or … 'That moves me', or 'No, I'm afraid that doesn't do anything for me.'

🔊 1.28

J = Jake; T = Tom

J: Hey, Tom, how was *The Lion King*?

T: I loved it … I'm not generally a fan of musicals …

J: No, me neither … I never feel particularly inspired by the music in them … which should really be the whole point of them … with a few exceptions perhaps … like *West Side Story* or *Grease* which have fantastic music … So what was so good about it?

T: Well, visually it's absolutely stunning, the opening scene particularly. All the animals – giraffes, wildebeest, zebra, antelope – congregate on the stage to set the scene, which is the plains of the Serengeti where the story takes place. And they're in these fabulous costumes: they're difficult to describe but the effect is that they actually seem to move like real animals. Everyone in the audience was spellbound …

J: But is the story the same as in the Disney film? I remember there were a couple of rather annoying characters in the film, like that bird, who's supposed to be there for comic effect, well at least I think it is, but actually after a while they begin to annoy you.

T: You mean Zazu. Yeah, I know what you mean about that kind of Disney character – often they can get on your nerves – but this production's different. It actually seems much more adult than the film … It's very well-done. I found the story really moving.

J: Mmm … and what about the music?

T: It's essentially the same score as the film – I think Elton John wrote most of it, but it's all based on African rhythms and vocals …

J: Doesn't really sound like my kind of thing.

T: Oh … well, I've got a lot of time for Elton John. I think he catches the mood of this really well. Have you heard *Circle of Life*?

J: Er … no, I don't think so …

T: Well, I'm not going to sing it … anyway I really recommend it. It's not cheap to go but if you get a chance you should. I can't bear the high prices they charge for musicals these days, but actually I didn't mind for this one … it was worth it.

Unit 5

🔊 1.31

Speaker 1

It's always been our dream to have our own place in the countryside which is self-sufficient. So recently we decided to buy a small piece of land in the hills. We're going to build a home out of natural materials and try to generate our own electricity using wind and solar power so that we won't need to buy in any extra electricity from outside.

Speaker 2

At the moment a lot of students use their own cars to get to the university which is four miles outside the city and not served by regular public transport. So we hope that this new rail link with trains running every half an hour will help reduce traffic congestion around the university and also reduce pollution.

Speaker 3

I think this is the first mobile device to offer simultaneous translation. It listens to the speaker and then displays a translation of what they are saying directly onto the screen – absolutely incredible. It will transform communication between people speaking different languages.

🔊 1.32

There used to be a lovely residential area right in the city centre, but, in the 1960s the local authority decided to redevelop it as a shopping district. This involved demolishing all the houses and making way for huge car parks so that shoppers from out of town could park their cars. What's strange is that no one really considered opposing the idea at the time. Even the residents seemed to accept that the area had to be modernised. If you proposed converting houses into shops on such a big scale today, I don't think you would be allowed to do it.

Anyway, the result was that they spoilt the character of the centre. People shopped there in the daytime but at night everyone avoided going there because it became a centre for drug dealing and crime. Now, 50 years later, the local authority wants to transform it into a mixed area again by building new homes. The trouble is that rents are so high that ordinary people, like the ones who were moved out originally, can't afford to live there anymore.

1.33

I = Interviewer; J = Journalist
I: I know you like exotic places – have you tried visiting India?
J : I was just there actually – in Kerala in the south-west. I was intending to go on to tour other parts of India, but Kerala was so fascinating I stayed on …
I: Were you on holiday?
J: No … well, it was meant to be a holiday, but actually it turned into more than that …
I: Oh dear …
J: Oh, no. I don't regret changing my plans … I became so interested in the place that I started to write an article about it for the newspaper I work for …
I: Really? Is it a travel article?
J: Not really. It's more sociological, I guess. I'm trying to show what a remarkable place Kerala is in the developing world. You see, it's a small state with a big population and the average income is only about $300 a year. Usually that would mean people having a fairly poor quality of life, but that's not the case. In fact Kerala stands out as a kind of model of social development. The population is highly literate and well-educated and they seem quite well-off, compared to other parts of India. They're healthy and live almost as long as Americans or Europeans; it seems that infant mortality is also very low. Also, women, who've umm … always traditionally been the head of the household, continue to be very active (and equal) participants in society.
I: Mmm … that's really interesting. I remember going there with my wife in the 1990s. But we were just tourists and my memories of it are as a very tranquil and beautiful place, with gorgeous beaches and lagoons …
J: Well, of course that's the part of it that tourists like to spend time visiting. But tranquil is not necessarily the adjective I would use. Trivandrum, the main city, where we stopped to visit an Indian journalist I know – a highly cultured man, by the way – is absolutely hectic. The people there are very politically engaged: they never stop debating; there are often strikes on the buses or parades of demonstrators – some medical students started protesting when we were there and went on protesting for four days.
I: So why do you think it's such a successful society?
J: Well, there are essentially two reasons, I think. The first is that the Keralites are naturally tolerant people: you find Hindus, Muslims and Christians all living peacefully alongside each other and foreigners are treated no differently to anyone else. And secondly, the government has invested a lot in health and education and goes on investing a lot. The land is incredibly fertile and well-organised – small farmers cultivate every inch of it so none is wasted, which I regret to say is not always the case in some developing countries.

I: Sounds fascinating. Please remember to send me a copy of the article when it's published.
J: Of course I will.

1.35

P = Patrick; A = Anna; I = Isabelle
P: OK, Anna, I believe you've prepared a brief summary of the Howard Park project … [Anna: Yup]. Would you just like to take us through the main points?
A: Yes, sure. Well, the Howard Park project began two years ago. We agreed to lend the local authority £750,000 to redevelop a green space in the Howard's Hill area of the city. The aim was to give the local residents a nicer park, first of all, but also some new recreation facilities: a mini-golf course, two tennis courts, a small café and a new children's play area. The play area was in terrible condition … full of rubbish … it was actually quite dangerous. So here we are two years on: what progress have they made? Well, they've done a good job of cleaning the area up: they've planted trees and laid new grass, so it looks much, much better. They've also built the café and the children's play area. However, they've also done some things that weren't part of the original plan. For example, they've built a fountain near the café and six months ago they also bought a sculpture, at a cost of £80,000 to place near the fountain. Now they've run out of money and are asking for a new loan of £250,000 to complete the tennis courts and mini-golf course. What do you think?
I: If you ask me, that's completely wrong. They've been spending money on things they had no right to. I don't think we should give them another penny.
P: Well hang on a minute. Let's not be too hasty. I agree that they should have told us about these other changes. But we need to consider if they are in the spirit of the original aims of the project …
A: That really depends on the opinion of the local residents. The way I see it, it's probably a good thing – if residents like it and it means they'll use the park more.
I: Well, I just find it arrogant of them, actually …
P: OK … so what ought we to do? Personally, I don't think we should lend them any more until we know what local people think of the work they've done already.
A: Yes, I'd go along with that. We need to ask them to conduct a survey of local opinion and then show us the results.
P: Exactly. Are we all agreed on that then?
I: Yes, I guess so … yes, that seems fair to me.

Unit 6

1.36

I only get three weeks' holiday a year so I always choose the places I go to carefully. I try to go to places with dramatic scenery … and unusual places. It can take time to get to these, but it's generally worth it. I've visited a few ice hotels in my time in Scandinavia, but Hotel de Glace is something special. It's a real work of art. The furniture and fittings are all made of ice – there's even an ice chandelier in the lobby – and the walls are decorated with pictures carved out of the snow. Once the sun goes down and all the coloured lighting is switched on, the effect is stunning. But … there is a but, I'm afraid – as a place to get a comfortable night, I'm not sure I'd recommend it. I know it sounds obvious, but the place is really cold. Unless you have a sauna before going to bed, you'll probably wake up in the

night feeling chilly, even in the special minus 40 degree sleeping bags you are given. I guess it's a bit like high class camping, if you like that kind of thing.

1.37

P = Presenter; K = Katie Samuel
P: … Now, have you ever thought of doing a bit of building work during your holidays? Or helping to look after animals on a wildlife reserve? You probably thought that sort of vacation was for eighteen year olds on their gap year, didn't you? But it seems more and more working adults are opting for volunteer vacations. With us today is Katie Samuel, author of *Good Travel*, a guide to alternative holidays. Katie, I can see that this might attract a few people, but for most of us, who only get a few weeks off a year … wouldn't they prefer a more relaxing option?
K: Well, that depends very much on how your volunteer vacation is organised. The good companies in this field are certainly conscious of the fact that this should be a rewarding travel experience … and not just a work trip.
P: But isn't the whole point of it to go and lend a hand to people in need of help? It's not really a holiday as we know it, is it?
K: Well, no, perhaps it isn't, but it is more like what real travel should be about: a cultural experience where each side gives something and takes something. A good example is a programme next to Kenya's Tsavo National Park, where volunteers help local people to find ways of making a living that don't involve poaching or killing local wildlife. So they help them to plant crops, build fences, develop ideas for tourist businesses and so on. In return the locals take them for bush walks, which are like mini-safaris, teach them about local wildlife, talk about the history of their community …
P: But the volunteers pay for the trip, don't they?
K: Yes, of course, they have to pay for their airfares, their living expenses and something to cover the organisation costs.
P: And do you need to be qualified to volunteer? I imagine organisations don't want people turning up to teach or build or whatever who have no idea of what they're doing, do they?
K: Again it depends … There are a few projects which are only open to people with professional experience … um … like people with a medical background … but for the most part, volunteers can be trained to do the work. The Cultural Restoration Tourism Project (CRTP), which helps to restore cultural heritage sites around the world, gives volunteers the chance to work with local architects and artists. They have a project restoring a 300-year-old monastery in Nepal where you can get training in doing wall paintings from a world-famous painter.
P: So, you could actually come back with a skill you didn't have when you left?
K: Absolutely. It might not be a skill you'll ever use again: helping to bottle-feed milk to orphaned lion cubs – that's a project in Zambia – is unlikely to be of direct use to you back at the office in the UK, but we all benefit from new and different experiences, wouldn't you agree?
P: Yeah, I'm sure that's true. So could you tell us a bit more about …

1.40
M = Mike; J = Jeff

M: Hi, I'm interested in helping out on the Great Continental Divide this summer. My friend did four days last summer. I can work for just a few days, can't I?

J: Absolutely. Anything from two days to two months.

M: That's great. I have about a week in June. How much does it cost to take part?

J: It's free.

M: Sorry? Don't I have to pay for my accommodation?

J: No, it's completely free. You just have to register by filling out a form and sending it to us.

M: I can't do that online, can I?

J: Sure, you can. It's on our website. You've visited our website, haven't you?

M: Yes, I've had a quick look. And where on the trail can I work?

J: New Mexico, Montana, Wyoming …

M: Don't you have something in Colorado? That's where I live.

J: Yes, we do. We have spaces in Winfield and a few in Mount Elbert.

M: And you give training first, don't you?

J: It's on the job training, unless it's very specific. We're looking for a chef at the moment. You don't want to be a chef, do you?

M: No. I just want to help build some trails …

1.41
M = Malcolm; P = Paul

M: Hi Paul, this is Malcolm, your host. You emailed me about staying next Thursday for a couple of nights.

P: Oh hi, hi Malcolm. Thanks for getting back to me. Is that still OK?

M: No, that's all fine. I just thought I'd give you a call to explain how to get here, because it's a bit complicated. How are you getting to Hamilton, first of all?

P: I'm coming in by train sometime in the afternoon.

M: OK. I wanted to pick you up, but my car's at the garage that day.

P: Hey, that's kind of you, but I can make my own way.

M: OK. Well I'm at work 'til about five thirty so feel free to come over any time after six.

P: That sounds perfect. And how do I get to you from the town centre?

M: Well you could just get a taxi, but it's about eleven kilometres from the centre, so it won't be cheap. Alternatively, you can hop on a bus to Stoney Creek. Look out for the Stoney Creek Arena on your right and get off there. It's only a twenty-minute ride. From there, Cherry Heights is another fifteen minutes on foot, straight up King St. Once you reach the crossroads at Gray Road, the easiest thing is to give me a call and I'll come out and meet you.

P: So bus to Stoney Creek, walk up King St to Cherry Heights and call from there?

M: Yup. Call when you get to the crossroads at Gray Road.

P: OK, got it. That sounds great. If I get held up in any way I'll let you know, but otherwise expect a call around six thirty.

M: Great. See you next Thursday then. Bye

P: Bye.

UPPER INTERMEDIATE
WORKBOOK

Paul Dummett

Unit 1 Relationships

1a A tradition in decline?

Reading friendships

1 Look at the photo. Then read the article. Which of the following statements best summarises the difference in the French and American attitudes to friendships?

a Most Americans have a lot of close friends.
b Americans are friendly with everyone; the French only with a few people.
c The French view friendship as something superficial.

2 Read the article again. Choose the correct option (a–c).

1 Which of the following relationships does the author NOT mention?
   a colleagues
   b fellow travellers
   c fellow shoppers

2 Psychologists believe that in modern society … have become weaker.
   a family relationships
   b friendships
   c all relationships

3 According to the article, 25% of Americans don't have … .
   a strong family bonds
   b a strong friendship
   c any friends at all

4 Americans are known for being … people.
   a lonely
   b family-oriented
   c friendly

5 French people are … about making friends.
   a careful   b worried   c relaxed

6 The author thinks that in the West, we ignore the … of friendship.
   a significance   b qualities   c security

3 Find nouns in the article derived from these adjectives.

1 true   ....
2 strong   ....
3 warm   ....
4 long   ....
5 deep   ....

A tradition in decline?

Is intimate friendship a relationship that is dying out in modern society? In our busy lives, we have many acquaintances and friends – the people we work with, our neighbours, the people we chat to at the local shop and so on. But how many really close friendships can we count? The truth for most of us is probably not many. Some psychologists say that while we still value strong family bonds, in recent times, friendships have lost the strength and importance that they had in the past.

According to a study published recently in the USA, friendships in America have been declining in quality and quantity since at least 1985. The study claims that 25% of Americans don't have anyone they could call a close friend. Yet, on the surface, Americans seem extremely friendly people. If you have ever visited the USA, you will be familiar with the warmth and hospitality that they show to complete strangers. Everyone can be treated as a 'buddy', even if they are just a casual acquaintance.

But in other cultures, acquaintances and friendships have different qualities. In France, for example, when you are trying to get to know a person, they may seem rather unfriendly and the length of time it takes to form a strong friendship seems greater than in other countries. This is because for the French there is still a clear distinction between a casual acquaintance and a true friend. Although France is changing and perhaps becoming more like America, there is no doubt that French people are still more private in their friendships and that they reserve real intimacy for their closest friends. This intimacy can be found in many non-western cultures too, where great importance is attached to the quality and depth of friendships. It is something that many of us in the West have forgotten and need to rediscover.

Glossary
die out (v) /ˌdaɪ ˈaʊt/ disappear
buddy (n) /ˈbʌdi/ a friend (colloquial)
intimacy (n) /ˈɪntɪməsi/ closeness in a relationship

Grammar present tenses review

4 Look at the article. Find examples of the following.

1 two progressive changes (present continuous)

_____

_____

2 two everyday activities (present simple)

_____

_____

3 two recent events with an impact on the present (present perfect simple)

_____

_____

4 one event that started in the past and continues now (present perfect continuous)

_____

5 Complete the questions from a survey on friendship. Use present tenses.

1 What person or people _____
_____ (you / spend) most time with recently?

2 _____ (you / consider) this person or people to be close friends?

3 How many really close friends _____ (you / have)?

4 Would you say your friendship circle _____ (increase) or not?

5 _____ (you/make) any new friends in the past month?

6 How long _____ (you / know) your closest friend?

7 How often _____ (you / see) this person?

8 Generally, what qualities _____ _____ (you / look for) in a friend?

Vocabulary friends: nouns and phrasal verbs

6 Look at the article again. Find the adjectives that collocate with these words. You may use the adjectives more than once.

1 a(n) _____ , _____ , _____
friendship

2 a _____ bond

3 a _____ , _____ friend

4 a _____ stranger

5 a _____ acquaintance

7 Which word in each group does NOT collocate with the single word next to it? Cross out the word.

1 a mutual *friend / respect / student / interest*

2 a fellow *student / companion / scientist / traveller*

3 a close *acquaintance / relationship / friend / relative*

4 a *flat / faithful / travel* companion

5 a(n) *odd / happy / blood* couple

6 a(n) *fair-weather / old / passing* friend

8 Complete the sentences. Use the best collocation from Exercises 6 and 7.

1 Travelling alone can have its advantages, but I always prefer to have a
_____ .

2 They are a very _____ :
Kate is a highly-educated scientific researcher and Dan is a professional footballer who left school when he was fifteen.

3 Relationships where one person thinks they are better than the other don't work, but in this case they have a great _____ for each other.

4 Malcolm is probably my best friend. We were _____ at university.

5 I don't really consider Ann to be a _____ : she's the mother of my brother-in-law's wife.

9 Complete the phrasal verbs. Choose the correct option.

1 I used to hang *out with / around* John a lot at college because we were both keen swimmers.

2 I'm meeting *with / up with* a group of colleagues on Friday. Would you like to join us?

3 I don't get *off / on* very well with my new boss. He's really difficult to work with.

4 Do you want to come *across / round* to my house and watch the football? It starts at 8 p.m.

5 It's very important to stand *by / with* your friends when they are in trouble.

6 Some people are very good at keeping *up with / on with* their old friends. I've lost touch with practically all the people I knew at college.

7 Jane and I were friends at school, but when we met we just seemed to pick *off / up* from where we left off 20 years ago.

8 It's your 30th birthday next month. What kind of celebration are you going *for / after*?

1b Young and old

Listening the ageing population

1 🎵 **1.1** Listen to an extract from a radio programme about the ageing population. Are the sentences true (T) or false (F)?

1 People are not having so many children as in the past.

2 People don't eat and exercise as healthily as in the past.

3 Older people are not as much at risk from deadly diseases as they were in the past.

4 The average age that anyone in the world can expect to live to is now around 80.

5 In the future, the money to support the old will come from the younger generation.

6 The ageing population will help bring families closer together.

2 🎵 **1.1** Complete the sentences with nouns. Then listen to the programme again and check.

Reasons for the ageing population

1 The birth _____ has declined over the last 20 years.

2 60 years ago, there was a baby _____ ; these 'baby boomers' are now reaching _____ age.

3 Improved _____ : people eat more healthily these days.

4 Healthier _____ : not only do people eat better, they are also more aware of the need to keep fit.

5 Advances in medicine have increased life _____ to around 80 in the developed world.

6 People are given routine _____ against life-threatening diseases, e.g. flu jabs for the elderly.

Grammar the passive

3 Rewrite the sentences from the active to the passive form.

1 Governments **are forcing** people to work longer.
People _____ to work longer.

2 Governments **have raised** the age of retirement in many countries.
The age of retirement _____ in many countries.

3 People **don't consider** someone to be old until they are about 80.
Someone _____ to be old until they are about 80.

4 The government **is encouraging** each family to have more children.
Each family _____ to have more children.

5 The government **reduces** taxes for families with more than two children.
Taxes _____ for families with more than two children.

6 The public **have not welcomed** the idea of working longer for less money.
The idea of working longer for less money _____ by the public.

4 Look at these sentences from the radio programme. Complete the sentences with the passive form of the verbs.

1 More _____ (know) these days about healthy and unhealthy eating.

2 Food producers _____ (oblige) to give consumers more information about the salt and fat content of their food.

3 In the past few years, people _____ _____ (educate) in the right way to exercise and keep fit.

4 Enormous progress _____ (make) in recent years in the field of medicine.

5 People _____ (also / give) routine vaccinations against diseases like flu.

6 The younger generation _____ _____ (now / outnumber) by the old.

5 Choose the correct option.

1 Life expectancy *is rising / is being risen* in many countries.

2 In the Middle East, the number of young people *is growing / is being grown*.

3 The idea of working longer *has not received / has not been received* well by people.

4 Some people say that advances in medicine *have gone / have been gone* too far.

5 It is unfair that young people *oblige / are obliged* to pay for the care of the old.

6 In some western countries, people *encouraging / are being encouraged* to have more children.

6 Pronunciation weak forms in passive verbs

a 🎵 **1.2** Listen to the sentences. Which parts of the verb in bold are NOT stressed? Circle the unstressed word.

1 People **are given** better protection against deadly diseases.

2 Some great advances **have been made** in medical science.

3 The problem of the ageing population **is being discussed** by many governments.

4 A satisfactory solution to this problem **has not yet been found**.

5 Working longer **is considered** to be one solution.

6 People **are expected** to work longer than in the past.

b 🎵 **1.3** It is possible to stress auxiliary verbs for emphasis. Listen to the phrases. Are the underlined words stressed (S) or unstressed/ weak form (W)?

	S	W
1 He <u>has been</u> told several times.	☐	☐
2 You <u>are</u> not allowed to smoke.	☐	☐
3 I <u>have been</u> given a new job.	☐	☐
4 She <u>is being</u> educated at home.	☐	☐
5 They <u>are</u> looked after very well.	☐	☐
6 The questions <u>are being</u> discussed.	☐	☐

7 Dictation old and young

🎵 **1.4** Look at the photo. The person is describing her family. Listen and write what she says. What is she looking forward to when she is older?

1 I think my parents' generation _____ _____

2 My parents _____ _____, but they both _____ _____ . So now they can relax and enjoy themselves.

3 They've said _____ and that we children _____

4 Considering that my husband and I _____

1c A dynamic society

Listening a study project in Vietnam

1 🔵 **1.5** Listen to an interview with a student who recently returned from a study trip to Vietnam. Which statement (a–c) best summarises her views about the different generations in Vietnamese society?

a   There is a deep cultural divide between the old and the young generations.

b   All generations are confused by the changes taking place.

c   The generations see things differently, but they all respect each other.

2 🔵 **1.5** Listen to the interview again. Are the sentences true (T) or false (F)?

1   Both the presenter and Lauren went on study trips as part of their university courses.

2   Vietnam is in a period of great economic and social change.

3   Lauren had the opportunity to meet a lot of ordinary Vietnamese citizens.

4   The older generation has suffered to reach where they are now.

5   Younger people are a little nervous about greater contact with the outside world.

6   The Vietnamese think it's very important to teach the young about the country's history.

7   Lauren felt that the different generations in the family couldn't understand each other.

8   The older generation is increasingly ignored by younger people.

3 Look at the phrases in bold from the interview. Choose the correct definition (a–c).

1   We were lucky to experience that **first-hand** …
   a   for ourselves
   b   for the first time
   c   something no one else has ever experienced

2   We **got to** meet …
   a   had the opportunity to meet
   b   were obliged to meet
   c   met by chance

3   They **take** this new wealth **for granted** …
   a   are suspicious of it
   b   are grateful for it
   c   assume it should be like this

4   They don't know **which way to turn** …
   a   the rules
   b   what to do
   c   where to drive

5   The generation in the middle **bridges the gap** …
   a   creates a space between two things
   b   joins two sides
   c   crosses from one side to another

6   The **30-somethings** …
   a   the 1930s
   b   a group of 30 objects
   c   people in their 30s

4 **Pronunciation word stress: *-ic* and *-tion/-sion***

a 🔵 **1.6** Listen to these words from the interview. Underline the stressed syllable in each word. What pronunciation rule can you make about words that end in *-ic* and *-tion*?

1 dynamic	4 generation
2 fantastic	5 restriction
3 economics	6 tradition

Rule: _____

b 🔵 **1.7** Practise saying these words, putting the stress on the correct syllable. Then listen and check.

specific	impression
italics	relation
terrific	interruption
scientific	transformation
characteristic	comprehension

1d What a nice surprise!

Real life meeting people you know

1 Look at the sentences. Some prepositions are missing. Insert the correct preposition, where necessary.

1 Fancy bumping _____ you here!
2 How's it all going _____ ?
3 What have you been up _____ lately?
4 I've been completely snowed _____ with work.
5 Being self-employed obviously suits _____ you.
6 Do you see much _____ Georgia these days?
7 How is your daughter getting _____ at university?
8 Do give _____ them my regards.
9 I'm _____ a bit of a hurry.
10 Good luck _____ the new job.

2 Grammar extra present perfect: simple and continuous

Look at the highlighted verbs in the sentences (1–4). Are they in the present perfect simple (PPS) or present perfect continuous (PPC) form?

1 He**'s moved** to New York for his job. _____
2 What **have you been doing** since I last saw you? _____
3 I **haven't seen** Hannah for ages. _____
4 She**'s been preparing** for her law exams.
_____

3 Look at the sentences in Exercise 2 again. Answer the questions.

1 Which tense emphasises how someone has spent their time recently? _____
2 Which tense emphasises a present result?
_____

4 Read the conversation. Choose the correct option.

Ben: Hi Sam. a _____ .
I've ¹ *wondered / been wondering* how you were.

Sam: Oh, hi Ben. b _____ .
I'm fine. I've ² *worked / been working* in Scotland for the last three months.

Ben: Well, c _____ .
You're looking very well. Have you ³ *decided / been deciding* to move up there?

Sam: No, it's just a temporary job. I've ⁴ *helped / been helping* to renovate an old castle. And d _____ ? Is Emily well?

Ben: Yes, thanks. She's just ⁵ *finished / been finishing* her nursing course.

Sam: Really? That's fantastic.
e _____ .

Ben: Well, f _____ .
I should probably go and do my shopping.

Sam: OK. Could I have your phone number again? I've ⁶ *lost / been losing* it.

Ben: Sure. It's 07945 699636.

Sam: Thanks. Well, speak soon, I hope.
g _____ .

5 🔊 1.8 Listen to the conversation in Exercise 4. Complete the phrases (a–g).

6 Pronunciation expressive intonation

🔊 1.9 Look at the phrases (1–6). Would you say them with an expressive intonation (E) or a flatter intonation (F)? Then listen and check.

		E	F
1	What a nice surprise.	☐	☐
2	Busy as ever.	☐	☐
3	How are things?	☐	☐
4	You're looking well.	☐	☐
5	Say hello to her from me.	☐	☐
6	Great to see you.	☐	☐

7 Listen and respond meeting people you know

🔊 1.10 Listen to comments where someone meets a friend by chance in the street. Respond with your own words. Then compare your response with the model answer that follows.

1

> Hi. What a nice surprise! How are you?

> I'm fine, thanks. Good to see you.

1e News from home

Writing an informal email

1 Complete the email to a friend who is working abroad. Use the sentences and phrases (a–g).

a   So keep your fingers crossed for me.
b   All the best,
c   How are you **getting on**?
d   Anyway, do send me your news when you **get** a moment to write.
e   What news from here?
f   I'm sorry I haven't written sooner.
g   Dear Esther

1 _____
2 _____ I hope everything is going OK. 3 _____ I've been really busy at work the last few weeks. Everyone has been asking about you. How is your Arabic coming on? I imagine you're able to **get by** with day-to-day conversations by now.
4 _____ Well, shortly after you left, I **got** a letter from a fashion designer in New York. They saw some of my work in a catalogue for the shop that I work for and they want me to fly over to New York for an interview. I'm trying not to **get** too excited about it in case they don't offer me a job, but as you know, it's always been my dream to **get** a job with a top designer.
5 _____
The other big piece of news is that Sarah is going to **get** married next year! I've met her boyfriend and he seems a really nice guy. They've fixed the date for 9th July. I hope you'll be back by then.
6 _____
It'd be great to hear how things are there.
7 _____
Sophie

Word focus *get*

2 Look at the verb *get* highlighted in the email in Exercise 1, either on its own or as part of a phrasal verb. Match the uses of *get* to a word with a similar meaning in the box.

be	become	doing	have	manage	
obtain	received				

_____   _____
_____   _____
_____

3 Look at the verb *get* in these sentences. Write a synonym for *get* in each sentence.

1   I'm sorry. I don't **get** what you're saying. Why do I have to wait? _____
2   Can you **get off** the phone? I'm trying to work.
_____
3   I **got** this jacket for £20 in the sales.
_____
4   Call me when you **get to** the station.
_____
5   We had to **get** a taxi because there were no buses. _____
6   It was a bad cold. It took me two weeks to **get over** it. _____
7   They **got** first prize in the dancing competition.
_____
8   Could you **get** the map from the car so that we can plan our route? _____

4 Rewrite this informal email.
1   First write the verbs in the correct tense.
2   Then see how many verbs you can replace with *get*.

Dear Jack,
I 1 _____ (receive) your email yesterday.
I 2 _____ (be) glad that you 3 _____ (arrive) there safely. It 4 _____ (sound) as if you
5 _____ (have) a really busy time.
Sorry to hear that you 6 _____ (be) delayed at the airport in the UK. I 7 _____ (hope) you
8 _____ (recover) now from the long journey to Chennai.
I hope the weather 9 _____ (not/become) any hotter too – 45 degrees Centigrade
10 _____ (sound) quite enough! I 11 _____ (not/think) I 12 _____ (ever/experience) temperatures like that.
Nothing much 13 _____ (happen) here since you left. I 14 _____ (try) to find a new job, but I 15 _____ (not/be) able to find anything suitable yet. I'll let you know when I
16 _____ (find) one.
Louis 17 _____ (help) me to write a CV and a covering letter, because I 18 _____ (not/really/understand) the whole job application process.
Anyway, fingers crossed.
Good luck with everything there and write again soon.
Love,
Theresa

Wordbuilding forming adjectives from nouns

1 Complete the table. Form adjectives from the nouns and verbs below.

care   conservation   control   child   decision   depend   difference   dominate   entrepreneur   fool
help   humour   industry   intellect   self   love   play   practice   respect   sense   study

-ful	-ish	-ive	-ious/-ous	-ent/-ant	-al	-ing
respectful	foolish	sensitive	studious	dependent	entrepreneurial	caring

2 Complete this interview about a family using adjectives from Exercise 1.

Are you a close family?
Yes, we are. We all have our own lives and careers so we are not ¹ _____ on each other, but we remain very close.

Why do you think that is?
We were brought up in a very ² _____ and loving environment and taught to look after each other.

Is there a clear head of the family?
It's quite a ³ _____ and traditional family in many ways. My father is certainly the ⁴ _____ figure – he gives the orders.

And do you all share a particular family trait?
We're all quite ⁵ _____ and down-to-earth people: good with our hands

Is there someone in the family you admire especially?
My uncle, who's a historian. He's more ⁶ _____ and quite a deep thinker, but he can also be very ⁷ _____ . He tells some very funny stories.

Has your family influenced your own path in life?
Yes. My father is an inventor and I think I have inherited his ⁸ _____ spirit. I set up my own business when I was 22. He's also very hard-working and we are ⁹ _____ types too.

Learning skills extending your vocabulary

3 You can extend your vocabulary by making word families. Look at the word *decide*. How many words can you think of that are related to it? Complete the words and expressions.

- different parts of speech: *decision* (noun), *decisive* (adjective), ¹ _____ (adverb)
- collocations: *make a decision*, ² _____ *a decision*
- opposites: *indecision*, ³ _____
- synonyms: *make up your mind, come to a* ⁴ _____

4 Now write a word family for another word. Choose two from the list.

fortune   immigration   influence   obey
respect   support

Check!

5 Do the quiz. Choose the correct option. All answers appear in Student's Book Unit 1.

1   Orang-utans are unusual in that they like to … .
    a   spend time with other animals
    b   share their food
    c   live independently

2   A fair-weather friend is someone who … .
    a   helps you in difficult situations
    b   makes a bad situation better
    c   is only a friend in good times

3   In which passive sentence is there NO agent?
    a   Bella has been raised in China.
    b   The right brands are selected by Bella.
    c   Her parents are confused by all the changes taking place in China.

4   The adjective from the noun *rebel* is … .
    a   rebelful   b   rebellient   c   rebellious

5   An expression for saying you are overloaded with work is to be … .
    a   snowed up
    b   snowed in
    c   snowed under

Unit 2 Storytelling

2a March of the Penguins

Reading a film documentary

1 Read the interview with a film director and answer the questions.

1 What is unusual about the lives of the penguins?

_____

_____

2 What is the theme of the film?

_____

Glossary
breed (v) /briːd/ have children
hatch (v) /hætʃ/ be born from an egg
chick (n) /tʃɪk/ a baby bird

2 Read the interview again and choose the correct option to complete the sentences.

1 The penguins make the long journey across Antarctica to *find food / have chicks*.

2 The mother penguins must hurry back from the ocean to feed *their young / the males*.

3 The director thinks the penguins' story was suited to film because it is *dramatic / romantic*.

4 It was easy to film the penguins because they are *friendly / predictable*.

5 The interviewer is surprised that the penguins can survive *out of water / in such hard conditions*.

Stefan Lovgren for
National Geographic News

March of the Penguins tells the remarkable story of emperor penguins who each year journey for hundreds of miles across the ice of Antarctica to reach their traditional breeding ground. After laying a single egg, the females return to the ocean for fish, leaving the males behind to guard the eggs, which they balance on top of their feet, even during snowstorms. After two months, during which the males eat nothing, the eggs begin to hatch. But if the mothers are late returning from the ocean with food, the chicks will die. French director Luc Jacquet spoke to us about the challenges of making *March of the Penguins*.

Your background is as a biologist. How did you become interested in penguins?
In 1992, I spent fourteen months at the French scientific centre in Antarctica doing research. In my career, I have also worked as a cameraman. I helped to shoot another film, *The Congress of the Penguins*, in 1995. I was also inspired by the sheer beauty of Antarctica, and I felt this was a great story for the movies. It has all the elements of great drama – love, life, death.

In the film, the narration comes from the penguins' perspective – we hear their thoughts. Why did you choose this storytelling technique?
I wanted to get away from the documentary genre and to write a story that made the viewer feel like he or she was really right there with the penguins.

How did you approach the penguins?
It was easy to get near them. They have never experienced any form of colonisation, so they're not scared of humans. They are also easy to work with because it's possible to anticipate everything they do – the route they will take, or how they will act in any given situation.

How would you describe the overall theme of the movie?
I wanted to tell things as I felt them, rather than as a scientist. It's about the struggle between life and death. The penguins have learned to live where no other creature can. This is what struck me the most. How do they do that? How do they manage?

The penguins are bad walkers. How did nature allow them to make this terrible trek across the ice?
That's a good question, and I haven't found an answer for it. But I think if you gave the penguins the option of spending all their lives underwater, they would take it.

3 Look at the interview again. Find words that mean:

1 to film _____
2 motivated _____
3 a type of film _____
4 to predict _____
5 made an impression on _____

Grammar past simple and present perfect simple

4 Look at the filmmaker's answers in the interview. Find examples of the following:

1 his experience in general (present perfect)
_____

2 something he did at a specific time in the past (past simple) _____

3 something the penguins did in the past that has a present result (present perfect)
_____

5 Complete the final part of the interview using the verbs in the present perfect simple and past simple forms.

> **Some would say you have to be crazy to spend more than a year in such an inhospitable environment.**
> I ¹ _____ (met) many explorers and adventurers in my life. Some of them ² _____ (spend) their careers climbing mountains, others like to cross the desert or the sea. I ³ _____ (always / feel) comfortable in the polar environment. On this visit, I ⁴ _____ (get) a particular sense of adventure. Yes, I ⁵ _____ (encounter) a lot of difficulties. But once I had been there for a while, my body ⁶ _____ (adapt) to the environment. Over time, I ⁷ _____ (learn) to deal with the terrific wind, which in some ways is worse than the cold temperatures. Everyone who ⁸ _____ (visit) the polar regions for any length of time will tell you this. What you have to do is to learn to minimise body movement. So I ⁹ _____ (not / run) anywhere when I was there. I just ¹⁰ _____ (do) everything carefully and slowly.

Vocabulary books and films

6 Complete the review of *March of the Penguins* using these words.

audience	accurate	cast	director
gripping	location	sentimental	scenes
storyline	touching		

The ¹ _____ Jacquet has made a visually stunning film. But some people may find his approach to the penguins is too ² _____ , because he has romanticised their story by giving them a human voice.

I found it more ³ _____ than many thrillers, and more ⁴ _____ than many romantic films. And all without a ⁵ _____ of human actors.

Filmed on ⁶ _____ in Antarctica, *March of the Penguins* paints an ⁷ _____ picture of how harsh life can be for these creatures. Behind the basic ⁸ _____ of the struggle for survival is a message for the ⁹ _____ about modern family life. It contains some extraordinary ¹⁰ _____ , such as the males protecting their eggs in a raging blizzard.

7 Pronunciation the letter *l*

🔊 **1.11** Look at these words. Write *S* if you think the letter 'l' is silent. Then listen and check.

1 talk _____
2 silk _____
3 bold _____
4 could _____
5 calf _____
6 installed _____
7 folk _____
8 wild _____
9 calm _____
10 film _____

8 Dictation describing books and films

🔊 **1.12** Listen to someone describing the book *A Week at the Airport*. Complete the sentences.

1 The _____ Alain de Botton's _____ , *A Week at the Airport*, is Heathrow airport.

2 The _____ that passes through the airport.

3 The _____ with travellers and airline staff.

4 _____ is that if you are looking for somewhere that _____ , you don't need to look any further than an airport.

2b True stories

Listening the Aron Ralston story

1 🔊 **1.13** Listen to adventurer Aron Ralston's story, which was recently made into the film, *127 Hours*. Which of these sentences summarises what he did?

a When he became trapped, Ralston panicked.
b When he became trapped, Ralston thought carefully about what to do next.
c When he became trapped, Ralston knew immediately what he had to do.

Glossary
boulder (n) /ˈbəʊldə(r)/ a large rock or stone
wedged (adj) /wedʒd/ caught between two surfaces e.g. two walls
multi-tool (n) /ˈmʌltituːl/ a tool like a Swiss army knife
numb (adj) /nʌm/ unable to feel anything

2 🔊 **1.13** Listen again and choose the best option.

1 Ralston went to Bluejohn Canyon:
   a to help prepare himself for a future mountain climb.
   b to do some mountain biking.
   c to do a bit of camping.

2 His hand became trapped when:
   a he stood on one of the boulders.
   b he dropped down onto a boulder.
   c he put his arm around a boulder.

3 Ralston's options were to:
   a wait for help or free his hand.
   b wait for help or cut off his hand.
   c free his hand or cut off his hand.

4 The first thing he tried was:
   a calling for help.
   b freeing his hand with his multi-tool.
   c chipping away part of his trapped hand.

5 After five days, Ralston finally:
   a walked out of the canyon.
   b was lifted out of the canyon by some tourists.
   c walked all the way out of the National Park.

3 Look at the verbs in bold. Match the verbs with the correct definition.

1 He **stretched** to reach a secure foothold.
   a extended his leg
   b stepped
   c bent his leg

2 The boulder **slid down** …
   a crashed
   b slipped
   c rolled

3 The boulder trapped his hand, **crushing** it.
   a causing it pain
   b destroying it with pressure
   c cutting it

4 He tried to **shift** the boulder.
   a move
   b break
   c get on top of

5 He **chipped away** at the rock.
   a scratched
   b rubbed
   c broke little pieces off

6 **Dripping** blood, he made his way back.
   a letting large amounts escape
   b letting drops fall
   c trying to stop the flow

Grammar past tenses review

4 Complete the story using the correct past tense form of the verbs in brackets.

On April 25, 2003, Aron Ralston
¹ _____ (drive) to Moab, Utah, where he mountain-biked the famous Slickrock Trail. He then ² _____ (make) his way to Horseshoe Canyon. When he
³ _____ (arrive), night
⁴ _____ (fall), so he made camp.

He ⁵ _____ (climb) into the canyon on April 26. He
⁶ _____ (go) about five miles when he came to a section where a series of large boulders ⁷ _____ (hang), wedged between the walls of the canyon.

He ⁸ _____ (not/tell) anyone where he was. It would be days before anyone realised that he was missing. Ralston
⁹ _____ (stand) on a small stone, facing the boulder that ¹⁰ _____ (crush) his hand. The pain was intense, but he was determined to stay in control …

Ralston ¹¹ _____ (wait) there for five days. But by the time the search teams started out, he ¹² _____ (already/decide) what he had to do …

5 Look at the sentences. If it got dark at 6.00 p.m., when did Ralston arrive in each case? Match the sentences (1–3) with the times (a–c).

1 When he arrived at Horseshoe Canyon, night fell. _____
2 When he arrived at Horseshoe Canyon, night was falling. _____
3 When he arrived at Horseshoe Canyon, night had fallen. _____

   a around 6.00 p.m.
   b 6.00 p.m.
   c 7.00 p.m.

6 Pronunciation contracted negative forms

🔊 **1.14** Listen and write down the missing word, either an auxiliary verb or a contracted negative form.

1 I _____ been there before.
2 You _____ allowed to smoke.
3 It _____ the first time this has happened.
4 She _____ the person I told you about.
5 They _____ as tired from the journey as I expected.
6 I _____ talking about what happened to me.
7 She _____ been waiting a long time.
8 I _____ spoken French for years.

7 Grammar extra present tenses for narratives

a Read this short review of the film *127 Hours*, the Aron Ralston story. What tenses are used to describe the plot of the film?

Film title: *127 Hours*

Rating: 8.5

Director: Danny Boyle (*Slumdog Millionaire*, *Trainspotting*)

Actors: James Franco, Kate Mara, Amber Tamblyn

Genre: Action film

Release date: November 2010

Synopsis: Aron Ralston, a 27-year-old hiker, is canyoneering in Utah's remote Bluejohn Canyon. An 800-pound boulder falls and traps his hand, making it impossible for him to move. He hasn't told anyone where he is going. Based on a true story.

▶ **GRAMMAR EXTRA present tenses for narratives**

We use present tenses to describe the plot of a book or a film and to review them.
In the film '127 Hours' Aron Ralston is canyoneering in Utah's remote Bluejohn Canyon.
An 800-pound boulder falls and traps his hand.
He hasn't told anyone where he is going.
This use of the present tense is sometimes referred to as 'the present historic'.

b Look at the grammar box. Then complete the synopsis of a book using the verbs in the correct tense.

Book title: *To the Ends of the Earth*

Author: Ranulph Fiennes

Genres: Autobiography; travel; adventure

Synopsis: The mountaineer and explorer Ranulph Fiennes ¹ _____ (give) a personal and gripping account of an expedition around the world from top to bottom. The adventures really ² _____ (begin) once the group ³ _____ (reach) Antarctica and tensions ⁴ _____ (grow) between the friends, while all the time conditions ⁵ _____ (get) worse.

2c Children's stories

Listening the stories of Oscar Wilde

1 💿 **1.15** Listen to a review of a collection of short stories by Oscar Wilde. Are the sentences true (T) or false (F)?

1 The stories were written for children.
2 The stories were published recently.
3 All the stories reveal something about human behaviour.
4 In the story of the Happy Prince, the statue of the prince can think, feel and speak.
5 The Happy Prince wants to help the little bird.
6 The Happy Prince has a happy ending.

Glossary
ostensibly (adv) /ɒstˈensɪbli/ apparently
swallow (n) /ˈswɒləʊ/ a kind of bird that migrates
eyesore (n) /ˈaɪsɔː(r)/ something unpleasant to look at

2 💿 **1.16** Complete the sentences. Then listen again to the first part of the review and check your answers.

1 The stories are suitable for _____ and _____.
2 They contain elements that you would find in a traditional _____.
3 At the heart of what makes them beautiful is their _____.
4 People who read the stories are _____ by them.
5 Oscar Wilde did not like to give _____.

3 💿 **1.17** Read the summary of the story of *The Happy Prince*. Then listen again to the second part of the review and choose the correct option.

The Happy Prince is ¹ *an elegant / a shabby* statue in the centre of an old town in northern Europe. Each day the prince ² *proudly ignores / watches closely* what is happening in the town. One day, ³ *he stops a little swallow / a little swallow stops off with him* on its way to Egypt for the winter. The prince ⁴ *asks / orders* him to take the gold and jewels from his statue to poor ⁵ *people / children* around the town. The swallow continues doing this for some ⁶ *days / weeks*. In the end, the swallow ⁷ *is exhausted / catches cold* and dies at the foot of the statue. When the town councillors see the statue without its gold and jewels, they decide to ⁸ *destroy / renovate* it.

Word focus *keep*

4 Look at the phrases with *keep* from the story of *The Happy Prince*. Match the phrases (1–4) with the correct meaning (a–d).

1 I still had to **keep back** the tears.
2 Oscar Wilde **kept from** giving moral lessons.
3 From where he stands, he can **keep abreast of** all that is happening in the town.
4 The swallow stays for some days **keeping** the prince **company**.

a spend time with
b prevent (someone) from doing something
c hold in and not release something
d stay in touch or up-to-date with

5 Complete the sentences using these phrases. You will need to use the correct form. There are two extra phrases.

keep abreast of   keep an eye on   keep track of
keep (someone) company   keep (someone) from
keep back   keep a secret   keep a promise

1 Thanks for your help and sorry if I _____ your work.
2 Those flowers are a thank you present from Sarah. I _____ her flat while she was away.
3 People visit my grandfather at the weekend, but during the week there is no one to _____.
4 My brother is travelling around the world and he sends me emails so I can _____ his progress.
5 Apart from a small amount of money that she _____ for emergencies, she spent everything she had saved.
6 It's not fair to ask someone to _____ if they know telling it will help someone they know.

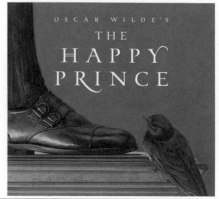

OSCAR WILDE'S
THE
HAPPY
PRINCE

2d I can sympathise

Real life reacting to stories

1 Look at these situations where things have gone wrong. Complete the sentences using the correct form of the verb.

1 My trousers got caught on a nail and _____ (tear).
2 The key _____ (break) in the lock as I was turning it.
3 The boy put his head through the railings and it got _____ (stick).
4 He had _____ (make) a big hole in his jumper.
5 The pipe _____ (freeze) because it was so cold.
6 When it warmed up again, the pipe _____ (burst).

2 Underline the words or phrases that can begin each reaction. Sometimes more than one answer is possible. Then match the reactions to the situations in Exercise 1.

a *How / What a / That was* nightmare!
b *How / What a / That was* good thinking.
c *How / What a / That was* embarrassing.
d *How / What a / That was* lucky.
e *How / Poor / What* a stroke of luck.
f *How / Poor / What* strange.
g *How / Poor / What* you!
h *How / What / That must have been* a relief.
i *How / What / That must have been* awkward.
j *How / What / That must have been* a disaster.

3 🔊 **1.18** Listen to two friends talking about a travel story. Answer the questions.

1 What was the problem?

2 How did they resolve the problem?

3 How did the speaker feel by the end of their ordeal?

4 🔊 **1.18** Listen again. Complete the reactions (1–6). Use phrases a–f.

a How stressful!
b Oh, that's awful.
c I think I would have done the same thing.
d Oh no. Poor you.
e I can sympathise.
f That was a stroke of luck.

1 _____ What happened?
2 _____ So did you leave her behind?
3 _____ And where were you?
4 _____ Did they make it in time?
5 _____ I hate being late when I'm travelling.
6 Did you? I don't blame you. _____

5 Pronunciation linking and assimilation

a 🔊 **1.19** The following phrases are either linked (1–4) or assimilated (the last letter of the first word is absorbed into the opening consonant of the second word). Listen and repeat.

1 large area
2 immediate action
3 open air
4 cry out
5 a burst pipe
6 Great Britain
7 hand baggage
8 bus shelter

b 🔊 **1.20** Now say these expressions. Then listen and check.

1 thick undergrowth
2 West Africa
3 dead end
4 climb up
5 pocket money
6 credit card
7 nice shoes
8 first class

6 Listen and respond reacting to stories

🔊 **1.21** Listen to five people telling you news. Respond with your own words. Then compare your response with the model answer that follows.

1

You'll never guess what happened to me yesterday on the bus. I started talking to this woman who I thought was Sue, my next-door neighbour, about my problems at work. But it wasn't Sue, it was a complete stranger!

How embarrassing! When did you realise it wasn't Sue?

2e 'Don't move!'

1 Writing skill using descriptive words

a Read this extract from a story and underline all the verbs and expressions that describe how people speak.

'Don't move,' she whispered, 'I think I can see an animal in the bushes.' 'I know,' Dominic replied anxiously. 'I can hear it too.' They stayed where they were, waiting to see what would appear from the bushes. Dominic, who was clearly very frightened, moaned quietly. 'Be quiet,' muttered Cat, 'or you'll attract its attention.' Just then, the branches parted and a tall man in white clothes stepped out into the clearing. 'Hello there!' he cried.

b Match the descriptive verbs (1–7) with the phrases (a–g).

1	he cried	a	she said wearily
2	she moaned	b	she said complainingly
3	she whispered	c	he said loudly
4	he screamed	d	he shouted at the top of his voice
5	he muttered	e	he said under his breath
6	she sighed	f	she said, not enunciating her words
7	she mumbled	g	she said softly

2 Writing skill extra punctuation

a Look at the sentences (1–4). Are the statements (a–d) true (T) or false (F)?

1 He said, 'What a surprise!'
2 'I know,' she said, 'that you don't like eating spicy food.'
3 'Do you agree?' he asked.
4 'I don't agree,' he said.

a You must put quotation marks at the beginning and end of each direct quotation.
b Question marks and exclamation marks belonging to the quotation must be inside the quotation marks.
c You always need a comma to separate the verb of saying from the direct quotation.
d If you break a sentence of a direct quotation and insert a verb of saying, you must put a comma after the verb and before the next set of quotation marks.

b Punctuate the following extract from a story with quotation marks and commas where necessary.

I don't think this is going to work Christopher sighed. We've been trying to build this canoe for three days and it still looks like a lump of wood. The wood's too hard he added. Actually, Christopher said Jen encouragingly we are making some progress. What we really need to do is find some better tools. Just then Tom screamed I've got it! Instead of using our penknives directly on the wood, why don't we make some better tools using our knives?

Writing a story

3 Write the opening paragraph of a story about two friends' encounter with a fierce animal. Follow these instructions:
• Begin with the most dramatic point in the narrative.
• Use descriptive verbs of speaking and moving.
• Use some direct speech. Make sure you punctuate it correctly.

Wordbuilding synonyms

1 Make pairs of close synonyms from the following words.

> **A** an author   an audience   a blockbuster
> a cinema   to edit   a film   a hero
> to publish   a remake   a sequel

> **B** a best-seller   to cut   a follow-up   a heroine
> a movie   a multiplex   a novelist
> a re-release   viewers   to release

2 Match words from Exercise 1 with the definitions.

1   a writer of stories ....

2   a leading female character ....

3   people who watch TV ....

4   a very successful book ....

5   to distribute a film for public viewing ....

6   to remove a scene from a film ....

7   a book or film that is the next part of the story ....

8   a cinema with many screens ....

9   a film which is distributed for a second time ....

10   an American word for a film ....

3 Look at these synonyms to do with speaking and movement. Choose the correct definition (a or b) for each.

1   We **trudged** for miles and miles in the baking heat. ....

2   We **stumbled** through the thick undergrowth, desperate to find a path. ....

   a   walk almost falling forward

   b   walk wearily

3   He **muttered** something about it not being fair. ....

4   Try not to **mumble**. It's very difficult to hear what you're saying. ....

   a   speak indistinctly because you don't want to be heard

   b   speak indistinctly

5   She **edged** towards the door and turned the handle slowly. ....

6   She **walked back slowly** to the window and looked out. ....

   a   move slowly

   b   move slowly and carefully

Learning skills pronunciation

4 Without good pronunciation, people can't understand you. Read these tips to help improve your pronunciation.

1   Don't speak too fast. It's better to be slow and clear than fast and misunderstood.

2   Practise saying phrases and short sentences rather than individual sounds. Listen to native speech and try to imitate the sounds you hear.

3   Record yourself and compare your pronunciation with a native speaker's.

4   Listen to songs in English and imitate exactly what you hear.

5   Practise your pronunciation every day. Choose phrases and texts you have learnt in the unit.

5 Look at these phrases from Unit 2. Follow steps 1–3 in Exercise 4 to practise pronouncing them.

   a   What a nightmare!

   b   That must have been a relief.

   c   I can sympathise with that.

6 Write a mini presentation on a topic of interest to you. Read it aloud and record yourself. Analyse your pronunciation and note your mistakes.

Check!

7 Do the quiz. All the answers are in Student's Book Unit 2.

> **1** **What kind of film or book are these?**
>
>   a   *Senna* ....
>   b   *The Frog Prince* ....
>   c   *The Lord of the Rings* ....
>
>
>
> **2** **What were these people's jobs?**
>
>   a   Peter Jackson ....
>   b   Wilhelm Grimm ....
>   c   Steve Winter ....
>
> **3** **What are these three English idioms?**
>
>   a   a narrow escape = a close ....
>   b   a lucky chance = a .... of luck
>   c   to get a little exercise = to .... your legs

3a No magic answer

Reading population growth

1 Read the text about the problem of overpopulation. What does the writer think the solution will be found through?
  a technology
  b population control
  c sharing of resources

2 Read the text and complete the sentences.

  1 The problem is not just how many people there are, it's how high their .... is.

  2 The economic optimists believe that resources .... as the population increases.

  3 In the last 60 years, food production has grown .... population growth.

  4 Parents in under-developed countries need .... to look after them in their old age.

  5 Bill Gates thinks that by improving health in poor countries we can limit population growth by ....

  6 For Joel Cohen, there are .... to help solve the problem of overpopulation.

No magic answer

For every problem we always hope there will be a magic answer that will make it go away. That's human nature. But problems like overpopulation are complex and demand complex solutions. First, let's outline a few basic facts.

Firstly, each person on the planet takes up space, consumes resources and creates waste. So the more people there are, the greater the problems of dwindling resources, overcrowding and pollution are going to be.

Secondly, rising standards of living – a product of economic growth – have exactly the same effects. Rich people have bigger houses, buy more consumer goods and generate more waste. So even if the population remains the same, economic growth will create similar problems.

But economic optimists don't worry about an increasing population because, according to them, people don't deplete resources, they create them. For them, more people mean more human intelligence and more brains to find clever ways to boost resources. One example they give is the 'Green Revolution'. Over the last 60 years, agricultural food production has grown dramatically – faster than the population, in fact. Through the engineering of better seeds and plants, which are more resistant to disease, experts predict that there will be enough food for all of us in the future.

Another example is the Gates Foundation's work in combating disease in poor countries through a programme of vaccination. You would think that saving lives through vaccination would actually increase the population, not decrease it. Parents in under-developed countries want to ensure that at least two children will be around to look after them when they are old. So they raise this probability by having more children. However, research shows that when you improve health in such communities, the population growth rate will fall within half a generation. Bill Gates believes that if we continue this work, the world population will peak at 8.3 billion by 2050 rather than the 9.3 billion currently predicted.

But of course technology alone is not the answer. It will help us to protect current resources and to find new resources, but we will also need to look at how we share these. Joel Cohen, a professor at Rockefeller University, put it nicely. He said that three schools of thought had a role to play in lessening the negative effects of overpopulation:

- 'The bigger pie school', who say that technology will increase resources.

- 'The fewer forks school', who say we need to reduce population growth and consumption.

- 'The better manners school', who say we should all share resources more equally.

The last, and probably the real answer, requires a different kind of faith: not in science, but in human nature.

Vocabulary verbs describing trends

3 Find verbs in the passage that describe things getting greater or smaller.

Greater	Smaller
1 r _____	7 d _____
2 b _____	8 d _____
3 g _____	9 d _____
4 i _____	10 f _____
5 r _____	11 l _____
6 p _____	12 r _____

4 Complete the sentences using an appropriate verb from Exercise 3. There is more than one possible answer for some of the sentences.

1 The author thinks that one way or another, we need to _____ the amount of resources we use.

2 The world's population is expected to continue to _____ until around 2050.

3 After that it will probably begin to _____ .

4 The economic optimists believe that whatever problems overpopulation causes, we will find a technological solution to _____ their impact.

5 One way to _____ the chance of having more children who will survive is simply to have more children in the first place.

6 Another way is to _____ the amount of money invested in health programmes in poor countries.

Grammar future forms review

5 Read these comments about the views expressed in the article. Choose the correct option.

1 'Bill Gates argues that if you improve health, people *will have / are having* fewer children. But what he doesn't say is that the result *will be / is about to be* more and more old people.'

2 'If we *will rely / are going to rely* on new technology to solve this problem, then heaven help us. New technology creates as many problems as it solves.'

3 '*I'll tell / I'm going to tell* you something – I *will be / I'm going to be* very surprised if the population growth rate *won't start / doesn't start* to fall in the next 20 years.'

4 'I'm from what the article calls "the better manners school". There are enough resources for everyone, but we *won't solve / don't solve* the problem until we *will share / share* them more equally.'

5 'I'm suspicious of people like Bill Gates. He made a fortune out of business and now he *will save / is going to save* the world.'

6 'Actually, *I'll go / I'm going* to hear Bill Gates speak at a climate change conference this week. It *will begin / begins* on Friday.'

6 Read the conversation about plans to attend a conference. Complete the sentences using the appropriate future form of the verbs.

Phil: Hi, Anna. ¹ _____ (you / go) to the 'Future Foods Fair' next weekend?

Anna: Yes, I am. How ² _____ (you / get) there?

Phil: I ³ _____ (probably / drive). What about you?

Anna: I haven't decided. Perhaps I ⁴ _____ (go) by train.

Phil: Don't do that – it's so expensive. I ⁵ _____ (give) you a lift.

Anna: That would be great. What time ⁶ _____ (you / leave)?

Phil: Well, the conference ⁷ _____ (start) at 10, so I thought about 8.30.

Anna: That sounds perfect. Do you imagine it ⁸ _____ (finish) by 6?

Phil: I hope so. I need to be back by 7.30.

7 Pronunciation /r/ and /t/ in American English

🔊 **1.22** Listen to an American speaking about Bill Gates and other philanthropists. Complete the text.

There's a group of philanthropists in the US – Gates, Buffet, Rockefeller, ¹ _____ – who have ² _____ a ³ _____ of money to good causes over the last ⁴ _____ ⁵ _____ .

The problem for them is that, because they're so rich and ⁶ _____ , people get suspicious of their ⁷ _____ . So when they ⁸ _____ up, they often do so ⁹ _____ , like they did a few years ago in ¹⁰ _____ .

3b Smart technology

Listening homes of the future

1 🔊 **1.23** You are going to listen to an interview with a researcher about smart homes of the future. Tick (✓) the items you think you will hear. Then listen and check.

kitchen gadgets ☐   visual media ☐

water use ☐   security ☐

GPS systems ☐   lighting ☐

sound-proofing ☐   hot water systems ☐

2 🔊 **1.23** Listen again and choose the best option (a–c).

1 The aim of the radio programme is to find out which technology … .
  a is going to be of practical use to us in the near future
  b is the most imaginative
  c will help us to be more environmentally-friendly

2 Intelligent fridges will be more popular when … .
  a they have been developed more
  b they can tell you about the condition of your food
  c they are less expensive

3 Ultrasonic showers are not likely to be used soon because … .
  a sonic waves do not clean the body particularly well
  b we still have plenty of water
  c they could be dangerous

4 The researcher thinks that in the future we could sound-proof rooms using … .
  a magnetic fields
  b high-tech insulation materials
  c energy fields

5 Which of the following will we NOT be able to do with a kitchen surface in the future?
  a watch TV
  b defrost a pizza
  c clean it by hand

6 In the future, we will be using electric lighting in our homes … .
  a in place of natural light
  b to simulate natural light
  c to help control our moods

3 Look at the words and expressions from the interview. Match the words or expressions in bold (1–8) with the correct definition (a–h).

1 new **gadgets**	a people who love technology
2 just a **gimmick**	b clever devices
3 **techies**	c distant
4 a **pipe dream**	d imitate or copy
5 remains to be **proven**	e protected from
6 a **remote** possibility	f fantasy
7 sound-**proof**	g thing that simply attracts attention
8 **simulate** the sunrise	h shown to be true

Grammar future continuous and future perfect simple

4 Read the sentences and choose the correct option.

1 In a few years, I'm sure we *will be hearing / will have heard* a lot more about this technology.

2 In the future, cookers *will be making / will have made* our meals for us.

3 We *will all be using / will all have used* intelligent fridges when food packaging is intelligent too.

4 In the next ten years, lack of water *will be becoming / will have become* a big issue, so we need to find alternatives.

5 In the future, people *will be using / will have used* energy fields that isolate a particular space from the rest of the house.

6 I don't think people *will be cleaning / will have cleaned* kitchen surfaces either in the future.

7 Soon, we *will be installing / will have installed* surfaces that can act as computer or TV screens in almost every room.

8 I think in ten years or so, that kind of technology *will be becoming / will have become* quite common in new-build houses.

9 Next year, our company *will be launching / will have launched* a new lighting system for bedrooms that simulates the sunrise.

5 Complete these predictions about the use of robots in the home of the future. Put the verbs into the future continuous or future perfect.

When people say that in the future robots
¹ _____ (do) all the boring chores around the home, most of us have an image of a human-shaped robot with a feather duster in its hand, which ² _____ (clean) the house while we sit with our feet up watching TV.

But if you move forward ten years, that is not actually the way technology ³ _____ (develop). In the future, robots in the home will take many forms. Vacuum cleaners that move around the room on their own are already available. In the future, we will see a lot of micro-robots, which ⁴ _____ (do) the kind of jobs that we tend not to do regularly. When we arrive home, micro robots ⁵ _____ (be) busy all day organising items in our cupboards or cleaning our drains. These robots will already be an integral part of the equipment we use: the fridge, kitchen sink, cupboard, etc. We ⁶ _____ (not / acquire) them as separate items.

Vocabulary information technology

6 Match the nouns to make collocations.

age	games	graphics	overload
programmer	security	storage	technology

1 information _____
_____

2 data _____
_____

3 computer _____
_____

7 Complete the sentences using one of the noun-noun collocations in Exercise 6.

1 The most serious issue of the next twenty years will be _____ : how we protect our personal and private information.

2 This post-industrial era that we now live in is called the _____ .

3 Augmented reality means projecting _____ onto our view of the real world.

4 Bigger _____ capacity means that portable devices can hold much more information than in the past.

5 People complain that we now have _____ . In other words, there is more information than we can absorb.

8 Dictation information overload

🔊 **1.24** Listen to three facts about the amount of information in the world. Write down the words you hear. Which fact surprised you most?

1 The weekday edition _____
_____
_____
_____

2 Around a thousand _____
_____
_____
_____

3 More information has _____
_____
_____

3c The simplest ideas are the best

Listening lifestraw

1 🔊 **1.25** Listen to a description of a device called *Lifestraw* and choose the best option (a–c).

1 *Lifestraw* protects against:
   a all stomach infections.
   b certain deadly diseases.
   c 90% of all bacteria.

2 It is operated:
   a with a pump.
   b with a small motor.
   c by sucking.

3 In order to get the best out of it, users need:
   a no training.
   b a day's training.
   c a little advice.

4 It does not solve the problem of:
   a purifying salt water.
   b travelling to get water.
   c drinking dirty water.

2 🔊 **1.25** Listen again and complete the sentences. Use numbers and figures.

1 In _____, the number of deaths from unclean water was _____ per day.

2 The filter traps _____ of water-borne bacteria.

3 Each straw cost approximately US $ _____ .

4 Each straw has a cleaning capacity of _____ litres of water.

5 The straw is _____ cm long.

6 Straws were used successfully in Haiti and Pakistan in _____ .

3 🔊 **1.25** Complete these facts about *Lifestraw*. Use the correct verb. Then listen and check.

1 *Lifestraw* _____ on a very simple principle.

2 It _____ protection against the killer diseases cholera and typhoid.

3 The filter _____ a substance called PuroTech Disinfecting Resin.

4 Each filter _____ up to a year.

5 It _____ very little, so it can be worn around the neck.

6 It doesn't _____ on electrical power.

4 Pronunciation *dis-*, *dys-* and *di-*

a 🔊 **1.26** Listen to these words. Is the underlined letter in each word pronounced /ɪ/ or /aɪ/?

	/ɪ/	/aɪ/
1 di̲saster	☐	☐
2 dy̲sentry	☐	☐
3 di̲arrhoea	☐	☐
4 di̲sease	☐	☐
5 di̲agram	☐	☐

b 🔊 **1.27** Practise saying these words. Then listen and check.

diabetes	discomfort	dysfunctional
distance	diamond	distribution
diary	dyslexic	disabled	diagonal

Vocabulary useful devices

5 Complete these sentences. The first letter has been given for you.

1 *Lifestraw* offers a n_____ solution to a serious, complicated problem.

2 Because you don't need to learn how to use it, it's an excellent example of a_____ technology.

3 For many people in developing countries, collecting water is a very time-c_____ process.

4 *Lifestraw's* appeal is that it's a very h_____ gadget – portable, useful and easy to operate.

5 Although it is simple for the user, inside it uses c_____ edge technology to filter out bacteria.

6 WaterAid is worried that *Lifestraw* is a quick f_____ for a more complex problem.

3d Computers

Vocabulary computing

1 Look at the icons. Match the words with the icons.

| attach | copy | cut | format | highlight | open |
| paste | save | search | select | sort | undo |

1 _____ 2 _____ 3 _____

4 _____ 5 _____ 6 _____

7 _____ 8 _____ 9 _____

10 _____ 11 _____ 12 _____

Real life asking for and offering help

2 🔘 **1.28** Listen to a conversation about a computer problem. Answer the questions.

1 What is the problem?
_____
_____

2 What are the two possible solutions?
1 _____
2 _____

3 Why doesn't the first speaker like the first solution?
_____
_____

3 🔘 **1.28** Complete the conversation. Use one word in each space. Then listen and check your answers.

Andy: Can you ¹ _____ me a ² _____ ? I'm having ³ _____ sending this document.

Meg: What do you want to do ⁴ _____ ?

Andy: Nothing very complicated. I'm ⁵ _____ to attach this document to an email and it won't let me.

Meg: ⁶ _____ me have a ⁷ _____ . OK, I see – the document's too large.

Andy: The ⁸ _____ is it's got a lot of photos in it, and I can't just cut them.

Meg: No, well you ⁹ _____ compress the photos.

Andy: What does that ¹⁰ _____ ?

Meg: I'll ¹¹ _____ you. Right-click on the photo … If you do that with all of them, that should do the ¹² _____ .

Andy: Yes, I ¹³ _____ , but then that reduces the quality of the photos. What ¹⁴ _____ do you suggest?

Meg: Have you ¹⁵ _____ dividing the document into three or four separate documents?

Andy: No, I'll give that a ¹⁶ _____ and see if it ¹⁷ _____ .

Meg: OK. Feel ¹⁸ _____ to ask if you want me to help you compress the photos after all.

4 Pronunciation stress in two syllable verbs

🔘 **1.29** In two syllable verbs, the stress usually falls on the second syllable. Listen and find the two words that do not fit this stress pattern.

| attach | compress | control | divide | highlight |
| involve | open | prepare | reduce | select | suggest |

5 Listen and respond asking for and offering technical help

🔘 **1.30** Listen to someone asking a friend for help with a computer problem. Respond with your own words. Then compare your response with the model answer that follows.

1

> Can you help me? My presentation slides look really boring!

> OK. What do you want to do exactly?

3e A technical problem

1 Writing skill being polite

Rewrite the sentences so that they are more polite. Use the bold words.

1 Is it OK if I bring your memory stick back on my way home from work tonight?
please _____
_____ ?

2 Where can I find a battery charger for my old phone?
happen _____
_____ ?

3 I want you to send me a brochure for your air conditioning units.
could _____
_____ ?

4 What is the phone number for Apricot Computers? I can't find it anywhere.
know _____
_____ ?

5 I want to know how to download photos from my X306 camera.
advise _____
_____ ?

6 What about reducing the price?
able _____
_____ ?

7 I need you to come over and fix my internet connection.
mind _____
_____ ?

8 What number should I call to get technical advice?
tell _____
_____ ?

Word focus *out of*

2 Complete the phrases with *out of* in these answers using the words below.

business	date	depth	interest
luck	order	question	way

a Sorry, I'm a bit out of my _____ there. I know about computers but not telephone connections.

b I regret to say that a discount is out of the _____ .

c Unfortunately, that's because they went out of _____ years ago.

d I'm afraid it's so out of _____ that probably no one stocks them anymore.

e I'm afraid our phone system is out of _____ at the moment. Please email me your number and we will call you back asap.

f Thank you, but please don't go out of your _____ .

g I will put one in the post to you today. Just out of _____ , where did you hear about our company?

h I'm afraid you are out of _____ there. We don't deal with the X306 range.

3 Match the requests (1–8) in Exercise 1 with the responses (a–h) in Exercise 2.

Writing short email requests

4 Write a short email to a friend about a problem you have with your computer. Use the notes below and polite requests.

- tried to call – no answer
- computer keeps crashing
- same problem you had?
- please email instructions to my work email about virus removal
- or call me

Wordbuilding prefixes

1 Match each prefix in box A to at least two words in box B to form words.

> **A** bio hyper mega micro semi ultra

> **B** byte chip conscious detached
> degradable diversity market
> sensitive sonic star violet wave

2 Which word is used to describe:

1 a very large shop? _____

2 a piece of cooking equipment? _____

3 a unit of computer memory? _____

4 a range of different plants and animals? _____

5 a piece of silicon with an electric circuit printed on it? _____

6 a house with another house attached on one side? _____

7 someone who is abnormally sensitive? _____

8 a kind of light? _____

9 above the range of human hearing? _____

10 a very famous entertainer? _____

11 non-polluting? _____

12 not fully awake or aware? _____

Wordbuilding compound nouns (noun + noun)

3 Match a noun from box A with a noun from box B and write the collocations.

> **A** address battery credit data
> information news repair travel

> **B** life manual protection card
> technology book story advice

_____ _____

_____ _____

_____ _____

_____ _____

Learning skills personalising new language

4 The best way to remember something is to make it relevant to you. Read the tips and answer the questions.

> **Grammar**
> Think about the grammar in this unit. Write sentences about:
> a where you are going to go on holiday next year.
> b what you are doing at the weekend.
> c what your next career step is going to be.
> d which person in your family will be the next to get married.
> e what you will be doing in five years' time.
> f what you hope you will have achieved in ten years' time.
>
> **Vocabulary**
> a Find four words from Unit 3 that relate to your life. What is their relevance?
> b Think, in your own language, about your own predictions for future technology. Can you translate all the terms you used? If not, look up the missing words in a dictionary.
>
> **Pronunciation**
> Think about any words in this unit that you found difficult to pronounce.
> a What were they?
> b Do they remind you of any words in your own language?
> c How do they sound different?
>
> **Writing**
> Think of something you really need some help with. Write a short email request in English to a friend asking for their help.

Check!

5 Complete the sentences. Then use the first letter of each word to make another word, which describes the problems in Student's Book Unit 3a. All the answers are in Student's Book Unit 3.

1 Another word for a device or tool is a _____ . (6)

2 Thomas Malthus said that people were 'basically _____'. (4)

3 In today's multi-media world, we all suffer from 'information _____'. (8)

4 A great scientific advance is often called a technological _____ . (12)

5 '_____ technology' provides the simplest and best solution to a problem. (11)

6 If you miss the opportunity to get something, you are 'out of _____'. (4)

Word: _____

4a What's on in London?

Vocabulary performance

1 Complete the sentences using the correct words.

> act   band   company   exhibition   gallery
> gig   musical   performance   play   show
> theatre   venue

1   We saw a great _____ last week. It was a kind of variety performance with different performers. The best one was a circus _____ who did some amazing tricks on a high wire.

2   I went to a _____ at that new music _____ on the High Street last night. It was a local jazz _____ called 'Take Two Project'. They were very professional, I thought.

3   Have you seen the photography _____ at the Oxford Art _____? There are some amazing pictures in it.

4   My daughter has joined a dance _____ who are going to go on tour next month. Their first _____ will be at the new _____ in the centre of town.

5   You know the _____ *Macbeth* by William Shakespeare. Well, the Victoria Drama Company have turned it into a _____, with singing and dancing.

What's on in London?

1 The Alternative Village Fete

This fete at the National Theatre Square on the South Bank brings a modern urban flavour to the traditional country village fete. Hosted by the organisation 'home live art', which has a reputation for producing art works in unusual environments, the programme includes live art, performance art which you can participate in with three National Theatre actors, communal country dancing, plus loads of food and other produce.

2 Notting Hill Carnival

The Notting Hill Carnival is the UK's biggest street party. Featuring a parade of floats and a variety of styles of Caribbean music, dance and food, the carnival celebrates London's multicultural heritage. Join the party and dance the day and night away! It takes place in the Notting Hill district of West London over the August bank holiday weekend.

3 Batman Live

Part theatre, part circus act and part pure visual and special effects spectacle, this show is produced by 'Warner Bros Consumer Products', which should, I suppose, tell you that it's not going to be a serious piece of drama. In fact, it's really eye candy served up for all the family. Although the actors do their best, the storyline is not very strong. The emphasis is on the visual, especially the set pieces, including a fantastic giant Joker's head.

4 This is Design

The Design Museum has used various examples from its collection to make an exhibition which looks at the impact that modern design has on our daily lives. The collection includes classic designs like the Swiss army knife and the Mini car, as well as more mundane objects, such as road signs and utility clothing. Most of the designs aren't new, but it's still a fascinating exhibition which challenges the viewer to take a closer look at things around us that we usually take for granted.

5 The Floating Cinema

At first appearance, this event, put on by artists Nina Pope and Karen Guthrie as part of the Create11 summer festival, seems to be just a screen mounted on a boat. But there's more to it than that. Some films are projected onto the walls of buildings next to the canal where the boat is situated and one or two are followed by talks or workshops so that you can learn about the making of them in more depth. You don't have to be able to swim to attend, but you may get wet – the weather forecast for the weekend isn't great!

Reading out and about

2 Read the *What's on* guide on page 124 quickly. Find the following information.

1 Two events where you are a spectator rather than an active participant.

2 Two events which you can dance at.

3 Two events which you can eat at.

4 An event where you can work with actors.

5 An event where you can hear an expert speak about their work.

6 An event where different ethnic groups come together.

7 An event that children and adults can enjoy.

8 An event that you wouldn't normally find in a city.

3 Find words in the guide for these definitions.

1 shared or enjoyed by everyone (para 1)

2 a moving platform for performers (para 2)

3 something good to look at, but without much usefulness (para 3)

4 everyday, normal (para 4)

5 seminar or discussion group led by an expert (para 5)

Grammar expressions of quantity

4 Complete the sentences with expressions of quantity. Use one word in each space.

1 There will be a small _____ of actors at the Alternative Village Fete.

2 There is _____ carnival in the UK as big as Notting Hill.

3 There were _____ amazing set pieces in the *Batman Live* show.

4 There are _____ of different classic designs on show at the Design Museum.

5 Hardly _____ objects at the 'This is Design' exhibition will be new for the viewer.

6 A _____ films are accompanied by talks and workshops to discuss them in detail.

5 Choose the correct option to complete the sentences.

1 I really enjoyed the Alternative Village Fete – I even did *little / a little* dancing.

2 There aren't *much / enough* events like this in London.

3 There's *a lot of / much* international interest in the Notting Hill Carnival. *A large number of / A large amount of* the visitors this year were tourists.

4 I agree with the reviews – there were *plenty of / much* special effects in the *Batman Live* show, but there were *no / any* strong elements in the story.

5 We visited the website, but there was *a lack of / a little* clear information about the programme.

6 You don't see *several / many* new things at this exhibition, but you still learn a lot.

7 Book now, because when I phoned there were *hardly no / hardly any* tickets left.

8 There was *a bit of / a small number of* rain at the beginning, but it didn't spoil the show.

6 Pronunciation weak form *of*

🔊 **1.31** Practise saying these sentences. Pay attention to the weak form of *of*. Then listen and check.

1 First of all, just a few words of thanks.

2 Most of the time, it's a bit of a laugh.

3 As a matter of fact, he's a friend of mine.

4 That's kind of you, but it seems like a lot of trouble.

5 Of course it was just a bit of fun.

6 In spite of that, there were a number of volunteers.

4b Art or vandalism?

Vocabulary types of artwork

1 Label the pictures.

> graffiti   installation   landscape   portrait   sculpture   sketch   still life

1 _____

2 _____

3 _____

4 _____

5 _____

6 _____

7 _____

Listening the graffiti debate

2 Look at the two photos of graffiti. Answer the questions.

1 Can you see any difference between them?

_____

2 Which do you find more attractive?

_____

3 🔘 **1.32** Listen to a radio discussion programme about whether graffiti is vandalism or art. Answer the questions.

1 What event in the news prompted this discussion?

_____

_____

2 What is the graffiti artist Handy's view of this event?

_____

_____

3 When is graffiti vandalism according to Guy Francis?

_____

_____

4 🔊 **1.32** Listen again and choose the correct option (a–c) to complete the statements.

1 In the second half of the programme, they will be discussing:
   a graffiti.
   b help at work.
   c unemployment.

2 Guy Francis is an expert on the subject because:
   a he used to be a graffiti artist himself.
   b he used to be a journalist who wrote about the arts.
   c he works for the *Daily News*, a graffiti magazine.

3 Handy thinks that whether graffiti is art or vandalism should not be decided by:
   a the gallery owners.
   b the public.
   c the courts.

4 According to Guy Francis, Tox's work was vandalism because:
   a it was very basic and poor art.
   b he broke into the property like a criminal.
   c the property owners didn't want graffiti on their property.

5 Tox's graffiti consisted of:
   a writing his name and the date.
   b writing imaginative images.
   c drawing his name in many different colours.

6 The graffiti artist Banksy's work:
   a is very popular.
   b is very cheap.
   c has upset many property owners.

Grammar determiners

5 Look at the first sentence in each pair. Then complete the second sentence so that it has the same meaning as the first.

1 I have notified all the people who were invited.
   I have notified every _____ .
2 I think that both methods work.
   I think that either _____ .
3 Almost no one came to the opening night.
   Hardly _____ .
4 We've spent every bit of our money.
   We've spent all _____ .
5 Each country has its own laws and rules.
   All _____ .
6 Everyone in the world is waiting to see what will happen.
   The whole _____ .

6 🔊 **1.32** Complete the sentences from the radio discussion using these determiners. Then listen and check.

all	any	both	each	either	every
no (x2)	whole				

1 Is _____ case different or are there measures we can take that will help _____ unemployed people get back to work?
2 There's _____ difference in this case.
3 Graffiti is either art or vandalism. You can't have it _____ ways.
4 If Tox had put his work in a gallery, there wouldn't have been _____ trouble.
5 _____ owner of that property complained.
6 All Tox does is to write his name over and over again. There are _____ imaginative images at all.
7 The _____ debate of whether it's art or not is a different matter.
8 _____ type of graffiti could be considered art.

7 Complete the passage. Choose the correct option.

There is ¹ *no / any* way of telling what is art and what is not art any more. There is a story about a man who dropped his wallet in a modern art gallery. When he went back to get it, he found ² *every / all the* visitors gathered around, admiring it. The message of the story is that ³ *the whole / all the* modern art world is a trick and ⁴ *each / either* viewer needs to be told whether something is art or not before they can admire it. But were the people wrong to admire the wallet? If they thought it was art, some people argue, then it was art. ⁵ *Both / Either* views are possible. What's yours?

8 Dictation Banksy

🔊 **1.33** Listen to a description of the work of the graffiti artist Banksy. Write down the words you hear. Then put the sentences in the correct order.

1 The message was clear: _____

2 Often it carries _____

3 Despite not _____

4 Banksy, who is _____

5 Banksy loves to _____

4c Music and me

Listening the importance of music

1 💿 **1.34** Listen to four people talking about what music means to them. Write down the type of music each one is talking about.

1 ....
2 ....
3 ....
4 ....

2 💿 **1.34** Read the sentences. Then listen again and match the speakers (1–4) with the correct sentences (a–f).

a Music is a way to escape from the boredom of your daily routine. ....
b Music can sum up what you are feeling. ....
c Music gives me a sense of belonging to a place. ....
d Music represents people's creative and independent side. ....
e Music is the most important part of our cultural identity. ....
f Music brings people together in celebration. ....

3 💿 **1.34** Listen again and complete the statements.

Speaker 1
1 .... music tells stories about .... life.

Speaker 2
2 In Brazil we have a big range of musical .... to draw on.

Speaker 3
3 Millions of .... have been able to express their feelings ... by listening to .... music.

Speaker 4
4 People figured out how to make new .... using old ....

4 Match these verbs with the phrases from the interviews.

| be connected to | (not) be important | discover |
| escape | seem true | think of |

1 It also **has to do with** our history
....

2 wanting to **break free** from the pressures of school ....

3 it **hit a chord** with us, for sure
....

4 people **figured out** how to make new sounds
....

5 they **came up with** something totally new
....

6 it **doesn't count for anything**
....

Word focus *cool*

5 Look at the sentences. Match the sentences (1–6) with the meanings of *cool* (a–d). Note the extra meaning (*OK/acceptable*).

a not warm   c calm
b stylish and   d OK/acceptable
   fashionable

1 Once you get past a certain age, you have no idea what's **cool** anymore.
2 I love September – bright sunny days and **cool** clear nights.
3 At school, I was the **coolest** person in the uncool group.
4 It's **cool** if you want to talk about it and it's **cool** if you don't.
5 It's not a good thing for a sportsperson to **lose their cool** in a moment of stress.
6 Her reaction to the idea of dancing was distinctly **cool**.

6 Match the beginnings of the sentences (1–4) with the endings (a–d).

1 Because he was 30 minutes late for the meeting,
2 I was worried that he would be angry, but
3 When he was young,
4 He's normally very calm, but on this occasion

a he was always trying to be cool.
b he said he was cool about it.
c he got a very cool reception.
d he lost his cool.

4d TV favourites

Real life describing likes and dislikes

1 🔊 **1.35** Listen to a conversation in which Ian and Sue discuss a TV documentary. Answer the questions.

1 What was the documentary about?

2 Why did Ian like it particularly?

2 🔊 **1.35** Listen again. Does Sue like (✓) or dislike (✗) the following.

1 nature documentaries in general ☐
2 the *Tribe* series ☐
3 people who make programmes about
  others living in difficult conditions ☐

3 🔊 **1.35** Complete the phrases Ian and Sue use to express their likes and dislikes. Use up to four words in each space. Then listen again and check.

1 Oh, a nature documentary … not really my
  _____ actually.
2 I never _____
  by them.
3 I'm _____ the
  presenter.
4 It _____ a bit
  actually.
5 I could _____
  _____ all day.
6 I guess I just get _____
  _____ people making these programmes.

4 Grammar extra word order with modifying adverbs

> **WORD ORDER WITH MODIFYING ADVERBS**
>
> • Adverbs that qualify adjectives come before the adjective.
>   I'm not **particularly** keen on reality TV shows.
> • Adverbs of intensity come before the main verb.
>   I **really** love musicals.
> • Never separate the main verb from its direct object.
>   I like **Bruce Parry** very much. (~~I like very much …~~)

Look at the grammar box. Then put the words in the correct order.

1 listen / all day / I / Bach / can / to

2 documentaries / anything / don't / for me /
  do / really

3 into / really / I'm / TV / not

4 particularly / on / keen / the presenter /
  not / I'm

5 I / get / reality TV shows / of / a bit / tired

6 TV / generally / watch / don't / much / I

5 Pronunciation disappearing sounds

a 🔊 **1.36** Listen to these words. Cross out the disappearing sound in each word.

1 documentary   5 separate
2 everywhere   6 restaurant
3 specifically   7 listener
4 interest   8 general

b 🔊 **1.36** Practise saying each word. Then listen again and check.

6 Listen and respond describing likes and dislikes

🔊 **1.37** Listen to the questions about your likes and dislikes. Respond with your own words. Then compare your response with the model answer that follows.

1

> *What do you think of mobile phones with loud music ringtones?*

> *They really get on my nerves, especially when one starts ringing on the train or bus.*

4e A comedy gig

1 Writing skill personalising your writing

Complete the features of personal and impersonal writing using these words.

active   avoid   contracted   formal
furthermore   I, we and you   it   passive
share   uncontracted

Personal tone	Impersonal tone
a Use pronouns (e.g. _____)	Use pronouns (e.g. _____)
b Use _____ verbs	Use _____ verbs
c Use _____ forms (e.g. *isn't*)	Use _____ forms (e.g. *is not*)
d Use phrasal verbs	Use _____ verbs
e Add personal details	_____ personal information
f Use conversational linking phrases (e.g. *what's more*)	Use formal linking phrases (e.g. _____)
g _____ your feelings	Be objective in your judgements

Writing an online review

2 Read the beginning of an online review for a comedy show. Underline examples of the features of personal writing (a–g) from Exercise 1. Label the features.

> I've got to admit that I'm not a big fan of stand-up comedy. I always think that it's a rather unnatural thing. The comedian stands up in front of an audience who stare at him or her as if to say, 'Come on, then, make me laugh.' The comedian then has a few minutes to make them laugh or the audience will start to get restless. It's all a bit too aggressive and combative for me. So when I went with an old school friend to see new British comedian Spencer Brown last Tuesday night at the Bristol Comedy Club, I wasn't really looking forward to it.

3 Read the next paragraph of the review, which contains some features of impersonal writing. Rewrite the underlined words and expressions using personal forms.

> [1] However, we quite enjoyed the show. And we [2] were not the only ones – [3] his act seemed to be liked by the rest of the audience too. Brown's technique is to [4] commence by telling a small joke – usually some amusing observation about daily life – which [5] it is imagined at first is the main joke. But [6] subsequently he builds on this by telling a joke [7] that is related to the first and then another. The effect of [8] combining jokes like this is that, even though each one may not be that funny by itself, the whole sequence is [9] in reality very funny.

1	_____	6	_____
2	_____	7	_____
3	_____	8	_____
4	_____	9	_____
5	_____		

4 Complete the review by writing the last paragraph. Include a personal recommendation and details of when this show is on.

Wordbuilding suffixes

1 Choose the correct suffix for each word. Then write the words.

1 snow -scape / -ness / -ism ....
2 metalwork -ist / -ship / -er ....
3 craftsman -ism / -ship / -ness ....
4 polite -ness / -ist / -ship ....
5 saxophone -ship / -er / -ist ....
6 romantic -ness / -ism / -scape ....

2 Write the correct nouns using the correct suffixes.

1 the style of art that created surreal paintings

2 someone who plays the guitar

3 someone who presents a show on TV

4 a painting of a city view ....
5 the state of being calm ....
6 the arts movement that championed modern things ....

7 a picture showing the Moon's surface

8 the ability to be a musician

9 someone who plays the trombone

10 someone who does carpentry

11 the quality of being direct ....
12 the state of being a companion

Learning skills asking about language

3 Sometimes to help you learn you will need to ask your teacher or a native speaker questions about the language. Look at the questions 1–6 and the answers a student has given.

1 Is 'mate' a slang expression for 'friend'? *Yes.*
2 Do you pronounce the 'g' in 'recognition'? *Yes.*
3 Why do you say 'rush hour' when the traffic isn't moving? *Everyone's rushing to get home.*
4 Is there a similar saying to 'to make two hits with one stone' in English? *Yes, 'to kill two birds with one stone'.*
5 Is 'You're welcome' an American or a British expression? *American, but the British use it too.*
6 Does 'I wonder if you can help me' sound too polite or is it OK? *It depends on the situation: it is very polite.*

4 Look at these words and phrases from the unit. Answer the questions.

1 Is 'cool' a slang expression?

2 How do you pronounce 'comfortable'?

3 Why do you say 'either way' but 'both ways'?

4 Is there a similar expression to 'it hits me on the nerves' in English?

5 Is 'hip-hop' an American or a British expression? ....
6 Does 'I can't bear ... something' sound too direct? ....

Check!

5 Do the quiz. All the answers are in Student's Book Unit 4.

1 COMPLETE THE QUOTES.

a 'Nature has done everything for Sydney, man nothing; man has done everything for .... , nature nothing.'

b '............................ art is an imitation of nature.'

c 'Rap doesn't belong to .... culture. It belongs here.'

2 WHAT ARE THESE WORDS BEGINNING WITH 'F'?

a the countable equivalent of 'little'

b traditional, local music ....

c a supporter or follower (especially of a sports team or pop group) ....

3 WHAT ARE THE OPPOSITES OF THESE THINGS?

a a personal tone

b a little bit of luck

c warm up ....

4 REARRANGE THE LETTERS TO MAKE WORDS.

a music: igg .... siclry ....

b art: ketsch .... luscerupt ....

c theatre: aply .... lamicus ....

Unit 5 Development

5a Urban development

Listening rebuilding New Orleans

1 🔊 **1.38** Listen to a local journalist describing the rebuilding work in New Orleans after Hurricane Katrina. Are the sentences true (T) or false (F)?

1 A lot of rebuilding work has taken place in the French Quarter.

2 More than half the residents who were evacuated from the city have returned.

3 One project is helping to build affordable homes.

4 The new homes are very simple, practical houses.

Glossary
levee (n) /ˈlevi/ a barrier to protect an area from flooding
spare (v) /speə/ save from something

2 🔊 **1.38** Listen to the journalist again and complete the sentences.

1 For most tourists who visit New Orleans these days, things seem to be _____ .

2 Most of the damage in New Orleans was caused by the _____ , not the _____ .

3 Most New Orleanians _____ their city.

4 The redevelopment plan for New Orleans has not been systematic or _____ .

5 The Lower 9th Ward was a pretty _____ area of New Orleans, even before the storm.

6 The new homes are _____ and environmentally-friendly.

7 The journalist thought the designs of the buildings were very _____ .

8 Some critics say that the houses are not _____ .

Grammar verb + infinitive or -ing

3 Look at the sentences from the report about the rebuilding work in New Orleans. Choose the correct option.

1 In the French Quarter, everything now seems *being / to be* back to normal.

2 In other areas, you keep on *seeing / to see* the effects of the disaster.

3 The city's levees failed *holding / to hold* the big tidal wave back.

4 About two-thirds of the residents have managed *returning / to return*.

5 A few people decided *resettling / to resettle* elsewhere.

6 One project proposed *building / to build* 150 affordable homes.

7 No one wants to risk *seeing / to see* their home flood again.

8 You can't help *wondering / to wonder* how many more homes could have been built.

4 Complete the table with these verbs. Some verbs can go in more than one category.

allow	ask	carry on	enjoy	get
help	hope	imagine	make	want

verb + *to* + infinitive	verb + *someone* + *to* + infinitive
verb + *-ing*	verb + *someone* + infinitive

5 Grammar extra verb + infinitive or -ing

a Put these verbs into the correct column in the table in Exercise 4 on page 132.

avoid	choose	finish	force	involve
learn	let	(not) mind	teach	

b Complete the text about volunteering in New Orleans using the correct form of the verb in brackets.

If you want ¹ _____ (visit) New Orleans as a tourist, but would also like to do something to help local people ² _____ (rebuild) their lives while you are there, you could work as a volunteer on a project. There are lots of organisations that allow visitors ³ _____ (participate) for a week or even a few days. If you don't mind ⁴ _____ (get) your hands dirty, you could do some labouring on a building project. Alternatively, you could choose ⁵ _____ (work) with children or help out at a local museum. Some of the projects might involve ⁶ _____ (learn) a few new skills, but no one will force you ⁷ _____ (do) something you feel uncomfortable with. And don't worry about not having fun. You will have plenty of time off and you'll also enjoy ⁸ _____ (meet) New Orleanians – something a regular tourist might find more difficult.

Vocabulary urban development

6 Complete the announcement by a city's Planning Committee. Use these words.

centre	district	housing	luxury
mall	pedestrianised	spaces	waterfront

On 2nd July, the City Council's Planning Committee met and agreed the following actions to **transform** the city:
- The centre should become a ¹ _____ zone to allow shoppers and visitors to walk around more freely.
- The old shopping ² _____ in Prince's Street, next to the river, will be **demolished**. The council will invite designs for a new ³ _____ development in its place. It wants the area to be **redeveloped** as a mixed residential area: some

⁴ _____ apartments and some affordable ⁵ _____ .
- It was also agreed that a lack of green ⁶ _____ **spoils** the appearance of the centre. The plan is to encourage companies to move to a new business ⁷ _____ in the north of the city and **convert** existing car parks into garden areas.
- The council also proposes to **modernise** the new leisure ⁸ _____ in the north of the city.

7 Match the verbs in bold in Exercise 6 with these verbs.

1 bring up to date _____
2 change completely _____
3 damages _____
4 knocked down _____
5 rebuilt _____
4 turn _____

8 Dictation a New Orleanian speaks

a 1.39 Listen to a New Orleans resident describing life since Hurricane Katrina. Write down the words you hear. Is the resident happy living in New Orleans?

The fact that _____

_____

_____

I'm a musician _____

_____

_____

But since Hurricane Katrina, _____

_____

_____

b Underline examples of verb + infinitive or verb + -ing in your answer in Exercise 8a.

5b Monterey Bay

Reading changing places

1 Read the article about Monterey Bay. Which of the following sentences are true of Monterey today?

   a   It has an important tourist industry.
   b   It is a cosmopolitan place.
   c   It has an important fishing industry.
   d   There is little sea-life left.

2 Read the article again. Are the sentences true (T) or false (F). Or is there not enough information (N) to say if the statements are true or false?

   1   In the last 150 years, Monterey's main industry has been tourism, then fishing, then tourism again.
   2   Canning was a process that was invented in Monterey.
   3   Carl Danielsen was born in Norway.
   4   A lot of immigrants came to Monterey to take advantage of the boom in fishing.
   5   The reason for the disappearance of the sardines is unclear.
   6   Otters like to eat abalone.
   7   It's impossible to make a living from fishing in Monterey these days.
   8   The essential character of Monterey hasn't changed because its industry still centres around the sea and sea-life.

3 Find words or phrases in the passage with the following definitions.

   1   in the meantime (para 1)

   2   be part of the good times (para 2)

   3   suddenly (para 3)

   4   senior and experienced people (para 3)

   5   establish, start (para 3)

   6   try out (para 4)

Glossary
abalone (n) /ˌæbəˈləʊni/ a small edible shellfish
canning process (n) /ˈkænɪŋ ˈprəʊses/ preserving food by putting it in a tin
otter (n) /ˈɒtə(r)/ a small river or sea animal

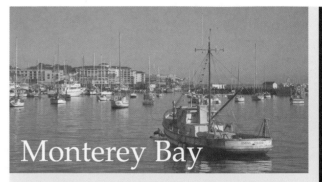

Monterey Bay

The history and development of Monterey Bay is a dynamic one. 150 years ago tourism was its main industry, as it is again today. But a lot of changes have taken place in the intervening period. Carl Danielsen, a fisherman in Monterey for the last 60 years, describes these changes.

'My father was a fisherman and his father before him. I first started going out to sea with my daddy when I was seven years old. In those days, there were a lot of sardines in the sea and Monterey took advantage of the newly-developed canning process, which meant that enormous amounts of fish could be preserved in a way that wasn't possible before. In the 1930s, Monterey was the world capital of the sardine canning industry and fishing was big business here. That was when my parents came over from Norway, along with other immigrants from Japan, China, Italy – you name it. Everyone wanted to join in the party. That's one of the reasons that Monterey is such a cosmopolitan place now.

Then in the 1950s, the sardines disappeared – just like that. No one knows why. Some people say it was because of overfishing; others say it was just part of the natural ocean cycle. One thing is for sure, and that is that fishing isn't the simple industry it was in the 1950s – I wish it was. There have been so many rules and regulations since then, controlling what and where you can fish. You can't collect abalone, for example, anymore – unless you're an otter, that is! Old-timers like me continue to fish, but it's not an easy life and many people have set up other businesses. Most are tourist-related, like boat trips, sightseeing trips and fishing trips, but all of them are connected with the sea and sea-life. We have a fantastic range of sea-life here: otters, whales, dolphins, and so on.

So today, tourism is the main industry here, but the essential character of the bay hasn't changed. The old canning factory has become an aquarium and a research centre for sea-life. There are lots of restaurants along the sea front, which do great business. I'd recommend any visitor to Monterey to sample the seafood. It's fantastic.'

4 Complete the sentences with the correct adjective. Use the nouns in brackets to help you.

1 Monterey is a _____ place. (dynamism)
2 In the 1930s, Monterey was a more _____ city. (industry)
3 Now it has become an _____ destination for tourists. (attraction)
4 The old harbour is well _____ . (preservation)
5 These days, fishing is strongly _____ . (regulation)
6 But the _____ character of the bay hasn't changed. (essence)

Grammar verbs with *-ing* and *to* + infinitive

5 Read the pairs of sentences. Do the verbs have a change in their meaning (C) or no change in meaning (NC)?

1 a When did they **start** to can sardines in Monterey?
  b When did they **start** canning sardines in Monterey? ____

2 a People **continued** to can sardines in Monterey until the 1980s.
  b People **continued** canning sardines in Monterey until the 1980s. ____

3 a I **stopped** to visit my aunt in California last year.
  b I **stopped** visiting my aunt in California last year. ____

4 a Did you **remember** to bring a guidebook?
  b Did you **remember** bringing a guidebook? ____

5 a I **like** to watch sea-life in the wild.
  b I **like** watching sea-life in the wild. ____

6 a I **prefer** to eat fresh fish to frozen.
  b I **prefer** eating fresh fish to frozen. ____

7 a He **went on** to work as a fisherman.
  b He **went on** working as a fisherman. ____

8 a Every fisherman **means** to get up early in the morning.
  b Being a fisherman **means** getting up early each morning. ____

6 Complete the sentences using the *-ing* form or *to* + infinitive.

1 Carl remembers _____ (go) fishing with his father in the 1950s.
2 In those days, preserving fish meant _____ (put) them into cans.
3 In the 1950s, fishermen had to stop _____ (catch) sardines.
4 Carl regrets _____ (say) that fishing is not a simple industry anymore.
5 Some older fishermen have gone on _____ (fish) to this day.
6 They try _____ (make) a living from it, but it's not an easy way of life.
7 Other fishermen stopped fishing _____ (go) into the tourist business.
8 Visitors to Monterey should try _____ (eat) the fresh seafood.

7 Choose the correct option to complete the text.

A lot of people visit Monterey Bay before going on [1] *visiting / to visit* San Francisco and Yosemite National Park in California. One thing they stop [2] *seeing / to see* are the otters which live in the harbour. While eating your lunch at a waterfront restaurant, you can watch them playing in the water or trying [3] *opening / to open* shellfish by breaking them against the fishing boats. Although the otters don't mean [4] *doing / to do* any harm, it annoys the fishermen because it means [5] *having / to have* to paint their boats more often!

8 Pronunciation rhyming words

🔊 **1.40** Make pairs of rhyming words. Match the words in box A with the word that rhymes from box B. Then listen and check.

A				
China	found	front	meant	ocean
placed	rule	way	whale	where

B				
drowned	hunt	minor	motion	sent
share	taste	they'll	tool	weigh

5c Sustainable development?

Listening eco-cities

1 🔊 **1.41** Read the sentences about eco-cities in China. Then listen to the interview with an architect. Are the sentences true (T) or false (F)?

1 China is a focus for eco-cities because it has so many new cities.

2 If you have the support of politicians, building an eco-city is relatively simple.

3 Construction workers already have the skills needed to build eco-cities.

4 Electric vehicles are favoured in eco-cities.

5 An eco-city must import as little energy, food and water from outside as possible.

Glossary
pipe dream (n) /ˈpaɪp driːm/ a fantasy that will never become reality
political will (n) /pəˈlɪtɪk(ə)l wɪl/ the support of politicians
skyway (n) /ˈskaɪweɪ/ a road in the air
UV light (n) /ˈjuːviː laɪt/ ultra-violet light

2 🔊 **1.41** Listen to the interview again and complete the facts.

1 Number of Chinese cities of one million-plus inhabitants by 2025: _____ .

2 In an eco-city there can be no _____ .

3 Chinese saying: 'Anything is _____ , but nothing is _____ .'

4 People who need to coordinate efforts: planners, architects, _____ firms and local _____ interests.

5 Another important consideration is the _____ that go into the building.

6 The layout should encourage people to _____ to work.

7 Transportation must be _____ .

8 No energy should be _____ .

9 Rain water is collected and made safe using _____ light.

10 Vegetables are grown in large _____ .

Word focus *pick*

3 Look at the phrases with the word *pick*. Choose the correct definition.

1 There's no shortage of good designs and clever ideas out there – you can **take your pick**.
   a relax   b choose from many
   c study them in your own time

2 Can I just **pick up on** something we mentioned earlier, which is the question of waste?
   a question   b highlight   c return to

3 The other difficulty is **picking your way through** all the bureaucracy and regulations.
   a examining   b being very careful with
   c finding a route through

4 Complete the sentences using the appropriate phrase with *pick* from the list below.

take your pick   pick holes in   pick on
pick up (x2)   pick your brains

1 I don't know why you always _____ me to do these boring administrative jobs!

2 The restaurant has been very quiet, but business will _____ in the spring.

3 Can you _____ me _____ from the train station at 5.30?

4 I don't mind which desk you sit at – _____ .

5 There are always people who will try to _____ a new eco-solution or idea and tell you why it isn't ecological.

6 Can I _____ about a venue for my parents' 25th wedding anniversary?

5 Pronunciation antepenultimate stress

a 🔊 **1.42** Often in words of three or more syllables, the stress falls on the third syllable from the end. Listen to the stress in these words and repeat.

photograph   photographer   analyse
analysis   analytical

b 🔊 **1.43** Underline the stressed syllable in these words. Then listen, check and repeat.

architect   architectural   electricity
energy   generate   material   minimise
political   sustainable   sustainability

5d A development project

Real life reaching decisions

1 Match phrases (1–6) from list A with phrases with a similar meaning from list B (a–f).

A		B	
1	I find it … that	a	That's absolutely right.
2	If you ask me, …		
3	Is everyone OK with that?	b	Not necessarily.
4	I'd go along with that.	c	I agree.
5	Let's not …	d	That seems … to me.
6	Exactly.	e	The way I see it, …
7	That depends.	f	Are we all agreed?
		g	We shouldn't …

2 Look at these phrases about urban features. Write the opposites.

1 private transport
   p_____ transport

2 luxury housing
   a_____ housing

3 out-of-town shops
   l_____ shops

4 built-up areas
   g_____ spaces

5 streets where cars can drive
   p_____ zones

6 places where people work
   l_____ facilities

3 🔘 **1.44** Listen to four conversations about reaching decisions. Who is speaking in each conversation? Write the correct letter (a–d).

Conversation 1 _____	a	bankers
Conversation 2 _____	b	councillors
Conversation 3 _____	c	neighbours
Conversation 4 _____	d	friends

4 🔘 **1.44** Listen again and circle the phrase you hear.

Conversation 1
Colin: *I find it incredible that / It seems incredible to me that* in a big city like this there aren't more leisure facilities. We've got one rather ancient swimming pool, a few tennis courts and a few children's playgrounds.

Jen: *I see your point. / I know what you mean.* I think we should get together and write a petition to the local council asking them to do something about it.

Conversation 2
Michelle: The problem is that no developer has any incentive to build affordable housing. They all make far more money from luxury homes. *If you ask me, / Personally*, I think it's a disgrace. *What's your view? / What do you think?*

Ruth: Well, *I agree, / I'd go along with that*, but I'm just not sure there's much that we, as a council, can do about it. *We ought to have / We probably need* to consider a completely different solution to the housing problem.

Conversation 3
Liz: So, the GFC is asking for a further loan to develop their food co-operative project. *What do you think we should do? / What's your view?*

Steve: *If you ask me, / The way I see it*, they have done a good job so far and made all their repayments on time. But *it's really a question of / it really depends on* what they need the money for.

John: *Exactly. / That's absolutely right.* So, we'll ask them to submit a more detailed proposal. *Is everyone OK with that? / Are we all agreed on that?*

Conversation 4
Alex: Have you seen the plans for that new house across the street? It looks awful: not at all like the other houses round here. *Personally, I think / If you ask me*, we should oppose it.

Nick: Well, *we shouldn't be / let's not be* too hasty. I think it would be better to talk to the new owners first about it. We want to try to keep on good terms with them.

5 Listen and respond reaching decisions

🔘 **1.45** Listen to five people expressing their views. Respond with your own words. Then compare your response with the model answer that follows.

1

> *What do you think of that new shopping mall they are building in the centre of town?*

> *Personally, I think it's horrible. I'd prefer to see more local shops.*

5e Urban sprawl

Writing an opinion essay

1 Read the paragraphs from an opinion essay on the topic 'Is urban sprawl a good thing?' Put the paragraphs in the correct order.

1 .... 2 .... 3 .... 4 ....

A

In the heart of the city, on the other hand, life for residents is tougher. They have no garden, there is more pollution, and probably also more crime and poverty. In addition, rents are high. Because of this, more and more people aspire to live in the suburbs and the city keeps spreading.

B

In 1965, two futurists predicted, 'By the year 2000, the area in the north-eastern United States between Boston and Washington DC, a distance of 450 miles, will form one big megalopolis.' They were wrong, but not far wrong! Towns and cities continue to grow outwards. As a result, the space they occupy grows bigger and the rural areas around them grow smaller. This is known as 'urban sprawl'. It seems to be a natural phenomenon, but is it a good one and should it be stopped?

C

There is nothing wrong with wanting to have the best of both town and country, but unless planners do something to reverse this trend, our city centres will become dark and dangerous places and eventually they will die. The only answer is to limit urban sprawl and refocus our efforts on making our city centres more pleasant places to live.

D

Urban sprawl takes place because people want to have the benefits of both city and country. In suburbia, they can have a nice home, a piece of land, a peaceful and safe environment, and convenient transport links into the city where, in all probability, they work.

2 Which of the following techniques does the writer use to begin the essay?

a giving a dramatic example of the problem (perhaps from your own experience)

b giving some statistics that illustrate the seriousness of the problem

c quoting what someone (often famous) has said about this problem

3 Rewrite the opening sentence(s) to this essay using one of the other techniques.

4 Find expressions in the essay that mean the same as the following.

1 As well as this (para A) ....

2 Consequently (para A and B)

....

....

3 in contrast (para A) ....

5 Writing skill linking words

a Look at the examples (a–d). Notice that the linking phrases need to be followed by a noun or the *-ing* form of the verb.

a **In addition to** this, cities are becoming more polluted.

b **As well as** this growth outwards, there is also more congestion in cities

c **Because of** growing outwards, cities are taking up valuable green space.

d **As a result of** cities growing outwards, we are losing valuable green space.

b Rewrite the sentences using the linking phrases given.

1 The house comes with three acres of land and a swimming pool.
As well as ....

2 People have moved out of the centre because crime has risen.
As a result of ....

3 We have a good bus service and excellent roads into the city centre.
In addition to ....

4 We are starting to redevelop city centres because there are restrictions on building on green spaces.
Because of ....

Wordbuilding adverb + adjective

1 Complete the sentences with these adverb + adjective phrases.

> cleverly designed   economically disadvantaged
> ethnically mixed   highly cultured   ill prepared
> long-term unemployed   politically correct
> upwardly mobile

1 It is very difficult for _____ _____ people to get back into work, because they lose confidence.

2 These days you have to be _____ _____ in your use of language so that you don't discriminate between people of different sex or race.

3 Nowadays, we say someone is _____ instead of 'poor'.

4 They are an _____ family: her father was a miner; her daughter is now a top criminal lawyer.

5 I was _____ for the meeting. Everyone else had read all the background information.

6 London is a very _____ city. You can find people from most parts of the world living there.

7 It's a _____ society in which it is common for ordinary people to visit museums and go to the theatre.

8 The houses, although small, are _____ with a lot of space inside.

Wordbuilding prefix *re-* with verbs and nouns

2 Complete the sentences using an appropriate verb with the prefix *re-*. Use the root words below to help you.

> adjust   build   decorate   do   read   train

1 They are trying to _____ their lives after the floods.

2 I think we need to _____ this room – the walls are a depressing colour.

3 He has left his job in banking and plans to _____ as a teacher.

4 When you return home after a long stay abroad, it takes time to _____ .

5 If your homework has too many mistakes in it, the teacher will ask you to _____ it.

6 It's such a great book. I've _____ it four times!

Learning skills critical thinking when you read

3 It is useful to apply critical thinking techniques when you read a text. Read these steps:

- Always scan the text quickly to get a general idea of the topic before you read it in detail.
- Look at who wrote it and for whom. Think about why they wrote the text.
- Read it carefully and note down the main points.
- Does the author develop a particular theme or argument? Is this presented logically?
- Do you agree or disagree with the argument?
- What other knowledge about the subject do you have? Does it fit with the arguments in the article?
- If you are interested in the topic, follow up your reading by researching more about the subject.

4 Look back at the article on page 58 of the Student's Book. Use the critical thinking techniques above and write your answers.

Check!

5 Do the quiz. You can find the answers in Student's Book Unit 5.

Quiz

1 Which of these does NOT describe a type of development?
  a personal
  b sustainable
  c life

2 Which of these is NOT in Dubai?
  a the world's tallest building
  b the world's biggest shopping mall
  c the world's busiest airport

3 Kerala is a happy society because the government has invested a lot in … .
  a agriculture
  b political involvement
  c health and education

4 Who were the main critics of the Nam Theun 2 hydro-power project?
  a the local villagers
  b environmentalists
  c the World Bank

5 Which of these phrases has the same meaning as *In addition*?
  a Then again
  b Furthermore
  c Consequently

Unit 6 Alternative travel

6a Staycations

Listening personal experiences

1 🔊 **2.1** Listen to four people talking about their idea of a staycation. Write the number of the speaker next to what's most important for them in a staycation. There are two extra items.

a planning your staycation ☐
b going back to a simpler way of life ☐
c changing your routine ☐
d getting help at home ☐
e spoiling yourself ☐
f filling the days with stimulating new experiences ☐

2 🔊 **2.1** Listen again and put the number of the speaker next to the activity they suggest. There are two extra activities.

a spending family time just chatting and playing ☐
b taking your children on day trips ☐
c learning a new sport ☐
d enjoying the experience of shopping for food ☐
e eating out often ☐
f getting a little exercise each day ☐

3 Look at the phrases in bold from the listening. Choose the correct definition.

1 By staying at home, you're not necessarily going to **switch off**.
   a forget about work
   b feel out of touch with the world
   c get more rest

2 I'm not trying to **be prescriptive**, but you must make some rules.
   a frighten you
   b tell you exactly what to do
   c be funny

3 My idea of a staycation is to **pamper myself**.
   a go to the health club
   b spoil myself
   c do healthy things

4 I organised things to do every day. Maybe my family thought I **overdid** it.
   a wanted to impress people
   b organised too much
   c spent a lot of money

5 Modern life shouldn't **dictate** your routine.
   a interfere with
   b destroy
   c control

Grammar *not*

4 Rewrite the phrases in bold in the negative form.

1 **Let's kid ourselves** that just by staying at home, you're going to relax.

2 **Answer** the phone – switch on the answer phone.

3 **You have to do** a big weekly shop, for example.

4 It would be easier **to do** things to keep fit.

5 **I think it's extravagant**, because I know I'm spending less than I would on holiday.

6 I hope **I overdid it**.

7 I tried **to let the children know** I was worried.

8 So **you really must let** modern life dictate what you do too much.

5 Rewrite the sentences using negative forms and the words given.

1 I won't have a coffee now, thanks.
_____ WANT

2 It doesn't seem to me to be a great idea.
_____ THINK

3 We shouldn't do anything to upset them.
_____ LET

4 I'm worried that I gave her the wrong impression.
_____ HOPE

5 You can give the book back to me when you like.

_____

_____ HAVE/IMMEDIATELY

6 Don't be late, please.
_____ TRY

7 It is forbidden to take food into the library.
_____ MUST

8 Have they decided to leave?
_____ STAY

Vocabulary travel

6 Complete the description of a holiday. Write one word in each space.

We had a great holiday, thanks. Up until September, I had only had two days [1]_____ all year. We booked a self-[2]_____ apartment in a little village in Pelion in the north of Greece. Pelion has lovely [3]_____ : wooded hills leading down to beautiful little coves and a crystal clear sea. Our apartment was in a village a little way up in the hills with a fantastic [4]_____ of the sea. We flew with one of the low-budget [5]_____ – I think our return flights were less than £100 each. We only took hand [6]_____ with us because on low-budget flights they charge extra for each bag you take. Then we rented a car to get us from the airport to our accommodation. It was quite a long [7]_____ but we went through very pretty [8]_____ . Coming back was expensive, though. The drive to the airport [9]_____ about three hours longer because of roadworks. So the car hire company charged us for an extra half day. Then the airline said my [10]_____ was too big and it would have to go in the hold – for an extra £80! I couldn't believe it.

Vocabulary phrasal verbs with *in* and *out*

7 Complete the sentences using the correct verb.

1 Shall we _____ in tonight and see what's on the TV? I'm too tired to go out.

2 Please _____ in and see us anytime. You're always welcome.

3 I don't like _____ out. I'd much rather just cook a meal at home.

4 Don't _____ out too late. You've got an interview in the morning.

5 You wouldn't believe the bureaucracy. We had to _____ in about ten forms!

6 The party starts at 8 p.m. Please bring a friend and come and _____ in the fun!

8 Dictation staycations

🔊 **2.2** Listen to a travel expert describing the trend in staycations. He makes four points. Write the words that you hear. Do you agree with him?

1 In tough economic times, _____

_____

_____

2 However, they _____

_____

_____

3 You don't have to _____

_____

_____

4 I don't think _____

_____

_____

6b Why volunteer?

Why volunteer?

Volunteering is one of the most rewarding ways you can make a real difference to people who live in very tough circumstances. Most people join us because they want to give something back and find they get much more in return.

VSO sends volunteers rather than money. We work on long-term, sustainable solutions. And volunteers are how we do it. Nothing compares with the satisfaction of translating generosity into practical, life-changing achievements.

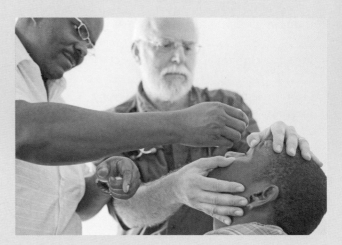

Our short-term roles give experienced professionals the opportunity to make a concentrated, high-impact contribution to the fight against poverty. You'll face fresh challenges, develop valuable new skills, and experience another culture in a way few people have the opportunity to.

Who can be a short-term volunteer?
Our placements tend to be consultancy-type roles, which are designed to achieve a specific goal or complete a set project, so they require highly skilled professionals who can hit the ground running. The majority of short-term roles last between four and six months.

For most of our roles, you will need at least five years' experience in your field of work, be able to stay for six months, and be ready to leave within eighteen months of applying – sometimes at short notice. VSO matches volunteers to placements where they are most professionally suited. It helps if you're flexible when considering where you're willing to work.

How we'll support you
This isn't 'voluntourism' – you don't have to pay to volunteer with VSO. We take care of all your expenses, from flights and insurance through to visas and accommodation. You even get a local living allowance. For more information, see our volunteering FAQs.

The skills we're looking for
We are currently looking for short-term volunteers in the following sectors: advocacy specialists, agricultural specialists, business and management specialists, financial specialists, fundraisers, IT specialists, monitoring and evaluation specialists, researchers, other specialist and one-off roles.

If you don't yet have the level of experience to undertake a short-term role, you can look at the long-term opportunities in your area of work.

Reading VSO

1 Read the information from the VSO website. Complete the notes about the short-term voluntary roles.

Type of work: [1] ....

Skills and experience required: [2] ....

Length of stay: [3] ....

Flexibility on dates: [4] ....

Costs: [5] ....

2 Read the information again and choose the correct option (a–c).

1 People who *want to give something back* means people who want to ... .
a repay VSO for giving them a job
b give money to the organisation
c make a contribution to society

2 Short-term volunteer jobs are open to people ... .
a who like project work
b with some work expertise
c who have already worked as consultants

3 *Hit the ground running* (paragraph 3) means ... .
   a start work immediately
   b be very adaptable
   c use your intelligence

4 When placing people, VSO especially takes into account a volunteer's ... .
   a wishes
   b willingness to work
   c work background

5 Which of the following volunteer costs does VSO NOT pay for?
   a travel
   b day-to-day expenses
   c hotel bills

6 The article suggests that long-term posts could be suitable for people who are ... .
   a less experienced travellers
   b less advanced in their careers
   c less confident

3 Read the information again and find adjectives that mean:

1 satisfying (para 1)
2 very difficult (para 1)
3 intensive (para 3)
4 new (para 3)
5 fixed (para 4)
6 not to be repeated (para 7)

Grammar negative and tag questions

4 Complete these negative questions for people who are thinking of becoming volunteers.

1 *Haven't you ever wondered* (you / ever / wonder) what it would be like to be a volunteer in another country rather than just a tourist?

2 You clearly care about others. Why _____ (you / translate) your concerns into concrete action?

3 _____ (you / would like) to use your skills to help others?

4 _____ (it / harm) your future career to take time away from work?

5 _____ (you / going to lose out) financially if you become a volunteer for nine months?

6 _____ (it / be) selfish to want to do this for your own personal development?

5 Look at the questions that a potential VSO volunteer asks. Complete them with question tags.

1 A: You don't organise two-week volunteer vacations, _____?
   B: No, we don't.

2 A: But the work would be suitable for a gap-year student, _____?
   B: Well, no. It's aimed at an older age group.

3 A: It isn't suitable for my 18-year-old daughter, then, _____?
   B: No, I'm afraid it isn't.

4 A: But you used to take younger volunteers, _____?
   B: Yes, but our policy has changed.

5 A: So, as a teacher, there might be possibilities for me to volunteer, _____?
   B: Absolutely, for a longer-term post.

6 A: And I'd have to be flexible about where and when I could go, _____?
   B: Well, of course, flexibility helps.

6 Pronunciation intonation in questions

2.3 Look at the questions. Does the intonation rise (R) or fall (F) at the end? Then listen and check.

	R	F
1 It's a fantastic idea, isn't it?	☐	☐
2 Wouldn't it be great if everyone did this?	☐	☐
3 Have you heard of VSO?	☐	☐
4 You can't really make that kind of long-term commitment, can you?	☐	☐
5 Didn't you do some volunteering when you were a student?	☐	☐
6 I don't have the right qualifications, do I?	☐	☐
7 Do you know any other organisations like VSO?	☐	☐
8 It would be interesting to talk to someone who's done it, wouldn't it?	☐	☐

6c Unusual trips

Listening a cruise with a difference

1 💿 **2.4** You are going to listen to a review of a cruise. Look at these words. Tick (✓) the items you would expect to find on a cruise ship. Then listen and compare which items are on the *NG Endeavour*.

a crane ☐   a microscope ☐
a kayak ☐   an inflatable rubber boat ☐
a casino ☐   restaurants ☐
shops ☐   guides ☐

2 💿 **2.4** Listen again. How does the review describe *NG Endeavour* cruises? Choose the correct the option.

1 entertaining / educational
2 reasonable / expensive
3 comfortable / uncomfortable
4 well-equipped / basic
5 exciting / monotonous

3 💿 **2.4** Complete the table with information about the *NG Endeavour*. Then listen again and complete any missing details.

Name of ship	NG Endeavour
Type of ship	Cruise ship converted from a ¹ .... trawler.
Fares	From ² .... to ³ .... a day
Special gadgets	⁴ .... ⁵ .... , Zodiacs
On-board staff	⁶ .... and expert ⁷ ....
Places it visits	Svalbard in the Arctic circle, the ⁸ .... and ⁹ ....
Eating facilities	one ¹⁰ .... room

4 Look at the transcript on page 154-155 and find words or expressions that mean:

1 spending time lazily and luxuriously (para 1)
....

2 fixed in a way that cannot be changed (para 2)
....

3 a good amount of (para 3)
....

4 rich (para 4) ....
5 easy to talk to (para 5) ....
6 during the whole (para 6) ....

Word focus *mind*

5 Rewrite the sentences using expressions with *mind*.

1 **If you were thinking of a cruise**, try one of Lindblad's expeditions.
.... (have in mind)

2 **If a bit of danger and excitement are not a problem for you**, Lindblad cruises are perfect.
.... (don't mind)

3 The cruises are amazing. **Admittedly**, they're not cheap.
.... (mind you)

4 **Remember that** these are not typical cruises.
.... (bear in mind)

5 I used to think that cruises were for the old and retired, **but I've got a different opinion** now.
.... (change one's mind)

6 **I want to go** on one of their cruises, **but it's quite expensive**.
.... (be in two minds)

6 Grammar extra negative expressions

a Look at these negative expressions.
a **Don't** judge a book by its cover.
b **No** problem.
c It **doesn't** matter.

b Complete these common expressions using the correct negative forms.

1 .... worry.
2 .... worries.
3 .... make sense.
4 .... way!
5 .... say a word.
6 .... work like that.

6d Navigation

Real life getting around

1 🔊 **2.5** Complete the sentences using prepositions. Then listen to a conversation between two friends and check.

1 I'll be coming _____ on the five o'clock train.
2 I can't pick you _____, I'm afraid.
3 How do I get _____ Sara's Café?
4 Just hop _____ any bus from the station.
5 Look _____ for the pier and get off there.
6 You'll see the café _____ your right.
7 If I get held _____, I'll call you.
8 I'll come _____ and meet you.

2 🔊 **2.5** Listen again and answer the questions.

1 Why can't Steve meet Joe at the station?

_____

_____

2 How will Joe get to the meeting point?

_____

_____

3 Where do they arrange to meet in the end?

_____

_____

3 Rewrite the sentences so that they have the same meaning. Use the words in brackets.

1 The easiest option is to take the bus.
_____ (thing)

2 Another possibility is to take a taxi.
_____ (alternatively)

3 I can get there on my own.
_____ (way)

4 It only takes fifteen minutes by bus.
_____ (ride)

5 I'm arriving by train.
_____ (coming)

6 If I am delayed, I'll let you know.
_____ (held)

4 Choose the correct word to complete the situations.

crossing	drive	flight	ride (x2)	walk

1 It's a twenty-minute _____ . (car)
2 It's a two-hour _____ . (plane)
3 It's a fifteen-minute _____ . (bus)
4 It's a twenty-minute _____ . (foot)
5 It's a ten-minute _____ . (taxi)
6 It's a one-hour _____ . (ferry boat)

5 Pronunciation intonation in sentences with two clauses

a 🔊 **2.6** Match the sentence halves. Then listen and check.

1 I'd prefer to drive,
2 It's not difficult to find,
3 I could come and meet you,
4 The bus is cheap,
5 You could take a taxi,

a but I don't finish work until 6.00 p.m.
b but it's quite a long way from the station.
c but it's a very scenic walk.
d but the car is behaving strangely.
e but it makes a lot of stops on the way.

b 🔊 **2.6** Practise saying the sentences using the correct intonation.

6 Listen and respond getting around

🔊 **2.7** Listen to a friend asking you for directions to your house from the town centre. Respond with your own words. Then compare your response with the model answer that follows.

1

> *Hi there. I'm coming in on the train tomorrow at two o'clock. What's the best way to get to your house from there?*

> *The easiest thing is to take the bus.*

6e Unfair charges

Writing a letter of complaint

1 Read the letter of complaint and answer the questions.

1 What is the woman's complaint?

....

....

2 What action does she want to be taken?

....

....

U-Fly Airlines
108 Pembroke Road
London
W8 7NP

24 Clifford Gardens
Oxford
OX3 2FG

Dear Sir/Madam

I am writing to register a complaint about having to pay extra charges to your airline on a recent flight to Spain (UZ485 from London to Seville on 3rd May). I feel that these charges were unjust.

At the time that I booked this flight, I read the terms about luggage carefully. The terms clearly stated that each passenger's hand luggage allowance was one bag measuring no more than 56 x 45 x 25cm and weighing up to 10 kilograms.

On arrival at check-in, I informed the member of the ground crew that my bag met these regulations, but she insisted that the coat that I was wearing should be placed in the bag. I attempted to pack the coat into my bag, but it would not fit, so I was instructed that I would have to pay £30 if I wished to take it onto the plane.

I was concerned that I was delaying other passengers, and consequently I opted to pay the money. Otherwise, I would certainly have disputed the charge, as I am now doing. It is perfectly reasonable to wear a coat onto a plane.

Given these circumstances, I would ask you firstly to refund the £30 to me and secondly to investigate the matter so that you can ensure that other passengers do not encounter the same problem.

Yours faithfully
Amelia Doyle

---

2 Answer these questions.

1 Where is the writer writing from?

....

2 What is her relationship to the recipient of the letter? ....

3 What is the tone of the letter (e.g. formal/ semi-formal)? ....

3 Writing skill formal language

a Find formal phrases in the letter with the same meaning as these less formal words.

1 complain ....

2 unfair ....

3 said ....

4 told ....

5 put ....

6 tried ....

7 wanted ....

8 chose ....

9 this situation ....

10 look into ....

b Rewrite the first paragraph of this letter of complaint using more formal language. Use these verbs to help you. You can change other words too.

consist	give	register	regret	serve
state	suffer			

Dear Sir/Madam

I'm writing to complain about the meal we got on our flight home last week – flight UZ332. On the booking confirmation it said that we would have breakfast and lunch. Well, breakfast was just a cup of tea and lunch was a tuna sandwich. By itself, this wouldn't have been a problem, but both my husband and I got food poisoning from the sandwich.

---

4 Now write the final paragraph of the letter, demanding some action from the airline.

Wordbuilding phrasal verbs with *in* and *out*

1 Complete the phrasal verbs using *in* and *out*.

1 Do **drop** _____ and see us the next time you're in town.

2 Stefan **dropped** _____ of college last year because he wanted to travel round the world.

3 Philippa and Sarah used to be business partners but they **fell** _____ over how to develop the business.

4 Chris **fell** _____ with the wrong crowd at college and started missing lectures.

5 Ben is **taking** Greta _____ to that new Thai restaurant tonight.

6 Sorry. Can you speak a little more slowly? I couldn't **take** it all _____ .

7 I'll **look** _____ and see my parents on my way home to make sure they're OK.

8 **Look** _____ ! You're going to bang your head on that door.

9 Is your old car still going? I thought it would have **given** _____ years ago.

10 I'm trying not to eat sweets, but it's very difficult not to **give** _____ to temptation.

2 Match the phrasal verbs from Exercise 1 with the definitions (a–j).

a have a disagreement _____
b absorb (information) _____
c pay someone a (short) visit _____

d pay someone a (short) visit to check they are all right _____
e become part of a social group _____

f be careful _____
g surrender _____
h arrange a social date with _____

i leave a course before it is finished _____

j stop working or functioning _____

Learning skills writing in English

3 Look at the diagram showing the important elements of writing. Complete the diagram with these elements.

| spelling   link the ideas   action wanted |
| examples |

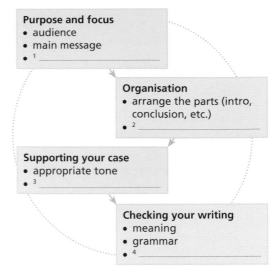

Purpose and focus
- audience
- main message
- 1 _____

Organisation
- arrange the parts (intro, conclusion, etc.)
- 2 _____

Supporting your case
- appropriate tone
- 3 _____

Checking your writing
- meaning
- grammar
- 4 _____

4 Look at the letter of complaint in Exercise 1 on page 146. Answer the questions.

1 What is the main message and where in the letter does this becomes clear?

_____

_____

2 What are the three main elements the letter includes?

_____

3 What phrases does the writer use to link the different ideas?

_____

4 What tone does the writer use?

_____

5 What details make the writer's case more persuasive?

_____

Check!

5 Answer the questions. All the answers are in Student's Book Unit 6.

1 How did Karen Ash have a Japanese holiday without leaving home?

_____

2 What are volunteers helping to build all across North America?

_____

3 Where can you pay to have an uncomfortable night and be treated unkindly?

_____

4 Where can you step right into a painting?

_____

5 What's a way to travel from place to place without ever paying for a bed to sleep in?

_____

Audioscripts

Unit 1

💿 1.1

P = Presenter, E = Expert

P: I'd like to ask you two questions: what is the real reason for the ageing population? And secondly, and more importantly, what effect is this having on relationships in society?

E: Well, there's not just one reason; there are a number of them. Firstly, the birth rate has declined over the last 20 years – fewer babies are being born. The second reason is that 60 years ago, there was a baby boom; these 'baby boomers' are now reaching retirement age. There's also no doubt about people's improved diet: more is known about healthy and unhealthy eating, and food producers are obliged to give consumers more information about the fat and salt content of their food. In fact, I'd say in general people have a healthier lifestyle: not only do they eat better, they have also been educated in the right way to exercise and keep fit. Lastly, we can't underestimate the enormous progress that has been made in the field of medicine. These advances have increased life expectancy to around 80 in the developed world. People are also given routine vaccinations against life-threatening diseases … for example, flu jabs for the elderly.

P: And what are the social consequences of this ageing population – that in the West the younger generation is now being outnumbered by the old?

E: The main result is that, in the future, a smaller number of young people will have to support this older population. For all of us, that means working longer, spending more time caring for old people, and paying more social insurance to fund their medical treatment. But of course, it also puts a strain on family relationships. Parents find that, having spent 20 years bringing up their own children, they then spend the next ten looking after their ageing parents – often both sets. That means less time together as a couple and less free time to enjoy with other friends and family. It's not easy …

💿 1.4

1   I think my parents' generation has been quite lucky.
2   My parents worked hard all their lives, but they both retired when they were 60 and they've been given good pensions. So now they can relax and enjoy themselves.
3   They've said that they don't want to be a burden on us, and that we children aren't expected to look after them when they get old.
4   Considering that my husband and I are now being asked to work until we are 68, I'm glad they said that.

💿 1.5

P = Presenter, L = Lauren

P: I know that Vietnam is a country which is developing incredibly fast and Lauren, you've just been sent on a three-week trip there as part of your university course …

L: That's right, yes.

P: … which sounds fantastic. I wish my economics degree had included that kind of trip, but … Can you just tell us a bit about how people in Vietnam are adapting to those huge changes and what it all means for them?

L: Sure. As you say, Vietnam is a very dynamic society right now. It's being transformed at an amazingly fast rate – both economically and socially. We were really lucky to get to experience that first-hand and get to meet so many different people of all ages, from all kinds of work backgrounds – politicians and government officials, farmers, and so many just … regular people too. And I've got to say – if anyone's thinking of going there – the people are amazing: really warm and friendly. But to answer your question, I think what you have is an older generation who are very conscious of their history. Many of them have been through two wars and are very aware of how much they've struggled to get to this point now of … of relative prosperity. And then there's a younger generation and they don't necessarily see all that effort. They kind of take this new wealth and opportunity for granted. I think they see the world opening up and they really want a part of it … And that's not always easy, because there are still some restrictions on access to information – Facebook and other social networking sites are closed down from time to time, for example. On the other side, the older generation desperately want their children and grandchildren to understand Vietnam's history and be proud of it … and of course to respect Vietnamese traditions.

P: And did you get a sense that people are confused by this? That they don't know which way to turn, as it were?

L: You know, not really. The sense I got was that the gap between old and young is being bridged by the generation in the middle – I guess the 30 and 40-somethings. We spent a day in a fishing community near the Mekong Delta and we had a meal with a family there, and all the generations were getting on fine together … I had the impression that the parents kind of balanced the home. The grandparents are really included and involved in things – they get to take care of the grandchildren and to teach them what they know. You could see that really clearly. And at the same time, the grandparents are definitely listened to and treated with respect by the parents and the children. I was really impressed by that, especially when you compare it with …

💿 1.8

B = Ben, S = Sam

B: Hi Sam. Fancy bumping into you here. I've been wondering how you were.

S: Oh, hi Ben. What a nice surprise. I'm fine. I've been working in Scotland for the last three months.

B: Well, it obviously suits you. You're looking very well. Have you decided to move up there?

S: No, it's just a temporary job. I've been helping to renovate an old castle. And how's it all going with you? Is Emily well?

B: Yes, thanks. She's just finished her nursing course.

S: Really? That's fantastic. Do give her my best regards.

B: Well, great to see you. I should probably go and do my shopping.

S: OK. Could I have your phone number again? I've lost it.

B: Sure. It's 07945 699636.

S: Thanks. Well, speak soon I hope. Good luck with the job.

💿 1.10

F = Friend, MA = Model answer

1

F: Hi. What a nice surprise! How are you?

MA: I'm fine, thanks. Good to see you.

2

F: So, what have you been up to lately?

MA: I've been working quite hard, but everything's going well.

3
F: Well, it obviously suits you. You're looking well.
MA: Thanks. So are you.
4
F: And do you see much of the old crowd these days?
MA: I've seen Polly a few times.
5
F: Well, I don't mean to be rude, but I need to get to the bank.
MA: No problem. Great to see you.

Unit 2

1.12
1 The setting for Alain de Botton's thought-provoking book, *A Week at the Airport*, is Heathrow airport.
2 The characters are you and me and every other typical passenger that passes through the airport.
3 The book is based on conversations that the author had with travellers and airline staff.
4 The idea behind it is that if you are looking for somewhere that can portray modern civilisation, you don't need to look any further than an airport.

1.13
On April 25, 2003, Aron Ralston drove to Moab, Utah, where he mountain-biked the famous Slickrock Trail. He then made his way to Horseshoe Canyon. When he arrived, night was falling, so he made camp. He was planning an ascent of Mount McKinley in Alaska, and this trip was part of his training. In the morning, he filled his backpack with water, candy bars and his climbing gear, and set out for Bluejohn Canyon.

He climbed into the canyon on April 26. He had gone about five miles when he came to a section where a series of large boulders were hanging, wedged between the walls of the canyon. He worked his way past these until he came to a boulder hanging over a drop of about three metres. Putting one hand around the boulder, which weighed about 800 pounds, Ralston stretched to reach a secure foothold below. As he did so, the boulder rotated, slid down and trapped his right hand between it and the canyon wall, crushing it completely.

His heart was beating fast and for the first few moments he threw his body repeatedly against the boulder to move it, but it refused to move. He forced himself to stop, breathe and then considered his situation logically.

He hadn't told anyone where he was. It would be days before anyone realised that he was missing. Ralston was standing on a small stone, facing the boulder that had crushed his hand. The pain was intense, but he was determined to stay in control. He only had two courses of action left to him: he could chip at the rock to free his hand; or he could cut off his hand.

His only tool was a cheap multi-tool. Over the next days, he worked to chip away at the rock with it, but the progress he made was minimal. He was wearing shorts, hiking boots and a fleece pullover. He had started with three litres of water. Now he was down to one.

Ralston had been waiting there for five days. But by the time the search teams started out, he had long since decided what he had to do. He packed his gear and arranged everything neatly in preparation for cutting

off his hand. The arm was numb, so he didn't feel anything, but it was still not an easy thing to do. The operation took over an hour. Dripping blood, he made his way back out of the canyon and began the long hike out of the National Park. After six miles, he was met by some tourists.

1.14
1 I hadn't been there before.
2 You are allowed to smoke.
3 It isn't the first time this has happened.
4 She was the person I told you about.
5 They weren't as tired from the journey as I expected.
6 I was talking about what happened to me.
7 She had been waiting a long time.
8 I haven't spoken French for years.

1.15

Part 1
Oscar Wilde's collection of short stories *The Happy Prince and other Stories* is ostensibly for children, but like all good children's literature, the stories have been written in a way that transcends age: their meaning is just as relevant for adults as it is for children. The stories contain elements of a traditional fairy tale – giants, speaking animals, perhaps a message too – but they are more than just good stories. They have a lyrical quality and a beauty … often this beauty lies in their sadness. I remember being quite upset by them as a child and when I re-read them to my children some 30 years later, I still had to keep back the tears. In fact, it's impossible not to be moved by them. When I said they had a message, I should qualify that by saying that Oscar Wilde kept from giving moral lessons. He simply threw light on human behaviour and then left the reader to make up their own mind. Let me give you an example – the story of *The Happy Prince*.

Part 2
The Happy Prince is a statue that stands high in the square of an old town in northern Europe. It's a fine statue covered in gold leaf and decorated with jewels for eyes and jewels in his sword. From where he stands, he can keep abreast of all that's happening in the town, good and bad. One day, a little swallow arrives, flying on its way south to a warmer climate in Egypt for the winter. He stops to rest on the shoulder of the Happy Prince and the prince asks him for his help. He persuades the swallow to take the gold and jewels from his statue to various people in need around the town: a little boy selling matches in the street, a poor artist in his cold attic room. The swallow stays for some days keeping the prince company and doing good errands for him until he has taken all the gold and jewels from the statue. Unfortunately for the swallow, it has got too late and too cold for it to continue its journey and it dies at the foot of the statue. The town councillors come by and see the statue all grey and plain-looking with a dead bird lying at its feet, and thinking it's an eyesore, they decide to pull it down and melt it so that the metal can be turned into something useful. The workers at the metal foundry find one part won't melt – the Happy Prince's heart – and they throw it on the rubbish tip where the dead swallow is lying.

1.16
See track 1.15, Part 1

1.17
See track 1.15, Part 2

1.18

A = Friend 1, B = Friend 2

A: How was the trip?

B: Well, we had a great time once we got there, but the journey there was a complete nightmare.

A: Oh, no. Poor you! What happened?

B: Well, about four hours before we were due to leave, Hannah realised that her passport was out of date.

A: Oh, that's awful. So did you leave her behind?

B: No, Paul took her straight to the passport office in London and someone had just cancelled their appointment, so they were able to get Hannah a new passport within an hour.

A: That was a stroke of luck. And where were you?

B: I went to the airport to wait for them and kept in touch with them by phone.

A: How stressful! Did they make it in time?

B: Well, they wouldn't have done but the plane was delayed by two hours, so in the end they got there with a bit of time to spare. But my nerves were completely destroyed by then.

A: I can sympathise. I hate being late when I'm travelling. Did the rest of the trip go OK?

B: Yeah, it was great, thanks. Costa Rica was fabulous. But I made sure we got to the airport four hours early for the flight back.

A: Did you? I don't blame you. I think I would have done the same thing …

1.21

F = Friend, MA = Model answer

1

F: You'll never guess what happened to me yesterday on the bus. I started talking to this woman who I thought was Sue, my next-door neighbour, about my problems at work. But it wasn't Sue, it was a complete stranger!

MA: How embarrassing! When did you realise it wasn't Sue?

2

F: I thought I'd lost my wallet this morning. But I'd actually left it on the table at a café and some kind person handed it in.

MA: That was lucky.

3

F: I feel really bad. Jeff asked me if he could borrow my camera and I said 'no'. The thing is he's really clumsy and it's a £600 camera.

MA: Don't worry about it. I think I would have done the same thing.

4

F: We had some people round to dinner last night and we spent so long chatting that I forgot to turn the oven off and all the food I had prepared was completely ruined. It was all dry and burnt.

MA: What a nightmare! What did you do?

5

F: My credit card got stuck in the cash machine. I phoned the bank and cancelled the card, and also left a note with my phone number in case someone managed to get it out.

MA: That was good thinking.

Unit 3

1.22

There's a group of philanthropists in the US – Gates, Buffett, Rockefeller, etcetera – who have contributed a lot of money to good causes over the last fifteen years. The problem for them is that because they're so rich and powerful, people get suspicious of their motives. So, when they meet up, they often do so secretly, like they did a few years ago in Manhattan.

1.23

P = Presenter, D = Didier Bertrand

P: I'm here with Didier Bertrand from the Research Department of GNH electricity company and today we're talking about 'smart homes' of the future. Everyone has heard about this type of technology in one form or another – robots that clean the house; cookers which will be making our meals for us – and, in a few years, I'm sure we will have heard a lot more. But what we'd all like to know is firstly, what technology is actually just around the corner – not just some techie's or researcher's pipe dream – and secondly, what things are actually practical and useful, and what are just gimmicks. So, first of all, welcome, Didier …

D: Hello.

P: Let's talk about what gadgets our homes will have and I'd like you to tell me if these are a reality, a possibility or just science fiction.

D: OK.

P: 'Intelligent' fridges.

D: Yes, intelligent kitchen gadgets and appliances are here already, but intelligent fridges are only in a few richer homes. I think we'll all be using them when food producers make the packaging intelligent too – so that the fridge can tell you when your food is going bad.

P: So, a reality then, that one. What about ultrasonic showers?

D: Well, the need is already here. In the next ten years or so, water shortages will have become a big problem, so we need to find alternatives. And we already know that sound waves are very effective at cleaning, but whether they're safe or not for humans remains to be proven. Ultrasound is certainly something we will be looking at, but …

P: A possibility then?

D: A remote one, I think, but a possibility, yes. There's another thing we are working on with sound.

P: What's that?

D: It's sound-proofing using energy fields. At the moment, if you want to sound-proof a room you use insulation, but in the future people will be using energy fields that isolate a particular space from the rest of the house. So you will be able to play music as loudly as you want in one room without disturbing anyone else.

P: That sounds amazing. What about surfaces in the house that are intelligent?

D: Yes, that's a very interesting area. We're working on several things – for example, kitchen surfaces that transmit heat – so that when you put a frozen pizza down in a certain smart, or intelligent, packaging, it'll defrost automatically. I don't think people will be cleaning kitchen surfaces either in the future – they'll be self-cleaning. And another area of development … we'll soon be installing walls and surfaces in each room that can act as computer or TV screens so that you can move around the house to do your computing or to watch TV.

P: That technology is quite real then?

D: Yes, I think in ten years or so, that kind of technology will have become quite common in new-build houses.

P: Wow! Anything else we haven't mentioned?

D: I think people will be able to control light much more intelligently. Our company will be launching a new system for bedrooms next year that simulates the sunrise.

P: I see, so you wake up gradually as the sun comes up … gets brighter.

D: Exactly …

1.24

1 The weekday edition of *The New York Times* contains more information than the average person in 17th-century England learned in a lifetime.

2 Around a thousand books are published internationally every day and the total of all printed knowledge doubles every five years.
3 More information has been published in the last 30 years than in the previous 5,000.

🎧 1.25

In 2007, the number of people dying from drinking unclean water was a shocking 6,000 per day. Diarrhoea is one of the biggest killers of children in the developing world, a situation that can be changed through the use of vaccines and the drinking of clean water. An ingenious invention, the *Lifestraw*, may be one answer.

Developed by the non-profit making organisation Vestergaard Frandsen, based in Switzerland, this simple device has won a number of awards including *Time Magazine's* Best Innovation of the Year.

Like all good inventions, *Lifestraw* works on a very simple principle. Water is sucked by the user through a filter that traps 99.9% of all water-borne bacteria, including salmonella and E. coli. As a result, it provides protection against the killer diseases cholera and typhoid, as well as common stomach infections like dysentery and diarrhoea.

The filter contains a substance called PuroTech Disinfecting Resin, or PDR, a material which kills bacteria on contact. Pre-filters made of textile fabric first remove particles up to 15 microns. Each filter lasts up to a year, and has a cleaning capacity of 700 litres of water. This equates to a typical daily intake of two litres of water per day. *Lifestraw* is only 30 cm long and being made of plastic, it weighs very little, so it can be worn around the neck without any discomfort to the wearer. Each device costs around US $6.

What are the limitations of *Lifestraw*? Not many it seems. It shouldn't be shared by users, of course. It isn't effective at filtering out metals such as iron and arsenic. And if you use it with salt water, you will reduce its life by about half. And people who are sensitive or allergic to iodine should seek advice before they use it. Other than that, there are only positives, the main one being that it doesn't run on electrical power but works simply through the mechanical action of sucking. There are some tips for making it work better, for example by sucking very steadily on the straw, or by periodically blowing some air and water back through it to clean out the filters, but basically it's obvious how it works.

Lifestraw was used successfully in the Haiti earthquake disaster of 2010 and the Pakistan floods of the same year. Like all ideas – particularly those aimed at solving humanitarian problems – it has its sceptics. The charity WaterAid said that while in principle it was a great idea, it did not solve the fundamental problem of access to water for many people in developing countries, which was one of distance, not cleanliness – many people have to walk up to 30 kilometres a day to get water.

🎧 1.28
A = Andy, M = Meg
A: Can you give me a hand? I'm having trouble sending this document.
M: What do you want to do exactly?
A: Nothing very complicated. I'm trying to attach this document to an email and it won't let me.
M: Let me have a look. OK, I see – the document's too large.
A: Hmm … I thought it might be. The trouble is it's got a lot of photos in it, and I can't just cut them.
M: No, well you can compress the photos.
A: What does that involve?

M: I'll show you. Right-click on the photo … then select format … then compress … then select 'print resolution'. If you do that with all of them, that should do the trick.
A: Yes, I see, but then that reduces the quality of the photos, doesn't it? What else do you suggest?
M: Umm … Have you tried dividing the document into three or four separate documents?
A: No, I'll give that a try and see if it works.
M: OK. Feel free to ask if you want me to help you compress the photos after all.
A: Yeah, OK. Thanks.

🎧 1.30
F = Friend, MA = Model answer
1
F: Can you help me? My presentation slides look really boring!
MA: OK. What do you want to do exactly?
2
F: Well, my slides are just full of text, and they look very plain and uninteresting. I want to make them more attractive.
MA: Let me have a look. Yes, I see. Well, you can add some animations.
3
F: What does that involve?
MA: Well, I'll show you. You have to select some of the text and then choose a way to animate it from the list of options.
4
F: That sounds a bit complicated. What else do you suggest?
MA: Have you tried just changing the font and the colour of the text?
5
F: No, that's a good idea. I'll give that a try.
MA: OK. Feel free to ask me if you need more help.

Unit 4

🎧 1.31
1 First of all, just a few words of thanks.
2 Most of the time, it's a bit of a laugh.
3 As a matter of fact, he's a friend of mine.
4 That's kind of you, but it seems like a lot of trouble.
5 Of course it was just a bit of fun.
6 In spite of that, there were a number of volunteers.

🎧 1.32
P = Presenter; H = Handy; G = Guy Francis
P: Welcome to the *Topical Hour*. In the second part of the programme, we'll be looking at the question of the long-term unemployed. Is each case different or are there measures we can take that will help all unemployed people get back to work? But first, following the news that the graffiti artist 'Tox' has been convicted of vandalism for his graffiti, we ask, 'When is graffiti art and when is it vandalism?' I'm joined by Guy Francis, former arts correspondent for the *Daily News*, and Handy, a graffiti artist himself. So both are experts in their own way on the subject. First of all, Handy, what was your reaction to this conviction?
H: I thought it was outrageous – he's gone to prison for his art. How can you say that one graffiti artist's work is vandalism and another's is art? Would you let the courts decide what artwork deserved to be shown in a gallery and what didn't? Of course not. There's no difference in this case.
P: Handy's right, isn't he? Graffiti is either art or vandalism. You can't have it both ways. Guy Francis.

G: Well, that's true, if the graffiti is in a place where the owner agrees to have it there. If Tox had put his work in a gallery, as Handy just suggested, there wouldn't have been any trouble. The fact is, he put his name all over public and private property. Every owner of that property complained and said that their property had been vandalised. In other words, Tox had caused criminal damage. People classed it as damage because all Tox does is to write his name and the year in numbers on the property over and over again. There are no imaginative images at all.

P: So, you're saying that if the owner of a property likes the work that a graffiti artist puts on his wall, then it's art.

G: Well, I'm saying in that case it's *not* vandalism. The whole debate of whether it's art or not is a different matter. If you take a famous and well-loved graffiti artist like Banksy, whose work sells for tens of thousands of pounds, you can't imagine the owner of a property complaining if some of Banksy's work appeared on his wall. Either type of graffiti could be considered art – but in the eyes of the law, whether or not it's vandalism is up to the owner.

🔊 1.33

1 The message was clear: is this how far we have come since the Stone Age?
2 Often it carries a political or social message, but in an amusing way that ordinary people can relate to.
3 Despite not calling himself an artist, his work has been shown in galleries and has sold for thousands of dollars.
4 Banksy, who is based in the UK, is perhaps the world's best-known graffiti artist.
5 Banksy loves to surprise. In 2005, a picture showing a primitive human being pushing a shopping cart appeared in the British Museum.

🔊 1.34

Speaker 1
You see, there are some places that have a strong tradition of a particular kind of music that, if you were born there, you just can't disassociate yourself from, wherever else in the world you may go. I was born in Mississippi and brought up on country music. Country music tells stories about real life: about love, pain, family, fortune and misfortune. Those are things that everyday folk can relate to and I think it's one of the last genres of music that's in touch with human feelings in that way. It's not just about money and having a good time (though of course that comes into it sometimes), or about politics. It's not insulting or angry in the way that rap music can be. It's about home.

Speaker 2
I think music often plays a more significant role in the culture of poorer communities. When you live in an area which is poor and deprived, you have to get your fun cheap. Music and dance can do that. That's why in Brazil dance music is such an important part of our culture. It's also to do with our history. There are so many different ethnic groups in Brazil that we have a big range of musical influences to draw on: local Indian instruments which are still used today, African rhythms, the melancholy songs of the Portuguese settlers. They've come together to create unique styles of music like samba, carimbó, bossa nova, maracatu. That mixture also brings people together. That's the power music has. You can see that so clearly at Carnaval.

Speaker 3
You don't have to be able to sing or play music to express your feelings through it. Millions of teenagers have been able to express their feelings of frustration at not being understood, or of boredom or anger, or of wanting to break free from the pressures of school and home, by listening

to rock music. They hear the very same sentiments they're feeling expressed in lyrics that are supported by a compelling tune or beat. I was brought up with punk rock, which was a kind of do-it-yourself, non-commercial, fast rock music. The music was saying, 'We reject all this commercial packaged stuff you're trying to sell us. Let's just keep the music simple and honest.' And it hit a chord with us, for sure.

Speaker 4
I love hip-hop. I love that it came from just ordinary, average people who wanted to make a better life for themselves from music. I love the innovative side of it too: that people figured out how to make new sounds using old technology – and some new technology too – but they took limited resources and came up with something totally new. No one ever demanded that hip-hop was played on radio or at clubs; there were no restrictions on what it could do or say. Forget the commercial version of hip-hop you hear today – 'cos it doesn't count for anything – the original hip-hop meant living free in an urban environment.

🔊 1.35

I = Ian, S = Sue
I: Hey, Sue, did you see that brilliant documentary on TV last night?
S: No. What was it about?
I: It was about the Amazon …
S: Oh, a nature documentary … not really my kind of thing, actually. I know I should take more of an interest, but I never feel particularly inspired by them. So what was so good about it?
I: Well I'm a big fan of the presenter, Bruce Parry – you must have seen him, he's been on TV a lot recently. Well, he travels the length of the Amazon interviewing different people who live and work around the river – so not just the indigenous tribes that have lived there for centuries, but also more recent settlers, like loggers and farmers.
S: Yes, I know Bruce Parry. He did that *Tribe* series where he went to live with different tribes in Africa and places. It got on my nerves a bit actually …
I: How can you say that? I have a lot of time for Bruce Parry. I could listen to him all day! Anyway, what I liked about this documentary was that he listened to everyone's side of the story – even the loggers who are tearing down the Amazon Forest. He doesn't make any judgements – the viewer is just left to make up their own mind …
S: Well, it sounds quite good … I guess I just get a bit tired of people making these programmes supposedly about other people living in difficult conditions, but more often it's just about them …

🔊 1.37

F = Friend, MA = Model answer
1
F: What do you think of mobile phones with loud music ringtones?
MA: They really get on my nerves, especially when one starts ringing on the train or bus.
2
F: Do you like graffiti?
MA: I'm not particularly keen on graffiti, but I've seen a few pieces that I like.
3
F: Do you like going to musicals?
MA: Yes, I love going to the theatre, but I don't get many opportunities.
4
F: What's your favourite TV programme?
MA: I'm really into watching sports. I'm a big fan of Formula One racing.

5
F: What kind of music do you listen to? Rock or something else?
MA: No, rock music isn't really my kind of thing. I'm into country and western music.

Unit 5

1.38

If you visit the famous French Quarter in New Orleans – which, after the airport, is probably the only part that most tourists see – everything now seems to be back to normal. That's because the French Quarter was largely spared when Hurricane Katrina hit in 2005. There was some damage, but it was fairly quickly repaired. But if you go to one of the residential areas south-east of the centre, it's a different story: you keep on seeing the effects of the disaster, even this long after the storm. There are a lot of homes and neighbourhoods which still have to be rebuilt. It wasn't the winds that did the damage, but rather the flood waters when the city's levees failed to hold the big tidal wave back. Huge numbers of people were forced to leave. A few people decided to resettle elsewhere, but most New Orleanians would never consider leaving their beloved city. About two-thirds of the residents have managed to return and little by little they are rebuilding the city.

The redevelopment plan has not been systematic or co-ordinated. There are some federal projects, some state projects, volunteer groups and also projects run by private benefactors. A particularly interesting project is taking place down in the Lower 9th Ward, an area that was pretty depressed even before the storm. A well-known film actor used his own money to create a non-profit organisation called 'Make it right'. Using architects from all over America, they planned to build 150 safe and environmentally-friendly homes in the area where ordinary local people could afford to buy or rent.

All the houses contain innovative design and safety features, because no one wants to see their home flood again. One solution is the 'float house' – the base of the house can rise on two guide posts and act as a raft in case of floods.

I visited some of them myself and was impressed by the imaginativeness of the architecture. At the same time, you can't help wondering how many more homes could have been built if they had used simpler designs and materials. It's a difficult issue. Here's someone genuinely trying to help people rebuild their lives, but is their vision too ambitious? Some critics think it's impractical.

1.39

The fact that most people have returned says a lot about how special this city is. The people who live here can't imagine living anywhere else.

I'm a musician and making a living in New Orleans has always been a challenge. We hoped to see more investment in jobs and tourism after the hurricane.

But since Hurricane Katrina, life has definitely become harder. I love this city, but these days, I'm forced to go out of town to find work.

1.40

China – minor	rule – tool
found – drowned	way – weigh
front – hunt	whale – they'll
meant – sent	where – share
ocean – motion	
placed – taste	

1.41

P = Presenter, J = Jim Bradstock
P: According to the McKinsey Global Institute, '350 million people will be added to China's urban population by 2025. China will have 221 cities with one million-plus living in them – Europe currently has 35.' That's a lot of people, a lot of energy and a lot of pollution. So the race is on to design and build sustainable cities that can generate their own energy, collect their own water and recycle their own waste. Pollution in these new eco-cities is not an option. I asked architect Jim Bradstock whether such cities are a realistic possibility or still some urban planners' pipe dream. Jim ...
J: There's a saying in China: 'Anything is possible, but nothing is easy.' The thing is that there are a lot of good designs and clever ideas – take your pick. But you also need the political will to make it happen, and a huge co-ordination effort by planners, architects, construction firms and local business interests to get the job done. Building a new eco-city – apart from being very expensive, of course – requires a lot of new skills that traditional construction workers just don't have. You also have to consider the sustainability of the materials. It's no good making a zero-energy house if you use enormous amounts of energy producing the concrete and other materials to build it. Each time you come up with an eco-solution, you find that you've created other problems that have to be dealt with.
P: Can we just focus on some of those solutions for a moment? Can you describe to our listeners some of the elements that make an eco-city sustainable?
J: Well, the first thing is the layout of the city. Business districts are placed close to where people live to encourage people to walk to work. Secondly, transportation is electric-powered: electric cars, electric skyway trains, and so on, so a number of clean generation methods are used to produce electricity in a non-polluting way.
P: Such as?
J: One idea is pavements that convert the energy of people's feet walking on them into electrical energy. But wind turbines and solar panels usually provide most of the energy. The key thing is that no extra energy should be imported from outside. That goes for food and water too. Houses collect all the rainwater that falls on or around them and then clean it using UV light so people can use it in the home. Large vertical farms that look a bit like skyscrapers grow vegetables and other crops ...
P: And can I just pick up on something we mentioned earlier and that's the question of waste. How do you deal with that because ...

1.44

Conversation 1
C = Colin, J = Jen
C: I find it incredible that in a big city like this there aren't more leisure facilities. We've got one rather ancient swimming pool, a few tennis courts and a few children's playgrounds.
J: I know what you mean. I think we should get together and write a petition to the local council asking them to do something about it.

Conversation 2
M = Michelle, R = Ruth
M: The problem is that no developer has any incentive to build affordable housing. They all make far more money from luxury homes. Personally, I think it's a disgrace. What's your view?
R: Well, I agree, but I'm just not sure there's much that we, as a council, can do about it. We probably need to consider a completely different solution to the housing problem.

Conversation 3
L = Liz, S = Steve, J = John
L: So, the GFC is asking for a further loan to develop their food co-operative project. What do you think we should do?
S: The way I see it, they have done a good job so far and made all their repayments on time. But it really depends on what they need the money for.
J: Exactly. So, we'll ask them to submit a more detailed proposal. Are we all agreed on that?

Conversation 4
A = Alex, N = Nick
A: Have you seen the plans for that new house across the street? It looks awful: not at all like the other houses round here. If you ask me, we should oppose it.
N: Well, let's not be too hasty. I think it would be better to talk to the new owners first about it. We want to try to keep on good terms with them.

🔊 1.45
F = Friend, MA = Model answer
1
F: What do you think of that new shopping mall they are building in the centre of town?
MA: Personally, I think it's horrible. I'd prefer to see more local shops.
2
F: I think that more money should be invested in leisure facilities for young people in the area.
MA: That's right. There's not enough for young people to do.
3
F: The trouble with having a business park out of town is that it encourages people to drive to work. What's your view?
MA: I know what you mean. But if you ask me, it's better than people driving into the city centre.
4
F: Do you think the council should pedestrianise the city centre?
MA: I think that depends on what they plan to do about public transport.
5
F: I find it amazing that no one developed the area around the canal. What they ought to do is make a nice area with shops and restaurants.
MA: I agree. It's an obvious area for development.

Unit 6

🔊 2.1
Speaker 1
Let's not pretend that just by staying at home, you're going to relax and switch off. If you're going to get a real break, you need to make a few rules and changes – a few don'ts, if you like. Tell your work that you are going away and you can't be contacted. Don't answer the phone – switch on the answer phone and listen to messages once a day to check that nothing urgent has come in. Change the weekly routine: you don't have to do a weekly shop, for example. Instead, make food shopping something that's fun and nice to do. Shop when you need to; go to the deli, the farmer's market and so on. Don't watch the same old TV programme that you watch each week. Don't do the cleaning – get a cleaner. I don't want to sound prescriptive, but unless you make some rules, you just won't relax properly.

Speaker 2
My idea of a staycation is to pamper myself for a week. I call it my 'home spa week'. I get up late. I go for a walk or a short run, and then I have a massage each day at the local health club. It would be easier not to do things to keep fit, but actually it makes me feel fantastic for the rest of the day. Then I take a late lunch – down by the waterfront usually – and spend the rest of the afternoon reading. Some evenings I spend the time preparing a meal very carefully; other times I go out to a show. I don't think it's extravagant, because I know whatever I do, I'm spending less than I would be if I went away on holiday.

Speaker 3
We had a staycation last year and I just organised loads of exciting things for the family to do every day. I hope I didn't overdo it. I think they enjoyed it. I'm just not one of those people who likes to sit still and do nothing when I'm on holiday. So we went to two theme parks; we went mountain biking in the Brecon hills; we even camped out in the garden one night. I think holidays are all about experiences and we certainly had some of those. We got lost on our bikes one day for about four hours. I tried not to let the children know that I was worried, but I was! Luckily we found the track again before it got dark.

Speaker 4
My advice for a staycation is just to keep it simple. It's an opportunity to enjoy the basic things in life and what nature has to offer. So you really mustn't let modern life dictate what you do too much. Do things with the family – take walks together, make meals for each other, play family games or just chat in the evenings – and don't get involved with anything even vaguely electronic, like computer games or the TV.

🔊 2.2
1 In tough economic times, people will try not to spend so much on luxuries and that includes holidays.
2 However, they don't want to go without a holiday altogether, because holidays are an important break from the stresses of work and daily life.
3 You don't have to go abroad to go on holiday. You can have a staycation instead. These have increased in popularity in recent years.
4 I don't think it's a bad trend because it means that people discover more about their own country, and at the same time, they boost the local economy.

🔊 2.4
If the saying 'Don't judge a book by its cover' was ever meant for a ship, then it should apply to the *National Geographic Endeavour*. The *Endeavour* was launched in 1966 as a North Sea fishing trawler and is very different from the modern lines of the cruise ships you see today swanning around the Caribbean. It looks more like a working ship, with a number of cranes for launching kayaks and other small boats. In fact, *NG Endeavour* is less of a cruise ship and more of an expedition ship that manages to mix comfort with exploration.

You won't find luxuries such as casinos, room service or in-cabin TVs on the *Endeavour*. Instead, you'll use the ship as a base camp while voyaging to some of the wildest locations on Earth, and you'll find that itineraries are never set in stone. Weather, wildlife and ice conditions always decide the afternoon's plans. Instead of shopping, you'll be kayaking among Antarctic icebergs or waking up at 2 a.m. to a ship's announcement saying that a polar bear has been spotted near the ship.

It's not cheap – fares of $500 to $1,000 a day – but you get value for your money: extraordinary experiences in the most remote regions on earth, a high degree of comfort and a healthy dose of excitement. It's equipped with sophisticated gadgets like the video microscope that magnifies images of sea-life up to 400 times; hydrophones that record whales singing underwater; and the Zodiacs or inflatable rubber boats that enable you to land just about anywhere. What else can you expect? Well, the passengers on *NG Endeavour* are mostly well-off, well-educated Americans in their 50s and 60s. At those prices, perhaps that's not surprising. Although there's only one shared dining room, and breakfast and lunch are buffets, the food is surprisingly tasty and varied.

Photographers from the *National Geographic* magazine accompany each voyage, and give passengers advice and instruction on how to take amazing pictures. *NG Endeavour* also employs expert naturalists as guides, who seem as excited as the passengers. Many of them have advanced degrees, all are very knowledgeable. Happily, they are also approachable and enthusiastic. You can get to know them on guided walks on shore, over meals, and in the bar at night.

Throughout the year, *NG Endeavour* sails from one end of the Earth to the other. From June to August, it's usually in Svalbard, way above the Arctic Circle, looking for polar bears. It then makes its way slowly south, through the Mediterranean for expeditions with a more historical and cultural focus, before heading to Antarctica, where it stays from November to March.

2.5
J = Joe, S = Steve
J: Hey, Steve. It's Joe. I'm just calling to say I'll be coming in on the five o'clock train this evening.
S: Fantastic … But I can't pick you up, I'm afraid. I'll be working then.
J: That's OK. I'll just make my way over to you at home – if that's all right.
S: Well, you could do that, but alternatively, since it's going to be a nice evening, why don't we meet up in town – say at Sara's Café down by the seafront?
J: Yeah, all right. That sounds nice. How do I get to Sara's Café?
S: Just hop on any bus from the station and ask the driver for King's Street.
J: OK.
S: Look out for the pier and get off there. Then walk down the front towards the city centre and you'll see the café on your right.
J: OK. If I get held up, I'll call you.
S: Actually, why don't you come and meet me at my office first? It's just as easy.
J: OK, where's that?
S: Well, get off at the same stop and walk in the same direction but turn down Ship Street. Call me when you get there and I'll come out and meet you.

2.6
1 I'd prefer to drive, but the car is behaving strangely.
2 It's not difficult to find, but it's quite a long way from the station.
3 I could come and meet you, but I don't finish work until 6.00 p.m.
4 The bus is cheap, but it makes a lot of stops on the way.
5 You could take a taxi, but it's a very scenic walk.

2.7
F = friend, MA = model answer
1
F: Hi there. I'm coming in on the train tomorrow at two o'clock. What's the best way to get to your house from there?
MA: The easiest thing is to take the bus.
2
F: OK. Is it far?
MA: No, it's only a ten-minute ride.

3
F: Great and how do I know when it's my stop?
MA: Look out for the big shoe factory on your left and it's the next stop after that.
4
F: OK, and what do I do when I get off the bus?
MA: Walk along the road until you see Harbord Road on your left. Turn down there.
5
F: Shall I call you when I get there?
MA: That's a good idea. Then I'll come out and meet you.
6
F: Great. Look, if I get held up, I'll call you. Otherwise, look forward to seeing you tomorrow.
MA: Yes, me too. Have a good trip.

Answer key

Unit 1

1a (pages 100 and 101)

1
b

2
1 b   2 b   3 b   4 c   5 a   6 a

3
1 truth   2 strength   3 warmth   4 length   5 depth

4
1 is dying out, you are trying, France is changing
2 we work with, we chat to, they reserve real intimacy
3 friendships have lost, you have ever visited
4 have been declining

5
1 have you spent *or* have you been spending
2 Do you consider
3 do you have
4 is increasing *or* has increased
5 Have you made
6 have you known
7 do you see
8 do you look for

6
1 intimate, close, strong   2 strong   3 close, closest, true
4 complete   5 casual

7
1 student   2 companion   3 acquaintance   4 flat
5 blood   6 passing

8
1 travel companion
2 odd couple
3 mutual respect
4 fellow students
5 close relative

9
1 out with   2 up with   3 on   4 round   5 by   6 up with
7 up   8 for

1b (pages 102 and 103)

1
1 T   2 F   3 T   4 F   5 T   6 F

2
1 rate   2 boom; retirement   3 diet   4 lifestyle
5 expectancy   6 vaccinations

3
1 are being forced
2 has been raised
3 isn't considered
4 is being encouraged
5 are reduced
6 hasn't been welcomed

4
1 is known
2 are obliged
3 have been educated
4 has been made
5 are also given *or* have also been given
6 is now outnumbered

5
1 is rising   2 is growing   3 has not been received
4 have gone   5 are obliged   6 are being encouraged

6a
1 (are) given   2 (have been) made   3 (is being) discussed
4 (has) not yet (been) found   5 (is) considered   6 (are) expected

6b
1 W   2 W   3 S   4 W   5 S   6 W

7
1 I think my parents' generation has been quite lucky.
2 My parents worked hard all their lives, but they both
   retired when they were 60 and they've been given good
   pensions. So now they can relax and enjoy themselves.
3 They've said that they don't want to be a burden on us,
   and that we children aren't expected to look after them
   when they get old.
4 Considering that my husband and I are now being asked
   to work until we are 68, I'm glad they said that.

1c (page 104)

1
c

2
1 F   2 T   3 T   4 T   5 F   6 T   7 F   8 F

3
1 a   2 a   3 c   4 b   5 b   6 c

4a
1 dynamic   2 fantastic   3 economics   4 generation
5 restriction   6 tradition
Rule: The penultimate syllable is always stressed.

4b
specific   italics   terrific   scientific   characteristic
impression   relation   interruption   transformation
comprehension

1d (page 105)

1
1 into   2 –   3 to   4 under   5 –   6 of   7 on   8 –   9 in
10 with

2
1 PPS   2 PPC   3 PPS   4 PPC

3
1 present perfect continuous
2 present perfect simple

4
1 been wondering   2 been working   3 decided
4 been helping   5 finished   6 lost

5
a Fancy bumping into you here
b What a nice surprise
c it obviously suits you
d how's it all going with you
e Do give her my best regards
f great to see you
g Good luck with the job

6
1 E   2 F   3 E   4 E   5 F   6 E

7
Students' own answers.

1e (page 106)

1
1 g   2 c   3 f   4 e   5 a   6 d   7 b

2
1 How are you **getting on**: doing
2 when you **get** a moment to write: have
3 you're able to **get by**: manage
4 I **got** a letter: received
5 I'm trying not to **get** too excited: become
6 to **get** a job: obtain
7 Sarah is going to **get** married: be

3
1 understand   2 put down   3 bought   4 arrive at *or* reach
5 take *or* catch   6 recover from   7 won   8 find *or* bring
or fetch

4
1 received *or* got   2 am   3 arrived *or* got   4 sounds
5 have had *or* have been having   6 were *or* got
7 hope   8 have recovered
9 hasn't become *or* hasn't got / doesn't become *or*
   doesn't get
10 sounds   11 don't think   12 have ever experienced
13 has happened   14 am trying *or* have tried *or* have been
trying   15 haven't been   16 find *or* get   17 helped *or* has
helped *or* has been helping   18 don't really understand *or*
don't really get

Wordbuilding / Learning skills / Check! (page 107)

1
-ful: respectful, helpful, playful
-ish: foolish, childish, selfish
-ive: sensitive, conservative, decisive
-ous: studious, humorous, industrious
-ent/-ant: dependent, different, dominant
-al: entrepreneurial, industrial, intellectual, practical
-ing: caring, controlling, dominating, loving

2
Possible answers:
1 dependent   2 caring/sensitive   3 conservative
4 dominant   5 practical   6 intellectual/studious
7 humorous   8 entrepreneurial   9 industrious

3
1 decisively   2 take   3 indecisive   4 conclusion

4
Students' own answers.

5
1 b   2 c   3 a   4 c   5 c

Unit 2

2a (pages 108 and 109)

1
1 They travel for hundreds of miles to breed.
2 The struggle between life and death.

2
1 have chicks   2 their young   3 dramatic
4 predictable   5 in such hard conditions

3
1 to shoot   2 inspired   3 documentary *or* drama
4 to anticipate   5 struck (me)

4
1 I have also worked as a cameraman.
2 I spent fourteen months at the French scientific centre in
   Antarctica. *and* I helped to shoot another film in 1995.
3 They have never experienced any form of colonisation,
   so they're not scared of humans. *and* The penguins have
   learned to live where no other creature can.

5
1 have met   2 have spent   3 have always felt   4 got
5 encountered   6 adapted   7 learned   8 has visited
9 didn't run   10 did

6
1 director   2 sentimental   3 gripping   4 touching   5 cast
6 location   7 accurate   8 storyline   9 audience   10 scenes

7
There is a silent 'l' in the following words: talk, could, calf,
folk, calm

8
1 setting for; thought-provoking book
2 characters are you and me and every other typical passenger
3 book is based on conversations that the author had
4 The idea behind it; can portray modern civilisation

2b (pages 110 and 111)

1
b

2
1 a   2 c   3 c   4 b   5 a

3
1 a   2 b   3 b   4 a   5 c   6 b

4
1 drove   2 made   3 arrived   4 had fallen   5 climbed
6 had gone   7 were hanging   8 hadn't told   9 stood
10 had crushed *or* was crushing   11 waited
12 had already decided

5
1 b   2 a   3 c

6
1 hadn't   2 are   3 isn't   4 was   5 weren't   6 was   7 had
8 haven't

7a
The tenses used to describe the film are: present simple,
present continuous and present perfect.

7b
1 gives   2 begin   3 reaches *or* has reached
4 grow *or* are growing   5 are getting

2c (page 112)

1
1 T   2 F   3 T   4 T   5 F   6 F

2
1 children; adults   2 fairy tale   3 sadness   4 moved
5 moral lessons

3
1 an elegant   2 watches closely   3 a little swallow stops off
with him   4 asks   5 people   6 days   7 catches cold
8 destroy

4
1 c   2 b   3 d   4 a

5
1 kept you from *or* have kept you from
2 kept an eye on
3 keep him company
4 keep track of
5 kept back
6 keep a secret

2d (page 113)

1
1 tore   2 broke   3 stuck   4 made   5 froze   6 burst

2
a What a
b That was
c How *or* That was
d How *or* That was
e What
f How
g Poor
h What *or* That must have been
i How *or* That must have been
j What *or* That must have been

Possible answers:
1 a *or* c   2 a *or* j   3 a *or* c *or* i   4 c   5 a   6 a *or* j

3
1 Hannah's passport was out-of-date.
2 She went to the passport office in London to get a new
   passport.
3 Very stressed.

4
1 d   2 b   3 f   4 a   5 e   6 c

6
Students' own answers.

2e (page 114)

1a
whispered, replied anxiously, moaned, muttered, cried

1b
1 c   2 b   3 g   4 d   5 e   6 a   7 f

2a
a T   b T   c F   d T

2b
'I don't think this is going to work,' Christopher
sighed. 'We've been trying to build this canoe for three days
and it still looks like a lump of wood. The wood's too hard,'
he added. 'Actually, Christopher,' said Jen encouragingly,
'we are making some progress. What we really need to do is
find some better tools.' Just then Tom screamed, 'I've got it!
Instead of using our penknives directly on the wood, why
don't we make some better tools using our knives?'

3
Model answer:
'Look out,' screamed Fergus, 'I think he's angry now.' The
two friends edged nervously backwards as the snake turned
its head to face them. Josh had thrown a large rock at it,
hoping that this would frighten it, but it seemed that it had
had the opposite effect. Now Josh was looking around for
something else to hit the snake with. 'Where's a stick when

you need one?' he muttered. 'Too late for that,' said Fergus.
'Let's get out of here.' And with that, he leaped towards the
trees and started running.

Wordbuilding / Learning skills / Check! (page 115)

1
an author – a novelist
an audience – viewers
a blockbuster – a best-seller
a cinema – a multiplex
to edit – to cut
a film – a movie
a hero – a heroine
to publish – to release
a remake – a re-release
a sequel – a follow-up

2
1 an author *or* a novelist   2 a heroine   3 viewers
4 a best-seller   5 to release   6 to cut   7 a sequel *or* follow-up
8 a multiplex   9 a re-release   10 a movie

3
1 b   2 a   3 a   4 b   5 b   6 a

4, 5 and 6
Students' own answers.

7
1
a a documentary
b a children's story *or* fairy tale
c a book-film adaptation

2
a film director *or* producer
b author *or* writer
c photographer

3
a shave
b stroke
c stretch

Unit 3

3a (pages 116 and 117)

1
c

2
1 standard of living   2 increase   3 more than *or* faster than
4 (two) children   5 one billion   6 three ways *or* three
schools of thought *or* three alternatives

3
Greater: rise, boost, grow, increase, raise, peak
Smaller: dwindle, deplete, decrease, fall, lessen, reduce

4
1 reduce   2 rise *or* increase *or* grow   3 decrease *or* fall
4 reduce *or* lessen   5 increase *or* raise *or* boost   6 increase

5
1 will have; will be
2 are going to rely
3 I'll tell; I will be; doesn't start
4 won't solve; share
5 is going to save
6 I'm going; begins

6
1 Are you going *or* Are you going to go
2 are you getting *or* are you going to get
3 'll probably drive *or* am probably going to drive

4 'll go
5 'll give
6 are you leaving *or* are you going to leave
7 starts
8 will finish *or* will be finished

7
1 etcetera   2 contributed   3 lot   4 fifteen   5 years
6 powerful   7 motives   8 meet   9 secretly   10 Manhattan

3b Smart technology (pages 118 and 119)

1
Items mentioned: kitchen gadgets, water use,
sound-proofing, visual media, lighting

2
1 a   2 b   3 c   4 c   5 c   6 b

3
1 b   2 g   3 a   4 f   5 h   6 c   7 e   8 d

4
1 will be hearing   2 will be making   3 will all be using
4 will have become   5 will be using   6 will be cleaning
7 will be installing   8 will have become   9 will be launching

5
1 will be doing   2 will be cleaning   3 will have developed
4 will be doing   5 will have been   6 won't have acquired

6
1 information age, information overload, information
technology
2 data security, data storage
3 computer games, computer graphics, computer
programmer

7
1 data security   2 information age   3 computer
graphics   4 data storage   5 information overload

8
1 The weekday edition of *The New York Times* contains more
information than the average person in 17th-century
England learned in a lifetime.
2 Around a thousand books are published internationally
every day and the total of all printed knowledge doubles
every five years.
3 More information has been published in the last 30 years
than in the previous 5,000.

3c (page 120)

1
1 b   2 c   3 c   4 b

2
1 2007; 6,000   2 99.9%   3 6   5 700   5 30   6 2010

3
1 works   2 provides   3 contains   4 lasts   5 weighs
6 run

4a
1 /ɪ/   2 /ɪ/   3 /aɪ/   4 /ɪ/   5 /aɪ/

5
1 neat   2 appropriate   3 consuming   4 handy
5 cutting   6 fix

3d (page 121)

1
1 sort   2 format   3 undo   4 copy   5 select   6 highlight
7 open   8 search   9 attach   10 paste   11 save   12 cut

2
1 He is having trouble sending the document. *or* He's trying
to attach a document to an email, but he can't.
2 1 Compress the photos; 2 Divide the document into three
or four separate documents.
3 It reduces the quality of the photos.

3
1 give   2 hand   3 trouble   4 exactly   5 trying   6 Let
7 look   8 trouble   9 can   10 involve   11 show   12 trick
13 see   14 else   15 tried   16 try   17 works   18 free

4
The two verbs which do not fit the stress pattern are:
highlight and open

5
Students' own answers.

3e (page 122)

1
1 Please could I bring your memory stick back on my way
home from work tonight?
2 Do you happen to know where I can find a battery
charger for my old phone?
3 Could you please send me a brochure for your air
conditioning units?
4 Do you know the phone number for Apricot
Computers (please)?
5 Please can/could you advise me how to download photos
from my X306 camera?
6 Would you be able to reduce the price?
7 Would you mind coming over and fixing my internet
connection?
8 Please could you tell me what number I should call to get
technical advice?

2
a depth   b question   c business   d date   e order
f way   g interest   h luck

3
1 f   2 d   3 g   4 c   5 h   6 b   7 a   8 e

4
Model answer:

Hi Jim

I hope all is well with you. I tried to call you earlier, but
I couldn't get any answer. I wonder if you could do me a
favour. My computer keeps crashing and I think it may
have the same virus that yours had a few weeks ago.
Would you mind emailing me the instructions about
how to remove the virus to my work email? Then I can
print them and try to see if it works. Alternatively, could
you call me some time? I'll be at home most evenings
this week.

Many thanks

Sam

Wordbuilding / Learning skills / Check! (page 123)

1
1 biodegradable, biodiversity
2 hypermarket, hypersensitive
3 megabyte, megastar
4 microchip, microwave
5 semi-conscious, semi-detached
6 ultrasonic, ultraviolet

2
1 hypermarket   2 microwave   3 megabyte
4 biodiversity   5 microchip   6 semi-detached
7 hypersensitive   8 ultraviolet   9 ultrasound
10 megastar   11 biodegradable   12 semi-conscious

3
address book
battery life
credit card
data protection
information technology
news story
repair manual
travel advice

4
Students' own answers.

5
1 gadget   2 lazy   3 overload   4 breakthrough
5 Appropriate   6 luck
Word: global

Unit 4

4a (pages 124 and 125)

1
1 show, act   2 gig, venue, band   3 exhibition, gallery
4 company, performance, theatre   5 play, musical

2
1 Batman Live, This is Design
2 The Alternative Village Fete, Notting Hill Carnival
3 The Alternative Village Fete, Notting Hill Carnival
4 The Alternative Village Fete
5 The Floating Cinema
6 Notting Hill Carnival
7 Batman Live
8 The Alternative Village Fete

3
1 communal   2 float   3 eye candy   4 mundane
5 workshop

4
1 number   2 no   3 several/some   4 plenty/loads/lots
5 any   6 few

5
1 a little   2 enough   3 a lot of; A large number of
4 plenty of; no   5 a lack of   6 many   7 hardly any
8 a bit of

4b (pages 126 and 127)

1
1 portrait   2 graffiti   3 installation   4 sketch
5 sculpture   6 landscape   7 still life

2
1 In the first photo, the graffiti has been drawn on
public walls. In the second photo, the graffiti is part of a
piece of artwork.
2 Students' own answers.

3
1 A graffiti artist was convicted of vandalism.
2 Handy thought it was outrageous.
3 When the owner of a property doesn't like it or want
it on their property. or When it's criminal damage.

4
1 c   2 b   3 c   4 c   5 a   6 a

5
1 person who was invited
2 method works
3 anyone came to the opening night
4 our money
5 countries have their own laws and rules
6 world is waiting to see what will happen

6
1 each; all   2 no   3 both   4 any   5 Every   6 no
7 whole   8 Either *or* Any

7
1 no   2 all the   3 the whole   4 each   5 Both

8
1 The message was clear: is this how far we have come
since the Stone Age?
2 Often it carries a political or social message, but in an
amusing way that ordinary people can relate to.
3 Despite not calling himself an artist, his work has
been shown in galleries and has sold for thousands
of dollars.
4 Banksy, who is based in the UK, is perhaps the world's
best-known graffiti artist.
5 Banksy loves to surprise. In 2005, a picture showing a
primitive human being pushing a shopping cart appeared
in the British Museum.

The correct order is: 4, 3, 2, 5, 1

4c (page 128)

1
1 country music   2 dance music   3 (punk) rock   4 hip-hop

2
Suggested answers:
a 3   b 1   c 1   d 4   e 2   f 2

3
1 Country; real
2 influences
3 teenagers; rock
4 sounds; technology

4
1 be connected to   2 escape   3 seem true   4 discover
5 think of   6 (not) be important

5
1 b   2 a   3 b   4 d   5 c   6 a

6
1 c   2 b   3 a   4 d

4d (page 129)

1
1 the Amazon River   2 He likes the presenter.

2
1 X   2 X   3 X

3
1 kind of thing   2 feel particularly inspired   3 a big fan of
4 got on my nerves   5 listen to him   6 a bit tired of

4b
1 I can listen to Bach all day.
2 Documentaries don't really do anything for me.
3 I'm not really into TV.
4 I'm not particularly keen on the presenter.
5 I get a bit tired of reality TV shows.
6 I don't generally watch much TV.

5
1 documentary   2 everywhere   3 specifically   4 interest
5 separate   6 restaurant   7 listener   8 general

6
Students' own answers.

4e (page 130)

1
a I, we and you; it   b active; passive   c contracted;
uncontracted   d formal   e Avoid   f furthermore
g Share

2
Possible answers:
[1] <u>I've</u> got to admit that [2] <u>I'm</u> [3] <u>not a big fan of</u> stand-up
comedy. [4] <u>I always think that</u> it's a rather unnatural
thing. The comedian [5] <u>stands up</u> in front of an audience
who stare at him or her as if to say, 'Come on, then, make
me laugh.' The comedian then has a few minutes to make
them laugh or the audience will start to get restless. It's
all a bit too aggressive and combative for me. [6] <u>So</u> when [7] <u>I
went</u> with an old school friend to see new British comedian
Spencer Brown last Tuesday night at the Bristol Comedy
Club, [8] <u>I wasn't really looking forward to it.</u>
1 contraction
2 contraction
3 personal details
4 share your feelings
5 active verb
6 conversational linking phrase
7 active verb
8 share your feelings

3
Possible answers:
1 But   2 weren't   3 the rest of the audience seemed to like
his act   4 start   5 you think at first   6 then *or* after that
7 that's   8 putting together   9 in fact *or* actually

4
Model answer:
The secret of the show's success is that Spencer Brown
really understands his audience and what people find
funny. Not only that, but he comes across as a nice guy
too. If you are in Bristol, I'd definitely recommend going
to see him. He'll be at the Bristol Comedy Club until
Saturday 10th December. You'll be smiling for weeks
afterwards!

Wordbuilding / Learning skills / Check! (page 131)

1
1 snow**scape**   2 metalwork**er**   3 craftsman**ship**
4 polite**ness**   5 saxophon**ist**   6 romantic**ism**

2
1 surrealism   2 guitarist   3 TV presenter   4 cityscape
5 calmness   6 modernism   7 moonscape   8 musicianship
9 trombonist   10 carpenter   11 directness   12 companionship

4
1 No, not really.
2 /ˈkʌmftəbl/
3 You use *either* + singular noun, but *both* + plural noun.
4 Yes, 'it gets on my nerves'.
5 American
6 Yes, it's quite direct.

5
1a Melbourne   b All   c American
2a few   b folk   c fan
3a an impersonal tone   b a lot of luck   c cool down
4a gig; lyrics   b sketch; sculpture   c play; musical

Unit 5

5a (pages 132 and 133)

1
1 F   2 T   3 T   4 F

2
1 back to normal 2 floods; winds   3 love   4 co-ordinated
5 depressed   6 safe   7 imaginative *or* innovative
8 practical

3
1 to be   2 seeing   3 to hold   4 to return   5 to resettle
6 building   7 seeing   8 wondering

4
verb + *to* + infinitive: help, hope, want
verb + *someone* + to + infinitive: allow, ask, get, help, want
verb + *-ing*: carry on, enjoy, imagine
verb + *someone* + infinitive: help, imagine, make

5a
verb + *to* + infinitive: choose, learn
verb + *someone* + *to* + infinitive: force, teach
verb + *-ing*: avoid, finish, involve, (not) mind
verb + *someone* + infinitive: let

5b
1 to visit   2 rebuild   3 to participate   4 getting
5 to work   6 learning   7 to do   8 meeting

6
1 pedestrianised   2 mall   3 waterfront   4 luxury
5 housing   6 spaces   7 district   8 centre

7
1 modernise   2 transform   3 spoils   4 demolished
5 redeveloped   6 convert

8a
The fact that most people have returned says a lot about
how special this city is. The people who live here can't
imagine living anywhere else.
I'm a musician and making a living in New Orleans has
always been a challenge. We hoped to see more investment
in jobs and tourism after the hurricane.
But since Hurricane Katrina, life has definitely become
harder. I love this city, but these days, I'm forced to go out
of town to find work.

Answer: Yes, the resident is happy living in New Orleans.

8b
1 can't imagine living   2 hoped to see   3 m forced to go

5b (pages 134 and 135)

1
Sentences a and b are true of Monterey today.

2
1 T   2 N   3 F   4 T   5 T   6 T   7 F   8 T

3
1 in the intervening period   2 join (in) the party
3 just like that   4 old-timers   5 set up   6 sample

4
1 dynamic   2 industrial   3 attractive   4 preserved
5 regulated   6 essential

5
1 NC   2 NC   3 C   4 C   5 NC   6 NC   7 C   8 C

6
1 going   2 putting   3 catching   4 to say   5 fishing
6 to make   7 to go   8 eating

7

1 to visit   2 to see   3 to open   4 to do   5 having

8

China – minor	placed – taste
found – drowned	rule – tool
front – hunt	way – weigh
meant – sent	whale – they'll
ocean – motion	where – share

5c (page 136)

1

1 F   2 F   3 F   4 T   5 T

2

1 221   2 pollution   3 possible; easy
4 construction; business   5 materials   6 walk
7 electric *or* electric-powered   8 imported
9 UV   10 farms

3

1 b   2 c   3 c

4

1 pick on   2 pick up   3 pick (me) up   4 take your pick
5 pick holes in   6 pick your brains

5b

<u>a</u>rchitect   archi<u>te</u>ctural   elec<u>tri</u>city   <u>e</u>nergy   <u>ge</u>nerate
ma<u>te</u>rial   <u>mi</u>nimise   po<u>li</u>tical   sus<u>tai</u>nable   sustaina<u>bi</u>lity

5d (page 137)

1

1 d   2 e   3 f   4 c   5 g   6 a   7 b

2

1 public   2 affordable   3 local   4 green   5 pedestrianised
6 leisure

3

1 d   2 b   3 a   4 c

4

1 I find it incredible that
  I know what you mean.
2 Personally,
  What's your view?
  I agree,
  We probably need
3 What do you think we should do?
  The way I see it,
  it really depends on
  Exactly.
  Are we all agreed on that?
4 If you ask me,
  let's not be

5

Students' own answers.

5e (page 138)

1

1 B   2 D   3 A   4 C

2

c quoting what someone (often famous) has said about this
problem

3

Possible answers:
(giving a dramatic example) You used to be able to drive
from Washington to Boston, a distance of 450 miles, through
rich, green landscape. Now the only green you see is the
paint on people's houses!

(giving some statistics) In the United States, the area
between Boston and Washington DC, a distance of 450 miles,
is now a massive urban region with a population of about
50 million – that's almost 17% of the US population on 2%
of the US land area.

4

1 In addition
2 Because of this; As a result
3 on the other hand

5b

1 … three acres of land, the house comes with a swimming
  pool. *or* … coming with three acres of land, the house has
  a swimming pool.
2 … rising crime, people have moved out of the centre.
3 … a good bus service, we have excellent roads into
  the city centre. *or* having a good bus service, we have
  excellent roads into the city centre.
4 … restrictions on building on green spaces, we are starting
  to redevelop city centres.

Wordbuilding / Learning skills / Check! (page 139)

1

1 long-term unemployed   2 politically correct
3 economically disadvantaged   4 upwardly mobile
5 ill prepared   6 ethnically mixed   7 highly cultured
8 cleverly designed

2

1 rebuild   2 redecorate   3 retrain   4 readjust   5 redo
6 reread

4

Possible answers:
• It doesn't say who wrote it, but it doesn't seem to be a
  travel article. The interest seems to be from a historical
  and urban development perspective.
• The main argument is that a fantastic city has grown
  up in a place you would not expect it, because of one
  person's dream and ambition.
• The writer doesn't say whether he/she likes what has
  happened to Dubai or not, but he/she seems uncertain
  that it will be a long-term success.
• I agree with the writer's argument. It seems an
  unsustainable development.

5

1 c   2 c   3 c   4 b   5 b

Unit 6

6a (pages 140 and 141)

1

b Speaker 4   c Speaker 1   e Speaker 2   f Speaker 3
The two extra items are a and d.

2

a Speaker 4   b Speaker 3   d Speaker 1   f Speaker 2
The two extra activities are c and e.

3

1 a   2 b   3 b   4 b   5 c

4

1 Let's not kid ourselves	5 I don't think it's
2 Don't answer	extravagant
3 You don't have to do	6 I didn't overdo it
4 not to do	7 not to let the children know
	8 you really mustn't let

5

1 I don't want a coffee now, thanks.
2 I don't think it's a great idea.
3 Let's not do anything to upset them.
4 I hope I didn't give her the wrong impression.
5 You don't have to give the book back to me immediately.
6 Try not to be late, please.
7 You mustn't take food into the library.
8 Have they decided not to stay?

6

1 off *or* holiday   2 catering   3 scenery   4 view
5 airlines   6 luggage *or* baggage   7 journey *or* drive *or* way
8 countryside   9 took   10 suitcase *or* bag

7

1 stay   2 drop   3 eating   4 stay   5 fill   6 join

8

1 In tough economic times, people will try not to spend so much on luxuries and that includes holidays.
2 However, they don't want to go without a holiday altogether, because holidays are an important break from the stresses of work and daily life.
3 You don't have to go abroad to go on holiday. You can have a staycation instead. These have increased in popularity in recent years.
4 I don't think it's a bad trend because it means that people discover more about their own country, and at the same time, they boost the local economy.

6b (pages 142 and 143)

1

1 consultancy-type roles   2 highly skilled professionals
3 four to six months   4 there isn't any flexibility   5 no costs

2

1 c   2 b   3 a   4 c   5 c   6 b

3

1 rewarding   2 tough   3 concentrated   4 fresh   5 set
6 one-off

4

1 Haven't you ever wondered
2 don't you translate
3 Wouldn't you like
4 Won't it harm
5 Aren't you going to lose out
6 Isn't it

5

1 do you   2 wouldn't it   3 is it   4 didn't you
5 mightn't there   6 wouldn't I

6

1 F   2 R   3 R   4 R   5 R   6 F   7 R   8 F

6c (page 144)

1

Items on *NG Endeavour*: a crane, a kayak, a microscope, an inflatable rubber boat, guides

2

1 educational   2 expensive   3 comfortable
4 well-equipped   5 exciting

3

1 fishing   2 $500   3 $1,000   4 video microscope
5 hydrophones   6 photographers   7 naturalists/guides
8 Mediterranean   9 Antarctica   11 dining

4

1 swanning around   2 set in stone   3 a healthy dose of
4 well-off   5 approachable   6 throughout

5

1 **If you had a cruise in mind**, try one of Lindblad's expeditions.
2 **If you don't mind a bit of danger and excitement**, Lindblad cruises are perfect.
3 The cruises are amazing. **Mind you**, they're not cheap.
4 **Bear in mind that** these are not typical cruises.
5 I used to think that cruises were for the old and retired, but **I've changed my mind** (now).
6 **I'm in two minds about** going on one of their cruises.

6b

1 Don't   2 No   3 It doesn't   4 No   5 Don't   6 It doesn't

6d (page 145)

1

1 in   2 up   3 to   4 on   5 out   6 on   7 up   8 out

2

1 He's working. *or* He's at work.
2 He'll get a bus, then walk.
3 At Steve's office.

3

1 The easiest thing is to take the bus.
2 Alternatively, I can take a taxi.
3 I can make my own way.
4 It's only a fifteen-minute bus ride.
5 I'm coming in by train.
6 If I get held up, I'll let you know.

4

1 drive   2 flight   3 ride   4 walk   5 ride   6 crossing

5a

1 d   2 b   3 a   4 e   5 c

6

Students' own answers.

6e (page 146)

1

1 She had to pay £30 to carry her coat onto the plane.
2 She wants a refund and she wants the airline to investigate the matter.

2

1 Oxford   2 customer – company   3 formal

3

1 register a complaint   2 unjust   3 stated   4 informed
5 placed   6 attempted   7 wished   8 opted
9 these circumstances   10 investigate

3b
Model answer:

Dear Sir/Madam

I am writing to **register a complaint** about the meal we **were served** on our flight home last week – flight UZ332. On the booking confirmation, it **stated** that we **would be given** breakfast and lunch. **However**, breakfast **only consisted of** a cup of tea and lunch a tuna sandwich. By itself, this would not have been a problem, but **I regret to say that** my husband and I both **suffered** food poisoning from the sandwich.

4

Model answer:

Given the circumstances, I would ask you to do two things. Firstly, please ensure that in future communication with passengers you make it clear what kind of meal will be served. Secondly, please ensure that the food which you provide is fresh and has not been stored in the wrong conditions.

Yours faithfully

Thomas Garcia

Wordbuilding / Learning skills / Check! (page 147)

1

1 in 2 out 3 out 4 in 5 out 6 in 7 in 8 out
9 out *or* in 10 in

2

a fall out (with) b take in c drop in (on) d look in (on)
e fall in (with) f look out g give in (to) h take out
i drop out (of) j give up

3

1 action wanted 2 link the ideas 3 examples 4 spelling

4

1 To complain about an extra charge; this point is made in the opening paragraph
2 Reason for writing; details or facts about the incident; action wanted
3 At the time; consequently; Otherwise; Given these circumstances
4 formal
5 She didn't want to delay other passengers; it's not unreasonable to wear a coat onto a plane

5

1 She took a Japanese holiday in her own city.
2 The Great Continental Divide cycling and hiking trail.
3 In a prison hotel.
4 In an art hotel, e.g. Propeller Island City Lodge, in Berlin.
5 couch surfing

CREDITS

Although every effort has been made to contact copyright holders prior to publication, this has not always been possible. If notified, the publisher will undertake to rectify any errors or omissions at the earliest opportunity.

Text:
The publisher would like to thank the following sources for permission to reproduce their copyright protected text:

National Geographic for extracts adapted from 'When Surya the orangutan meets a hound dog by the river, the two carry on like long lost friends', http://channel.nationalgeographic.com/; 'Guardians of the Fairy Tale: The Brothers Grimm' by Thomas O'Neill, http://www.nationalgeographic.com; 'The Big Idea', http://ngm.nationalgeographic.com/; 'Dubai' by Afshin Molavi, January 2007, http://ngm.nationalgeographic.com/; 'Interview: "March of the Penguins" Director Luc Jacquet' by Stefan Lovgren, 24 June 2005, http://news.nationalgeographic.com. Reproduced with permission; Australian Council for figures and text from the report 'More than bums on seats: Australian participation in the arts', www.australiacouncil.gov.au; VSO for an extract from 'Why Volunteer?', http://www.vso.org.uk/volunteer/why-volunteer/, reproduced by permission of VSO.
In some instances we have been unable to trace the owners of copyright material and we would appreciate any information that would enable us to do so.

Photos:
The publisher would like to thank the following sources for permission to reproduce their copyright protected photos:

Cover: Paul Cheung/My Shot/National Geographic Image Collection

Inside: 6 tr Image Source/Alamy, 6 cl Barcroft Media/Getty Images, 6 cr Patrick Aventurier/Getty Images, 6 bl Tim Laman/National Geographic Image Collection, 6 br Michael Nichols/National Geographic Image Collection, 7 l Insadco Photography/Alamy, 7 r Aurora Photos/Alamy, 8 tl Shivji Joshi/Shivji Joshi, 8 tc Dario Mitidieri/Hulton Archive/Getty Images, 8 tr Shutterstock/Shutterstock, 8 bl David Doubilet/National Geographic Image Collection, 8 bl Nigel Swinn/National Geographic My Shot/National Geographic Image Collection, 8 bc George Steinmetz/National Geographic Image Collection, 8 br Jodi Cobb/National Geographic Image Collection, 8 cbc Reuters/Stringer China/Reuters Media, 8 cbc Reuters/Stringer China/Reuters Media, 8 cbr Robert Harding Travel/Photolibrary Group, 8 ctl Emanuele Picchirallo/National Geographic My Shot/National Geographic Image Collection, 8 ctc George Steinmetz/National Geographic Image Collection, 8 ctr Hemis/Alamy, 9 Shivji Joshi/Shivji Joshi, 10 Stevi Calandra/National Geographic Channel/National Geographic Image Collection, 12/13 Randy Olson/National Geographic Image Collection, 15 Paul Thompson/National Geographic Image Collection, 16 Corbis RF/Alamy, 17 Bartosz Hadyniak/Getty Images, 18 Edwin Levick/Hulton Archive/Getty Images, 20 Joel Sartore/National Geographic Image Collection, 21 Dario Mitidieri/Hulton Archive/Getty Images, 22 Adam Woolfitt/Corbis UK Ltd, 24 Steve Winter/National Geographic Image Collection, 27 Joel Sartore/National Geographic Image Collection, 28 Oote Boe Photography/Alamy, 29 Shutterstock/Shutterstock, 30 John Springer Collection/Corbis UK Ltd, 32 Beverly Joubert/National Geographic Image Collection, 33 Shutterstock/Shutterstock, 34 Randy Olson/National Geographic Image Collection, 36/37 Oliver Uberti/National Geographic Image Collection, 38 r Renee Comet/National Geographic Image Collection, 38 r Renee Comet/National Geographic Image Collection, 38 cl Renee Comet/National Geographic Image Collection, 38 cr Renee Comet/National Geographic Image Collection, 39 Kenneth Garrett/National Geographic Image Collection, 44 Amy White & Al Petteway/National Geographic Image Collection, 45 Emanuele Picchirallo/National Geographic My Shot/National Geographic Image Collection, 46 Annie Griffiths/National Geographic Image Collection, 48 Alexandre Orion, 51 David Alan Harvey/National Geographic Image Collection, 52 Stephen Morrison/epa/Corbis UK Ltd, 53 Justin Kase zfivez/Alamy, 54 Patrick Aventurier/Getty Images, 56 Stephen Sharnoff/National Geographic Image Collection, 57 George Steinmetz/National Geographic Image Collection, 58 Smar Jodha/National Geographic My Shot/National Geographic Image Collection, 60 l Frans Lanting Studio/Alamy, 60 r Michael Melford/National Geographic Image Collection, 63 Chien-Chi Chang/National Geographic Image Collection, 64 Shutterstock/Shutterstock, 66 Image Source/Alamy, 69 Hemis/Alamy, 70 Chris Johns/National Geographic Image Collection, 72 Minden/Frank Lane Picture Agency, 73 Ivo Roospold/Alamy, 75 t Ian Trower/Age Fotostock/Photolibrary Group, 75 b Juergen Henkelmann Photography/Alamy, 75 cb Sextantio Press, 75 ct Richard Nowitz/National Geographic Image Collection, 76 Keenpress/National Geographic Image Collection, 78 Insadco Photography/Alamy, 80 Farrell Grehan/National Geographic Image Collection, 82 tl Renee Comet/National Geographic Image Collection, 82 bl Renee Comet/National Geographic Image Collection, 82 br Renee Comet/National Geographic Image Collection, 82 Renee Comet/National Geographic Image Collection, 100 Jana Asenbrennerova/National Geographic Image Collection, 102 Shutterstock, 103 Philip Lee Harvey/Alamy, 104 Stephen Bures/Alamy, 105 Robert Fried/Alamy, 107 Shutterstock, 108 Frans Lanting/National Geographic Image Collection, 110 Lee Cohen/Corbis/Corbis UK Ltd, 112 Laura Stuzman/Sleeping Bear Press, a part of Cengage Learning/Cengage Learning (EMEA) Ltd, 114 John Lund/Drew Kelly/Getty Images, 115 tr Joel Sartore/National Geographic Image Collection, 115 br Dario Mitidieri/Getty Images, 115 l New Line/Saul Zaentz/Wing Nut/Kobal Collection/Kobal Collection, 116 iofoto/Shutterstock, 118 Catherine Karnow/National Geographic Image Collection, 119 Stefano Cavoretto/Alamy, 120 Renee Comet/National Geographic Image Collection, 124 Shutterstock, 126 tl Shutterstock, 126 tr Shutterstock, 126 tcl Shutterstock, 126 tcr LM Otero/AP/Press Association Images, 126 cl Shutterstock, 126 cc Shutterstock, 126 cc DEA / PEDICINI/Getty Images, 126 bl Joseph O. Holmes / portfolio.streetnine.com/Getty Images, 126 br Shutterstock, 128 Jodi Cobb/National Geographic Image Collection, 129 Shutterstock, 132 James Nielsen/Getty Images, 134 Terry Donnelly/Alamy, 135 Enrique R Aguirre Aves/Getty Images, 136 ssguy/Shutterstock, 138 David R. Frazier Photolibrary, Inc./Alamy, 140 Eye Candy/Alamy, 141 Netfalls - Remy Musser/Shutterstock, 142 Randy Plett/Getty Images, 144 Gordon Wiltsie/National Geographic Image Collection, 145 Shutterstock

Illustrations by Bob Lea p42; David Russell p40; Kevin Hopgood Illustration p120; National Geographic Image Collection p7